Writing for Young People

Writing for Young People

Critical Readings and Discussions on Craft

ELEN CALDECOTT

BLOOMSBURY ACADEMIC
LONDON • NEW YORK • OXFORD • NEW DELHI • SYDNEY

BLOOMSBURY ACADEMIC

Bloomsbury Publishing Plc, 50 Bedford Square, London, WC1B 3DP, UK
Bloomsbury Publishing Inc, 1359 Broadway, New York, NY 10018, USA
Bloomsbury Publishing Ireland, 29 Earlsfort Terrace, Dublin 2, D02 AY28, Ireland

BLOOMSBURY, BLOOMSBURY ACADEMIC and the Diana logo are
trademarks of Bloomsbury Publishing Plc

First published in Great Britain 2026

Copyright © Elen Caldecott, 2026

Elen Caldecott has asserted her right under the Copyright, Designs and
Patents Act, 1988, to be identified as Author of this work.

For legal purposes the Permissions on p. x constitute an
extension of this copyright page.

Cover Design and Illustration © Gita Govinda Kowlessur

All rights reserved. No part of this publication may be: i) reproduced or transmitted in
any form, electronic or mechanical, including photocopying, recording or by means of
any information storage or retrieval system without prior permission in writing from the
publishers; or ii) used or reproduced in any way for the training, development or operation
of artificial intelligence (AI) technologies, including generative AI technologies. The rights
holders expressly reserve this publication from the text and data mining exception as per
Article 4(3) of the Digital Single Market Directive (EU) 2019/790.

Bloomsbury Publishing Plc does not have any control over, or responsibility for, any
third-party websites referred to or in this book. All internet addresses given in this
book were correct at the time of going to press. The author and publisher regret
any inconvenience caused if addresses have changed or sites have ceased
to exist, but can accept no responsibility for any such changes.

A catalogue record for this book is available from the British Library.

A catalog record for this book is available from the Library of Congress.

ISBN: HB: 978-1-3504-1312-2
PB: 978-1-3504-1311-5
ePDF: 978-1-3504-1313-9
eBook: 978-1-3504-1314-6

Typeset by Integra Software Services Pvt. Ltd.
Printed and bound in Great Britain

For product safety related questions contact productsafety@bloomsbury.com.

To find out more about our authors and books visit www.bloomsbury.com
and sign up for our newsletters.

To Madi and Noah, gyda cariad mawr.

Contents

Permissions Page x

Introduction 1
        Cited Work 5

Chapter One 7
        Section 1: *This Is Not My Hat*, Written and Illustrated by Jon Klassen, A Critical Discussion 8
          Cited Works 18
        Section 2: An Interview with Jon Klassen 20
        Section 3: *This Is Not My Hat*, Writing Exercises 27
          Exercise A – Multi-Modal Stories 27
          Exercise B – Using Spreads 28

Chapter Two 29
        Section 1: *Dave Pigeon*, Written by Swapna Haddow and Illustrated by Sheena Dempsey, A Critical Discussion 30
          Cited Works 41
        Section 2: An Interview with Swapna Haddow 43
        Section 3: *Dave Pigeon*, Writing Exercises 48
          Exercise A – Pacy Plots 48
          Exercise B – Plot Engines: Character Goal, Internal Desire Fuelling Outward Action 49
          Exercise C – Plot Impediments, the Forces of Antagonism 49
          Exercise D – Writing Funny through Unlikely Metaphor 50

Chapter Three 51
        Section 1: *The Strangeworlds Travel Agency* by L.D. Lapinski, A Critical Discussion 52
          Cited Works 61

Section 2: An Interview with L.D. Lapinski 63
Section 3: *The Strangeworlds Travel Agency*, Writing Exercises 69
  Exercise A – Emotional World-building 69
  Exercise B – Revealing Character (after Anderson) 70
  Exercise C – Action! 70
  Exercise D – Psychic Distance 71

Chapter Four 73

Section 1: *October, October* by Katya Balen, A Critical Discussion 74
  Cited Works 83
Section 2: An Interview with Katya Balen 85
Section 3: *October, October*, Writing Exercises 91
  Exercise A – Rhetorical Devices 91
  Exercise B – Symbolism 92
  Exercise C – Word Archaeology 92

Chapter Five 95

Section 1: *Other Words for Home* by Jasmine Warga, A Critical Discussion 96
  Cited Works 106
Section 2: An Interview with Jasmine Warga 107
Section 3: *Other Words For Home*, Writing Exercises 113
  Exercise A – Narrative Verse 113
  Exercise B – The Character's Questions 114
  Exercise C – The Eyes of a Child 114
  Exercise D – Transnational Creativity 115

Chapter Six 117

Section 1: *When The World Was Ours* by Liz Kessler, A Critical Discussion 118
  Cited Works 127
Section 2: An Interview with Liz Kessler 128
Section 3: *When the World Was Ours*, Writing Exercises 135
  Exercise A – Whose Story? 135
  Exercise B – The Author's Positionality 136
  Exercise C – History and Peritext 137

CONTENTS

Chapter Seven 139
    Section 1: *The Knife of Never Letting Go* by Patrick Ness,
    A Critical Discussion 140
        Cited Works 149
    Section 2: An Interview with Patrick Ness 151
        Cited Work 156
    Section 3: *The Knife of Never Letting Go*, Writing Exercises 157
        Exercise A – Genre Tropes 157
        Exercise B – High Concept Premise 158
        Exercise C – A Guiding Principle 158

Chapter Eight 161
    Section 1: *Ace of Spades* by Faridah Àbíké-Íyímídé,
    A Critical Discussion 162
        Cited Works 171
    Section 2: An Interview with Faridah Àbíké-Íyímídé 173
    Section 3: *Ace of Spades*, Writing Exercises 179
        Exercise A – Narrative Channels 179
        Exercise B – Symbolic Palette 180
        Exercise C – Juggling Conflict to Maintain Tension 181

Bibliography 182
Index 188

Permissions Page

Copyright © 2012 Jon Klassen from *This Is Not My Hat*. Written and illustrated by Jon Klassen. Reproduced by permission of Walker Books Ltd, London SE11 5HJ www.walker.co.uk.

The extract from *Dave Pigeon* by Swapna Haddow is reproduced by kind permission of Faber and Faber Ltd: © Swapna Haddow 2016.

The extract from *The Strangeworlds Travel Agency* by L.D. Lapinski is reproduced by kind permission of Hachette Children's Group: © L.D. Lapinski 2020.

The extract from *October, October* by Katya Balen is reproduced by kind permission of Bloomsbury Publishing (World Rights excluding USA, Canada, and Philippines): © Katya Balen, 2021, *October, October*, Bloomsbury Publishing Plc. The extract from *October, October* by Katya Balen (USA, Canada, and Philippines) is reproduced by kind permission of Katya Balen and Felicity Bryan Associates: © Katya Balen 2020.

The extract from *Other Words for Home* by Jasmine Warga is reproduced by kind permission of HarperCollins: © Jasmine Warga 2019.

The extract from *When The World Was Ours* by Liz Kessler is reproduced by kind permission of Liz Kessler and Felicity Bryan Associates: © Liz Kessler 2021.

Text © 2008 Patrick Ness from *The Knife of Never Letting Go Written* by Patrick Ness. Reproduced by permission of Walker Books Ltd, London SE11 5HJ www.walker.co.uk.

The extract from *Ace of Spades* by Faridah Àbíké-Íyímídé is reproduced by kind permission of Usborne: © Faridah Àbíké-Íyímídé 2021.

Introduction

When I began my Master's in Creative Writing for Young People, way back in 2006, it's fair to say that I got in on the ground floor. I was part of only the second cohort to take the specialist degree at Bath Spa University, and that degree was one of only a small handful available in the UK. At that time there was only Bath Spa and Winchester, plus the option to study writing for young people as a pathway at Nottingham Trent and Manchester Met. Professor Julia Green, the Bath Spa Course Director, recalls, 'There was a sense that we were all breaking new ground, carving out a space for writing for young people in university settings, taking it seriously as an area for academic study' (Green 2023:3). For a new student – me – it seemed like the space we were carving out was made of granite and I had only a plastic fork to dig with. I was returning to university after working in bars and cinemas (and even as a museum security guard) I was regularly overwhelmed.

I remember reading the textbooks we'd been assigned and crying over them. I didn't understand them. And no wonder. They were the piecemeal texts of a brand-new discipline, drawn from English Literature, from Childhood Studies, from Cultural Studies, from Education. Wonderful, cognate fields all. But not fields that are easy to leap into without an undergraduate degree to give you a solid foundation.

And so, for the most part, my peers and I grabbed at the novels on our set text lists and devoured those instead. Creative Writing is, after all, a practical field and we turned to practitioners as our models. In seminars, we discussed how scenes had been constructed, how characters fashioned from nothing but artfully arranged typeface. It was alchemy. I vividly remember reading the scene in *Northern Lights* where Iorek Byrnison battles for supremacy of the bears, and marvelling over the sentence structure, the choice of words; we pointed such wonders out to each other in the seminar, desperate to learn the dark art ourselves. In time, this attentive reading, which I now know as 'reading-as-a-writer', has come to be a foundational methodology of Creative Writing for Young People, as it has been in the wider field of Creative Writing.

But, in time too, I have come to value the role literary studies, childhood studies, and our other academic cousins, can play. By having theoretical lenses through which to consider our writing, we get closer to saying exactly what it is we hope to say. We communicate better. The theory that felt unwieldy and overwhelming twenty years ago is being assimilated into the field in a way which feels generative and productive. It's offering the best of what it means to be interdisciplinary; we listen, we learn, and we turn our insights into more thoughtful art. I'm seeing this in PhD projects and in the wonderful papers presented at Creative Writing conferences, as well as in the art that is being produced by writers inside and outside the academy. Writers for young people are engaging with Creative Writing theory (for example, narrative theory, technical theory and so on), but I've also seen post-humanism, feminism, artificial intelligence, Gothicism, ideas about the Anthropocene – and so much more – work in service to creative writing. And the art is better for it.

Which leads me to this book. I am, above all, a creative writer. My main readership is young people. But I am also a writing teacher. I do that in university settings. And I wanted a book that I would be able to share with students that uses our primary methodologies, but also makes room for other lenses, where they are useful, where they can help us to be better writers. I wanted a book that stood on the now not-so-newly broken ground and offered a cartography of it that makes sense to creative writers for young people. You're reading the results of that now. I read-as-a-writer, but also, where it feels useful and generative, as an artist, I ask the neighbours in other fields if I can borrow their tools for a bit, to bring in the current debates, concerns and theories concerning the cultures of childhood and young adulthood.

I struggled to decide on a voice for this book. Am I more artist or academic in this endeavour? Should I use the prose style that is my natural writing voice? Should I adopt the academic voice that I found so impenetrable all those years ago? I wavered between the two, neither feeling quite right for the project at hand. Then, I remembered that I have a third voice, a teacherly voice. I have been consciously trying to bring my whole self into my classrooms over the past few years: to be funny and encouraging when needed, but not avoid jargon and technical terms when they are the correct way to describe something (and I have delivered sufficient context for it to be understood). So, in this book, you'll find a lot of the 'I' voice. Everything is just my opinion, after all; it's what I think – and you are welcome to disagree with me on any point. But I also try to frame things as I would if I were talking to a keen student who might need to use these terms confidently themself one day.

I intend that the structure of this book acknowledges some of these tensions.

Each chapter is divided into three parts: a critical discussion, an interview and exercises. The critical discussion takes an extract from a book and takes

INTRODUCTION

a deep dive into the writing techniques used, the wider context in which the art sits, and how those things might influence the other. These sections use the tools of the academy: I cite my sources, I refer deferentially to everyone by their surname; it's here that I use the academic methodologies of close reading, reading-as-a-writer and imbricated (woven in) theory. I follow this with an interview with an author. In these sections, I'm a curious artist, being given the opportunity to ask questions of someone I admire; these sections are natural conversations with only some of the 'umms' and 'ahhs' taken out. Finally, each section ends with a set of exercises for you, the reader, to try. Because, at the end of the day, writers learn by writing. Praxis – *doing* – is the ultimate methodology in our discipline; we write. Every time we write, we learn something and everything we learn feeds into our next piece of writing. I hope that this book is practical as well as theoretical.

The books I've chosen to discuss are varied in terms of their audience and genre; the authors are varied in terms of their backgrounds, their career paths so far and their geography. However, there are some limitations to the choices made that I want to address.

The books I've chosen are all well-known in the anglosphere because they are published by major houses with international reach. In one sense, this is good, the works shouldn't be too hard for readers to access if they want to consult the original. The drawback – and it's a big one – is that emergent book markets aren't well represented and authors with a more localized reach are absent. I felt that my level of expertise is insufficient to do justice to work produced in settings and circumstances with which I'm unfamiliar. In the future, a more collaborative edited work might be possible to harness the insights from local and regional writing. The same is true for books in translation; there are none present in this volume. Again, this is my limitation; I don't feel qualified to talk about the decision-making processes of translators rather than original writers.

Other limitations have come about through happenstance. I have selected up to 300 words from my chosen texts and I have to limit myself to the topics that can be discussed using those extracts. So, historical fiction is represented here, but romance is not. I've been able to discuss portal fantasy, but magical realism hasn't got a look-in. I am also, far too often, only able to gesture at the existence of a theory or issue, rather than exhaustively explore its various facets, which would be possible were word count no object. To return to the metaphor of the cartographer, I am sketching the outlines of the major landmarks; street view just isn't possible within the scope of this book. I hope that, having been made aware of a technique or theory that interests you, the cited works lists will help you seek out that extra degree of granularity.

I'm also a writer with my own positionality; I have personal tastes that shape what I look for in a text. I have a personal history and set of biases that influence what I see in a text. As I discuss each extract my own particular train of thought will move in a direction influenced by my own writerly concerns. I am fascinated by the narrator, for example, and maybe talk one (or two) too many times about psychic distance. I am particularly interested in social justice issues; a different critic might have chosen to foreground other critical lenses: the ecocritical, the psychogeographic, the economic, or dozens of others. As you read, there may be elements of context, technique or style that leap out to you that I fail to mention. Only know that while I may aim for comprehensiveness, I know that I will fall short.

A final limitation I fear is that this book might prove just as overwhelming to new writers in the academy as the textbooks I read in the 2000s. I hope it won't, but it is a possibility. I fear this because I have heard students say, as they analyse a text, 'this isn't what I'm thinking about when I write'. So, I want to say now, loud and clear, that this isn't what *anyone* thinks about when they write. We might feel that the scene needs more emotion, but we won't – necessarily – think 'I need to adjust the degree of psychic distance to close-in.' As we write we might feel that something is a bit off with our world-building, but we won't – necessarily – think, 'The positionality of my narrator is too ethnographic and that problematizes their relationship with the experience.' We just don't think in these ways as we're mid-flow. However, I do believe that being able to 'code switch' between these different ways of thinking does make us better writers. It's just that the analytical thinking might come later, with the edits. Or maybe it isn't visible to us at all, it might simply settle in our unconscious, helping, silently, to shape what we make. The difference between English Literature and Creative Writing, as disciplines, is that the text is fixed in English Literature, whereas in Creative Writing it is still mutable, changeable, alive, and so can grow and change in response to the stimuli we writers subject ourselves too. It's organic. So, I hope that these discussions, interviews and exercises will be interesting stimuli that help your work grow in interesting new ways.

There are eight chapters in this book.

We begin with a modern-classic picturebook in Chapter 1 with a deep dive (pun intended!) into the murky waters of *This Is Not My Hat* by Canadian writer-illustrator Jon Klassen. We find that the structures in both the images and the text support an understanding of childhood as just one stage in the ageing process. This is a position Jon puts warmly in our interview.

In Chapter 2, we consider archetypes and postmodernism as drivers of comedy for readers wanting easily digestible pleasure from their Early Readers. The subject of the discussion is *Dave Pigeon* written by New Zealand-based writer Swapna Haddow and illustrated by Sheena Dempsey. This is followed by our interview in which Swapna shares her path to publication.

British writer L.D. Lapinsky's debut novel, *The Strangeworlds Travel Agency*, comes under discussion in Chapter 3. We take a closer look at middle grade writing, adultification and how working-class joy might serve as a strategy of resistance. But we also consider how colonialism might be inevitably linked to the portal fantasy. L.D. takes on this question with huge insight in our interview.

We stay with a British writer in Chapter 4, with Katya Balen and *October, October*. In this chapter we consider how poetic and rhetorical devices can work in tandem with ecological themes and how that might reflect or subvert ideas of Romantic childhoods. In our interview, Katya suggests how leaning into her weaknesses makes her a better writer.

We turn to verse novels in Chapter 5 and American writer Jasmine Warga's *Other Words for Home*. There are important stylistic decisions under discussion, taking a closer look at both the 'verse' and the 'novel' sides of the coin. I also explore transnational writing and how powerful the image of the threshold can be in writing for young people. In our conversation, Jasmine shares how finding the voice was the key to writing the book.

In Chapter 6, we age up to teen/YA fiction with British writer Liz Kessler's historical novel *When the World Was Ours*. With this text, we have the opportunity to discuss how peritextual elements shape our reading, the compromises historical writers might decide to make and the duty that comes from writing about material that is close to home. Liz generously shares some of her thoughts on this in our interview.

Our second modern classic is the fantasy coming-of-age novel *The Knife of Never Letting Go* by American author Patrick Ness. We see the tight relationship between characterization and world-building in our discussion of the text and how a high-concept premise can be a rolling snowball creatively. Patrick picks up on this and discusses writing truth, even in fantasy, in our interview.

Finally, we end with another debut. This time, *Ace of Spades* by British author Faridah Àbíké-Íyímídé. In this chapter, we consider how Dark Academia can be critiqued from within and how conflict is used to create a page-turner. In our interview, Faridah shares her thoughts on writing intersectional LGBTQ+ characters.

We often hear that writers are like magpies, with the aphorism 'good writers borrow, great writers steal' ascribed to all the usual witty suspects. We take the bits that are useful and use them to expand or undergird our art. I hope that this book serves that function for as many readers as possible. Take what's useful. Write.

Cited Work

Green, J. 2023, 'On Writing for Young People Conference 2023, Keynote Speech', *Leaf Journal*, vol. 1, no. 2, pp. 1–8.

Chapter One

SECTION 1: *THIS IS NOT MY HAT*, WRITTEN AND ILLUSTRATED BY JON KLASSEN, A CRITICAL DISCUSSION

Note: this chapter contains spoilers for *This Is Not My Hat*.

We are going to begin at the beginning, with the sort of book that often represents a child's first encounter with literature: the picturebook. This is a warm and cosy place to start. We can imagine a child tucked in the crook of a grown-up's arm, sharing the delight, thrill or intrigue of a story, gasping at the danger and giggling at the jokes.

But beginning here, with picturebooks, offers a couple of additional benefits. First, it allows me to structure this book chronologically, following the development of young readers from infancy through to young adulthood – this is a very common way that university courses on children's books are structured too. Second, it allows me to demonstrate how reading-as-a-writer can work as a methodology using some very *obvious* structures – the shapes, colours and textures of *illustrations* as well as words. When I point something out and say 'this shape here', it is clear what I'm talking about. If I began with the written word, without laying this groundwork, it might not be so obvious what I mean when I say 'this structure here' (as I will in subsequent chapters). So, we're killing two birds with one stone … or catching two fish with one net, perhaps.

Because our first text is the wonderful picturebook *This Is Not My Hat* by Jon Klassen, which is a dramatic tale of two fish foes. This is Klassen's second picturebook as a writer-illustrator, although he had illustrated books for other writers previously. *This Is Not My Hat* is the story of a little fish (unnamed in the text, but henceforth Little Fish and gendered as male, by me, following the interview with Klassen), a self-delusional fish, who has stolen a hat from a big fish (henceforth Big Fish) and hopes to get away with the crime. Little Fish maintains a monologue as he flees, attempting to convince perhaps us, perhaps himself, that he will evade justice. Meanwhile, the reader is aware, Big Fish is moving inexorably towards Little Fish. He will, by the picturebook's end, have caught up with Little Fish and given in to the temptation of vigilante justice in reclaiming his hat. The fate of Little Fish happens off-stage but is not – we assume – good.

In this chapter, we will look closely at a double-page spread from the picturebook, reproduced below, drawing in additional supporting elements from elsewhere in the text, as needed.

FIGURE 1 Spread Twelve from *This Is Not My Hat* © Jon Klassen 2012.

This is a double-page spread from *This Is Not My Hat*. A spread is the term used to indicate both the verso (left-hand page) and the recto (right-hand page) when a book is open. It is crucial to think in spreads when writing a picturebook because the child reader is likely not following the printed text, as an adult might, from top-left to bottom-right. Instead, freed from having to read, their eyes rove across the whole page, taking in all the details at once. This fact has narrative implications that a writer must bear in mind. For example, there would be no point in setting up a visual gag on the verso if the punchline is displayed on the recto – the joke would be spoiled by the too-early reveal.

This goes some way to explaining why I have used the compound spelling 'picturebook' so far in this chapter, rather than 'picture book' (which my word processing programme insists is correct). I am led in this preference by Nikki Gamble (2019:187), herself influenced by Lewis (2001). The compound spelling acknowledges that the pictures and the text are indivisible in picturebooks; the story is told multi-modally, with the images and words contributing discrete elements to the overall narrative. More than these two modes, however, there is also a potential adult mediator present – the parent, carer or teacher sitting alongside our imagined child audience – reading the story aloud. That adult might be 'doing the voices', creating an audio element; they might be interruptible, allowing the child to ask questions and explore the book as they might a sandbox game; they might ask the child questions as they read, inviting commentary or collusion as the story is curated between them. The compound noun is intended to go some way towards acknowledging the hinterland of image, text, sound, performer, audience and associated paratextual elements that are all *picturebook*. Karen Coats (2017:150) goes even further, to include 'the weight, sheen, and texture of the paper … even the smell of the ink … constitute … the "ecology" of the picturebook experience'.

Much of this ecology is outside a writer's control. We can't insist that the adult reading the book to a child must welcome interruptions. It is unlikely – if we are working with a publishing house – that we will have much input into the way the book looks or is laid out. We can't influence the paper weight or ink quality in subsequent reprints or editions. So, although we acknowledge the ecology, we can't insist it is as we would create it were we in complete artistic and publishing control. However, Jon Klassen, as a *writer-illustrator*, has a higher degree of creative control than a writer alone would have. So, let's look more closely at the ecology of *This Is Not My Hat*.

The spread we are looking at is spread number twelve of sixteen. It is unusual to have sixteen spreads in a picturebook. A much more common number is twelve. This is because, in manufacturing, a picturebook is typically made of two signatures. A signature is one large piece of paper folded and cut to create sixteen sides. So, typically, a picturebook is made up of two signatures glued together to make thirty-two pages. Many of these pages are unavailable to the writer – they are reserved for the title page, the copyright page and so on. It is safest to assume twelve spreads are available when crafting a picturebook story. However, *This Is Not My Hat* needed an extra half-sheet, taking it to 2.5 signatures, or sixteen spreads. The reason for this need will become clear over the course of this discussion.

As we discuss this spread, I will follow a discourse framework proposed by Serafini (2010) who suggested that analysis of illustrated text could best be achieved by considering three concentric circles of conceptual ideas: perception; structural and ideological. This is to say, as we look at a picturebook text we should ask: what can we see; what might the perceived objects mean when positioned in relation to each other, and what ideas or beliefs do these meanings imply more generally? As Serafini states, these lenses are shifting and interlocking ways of discussing the text. Ultimately, a picturebook is always more than the sum of its parts. So, with that warning in mind, let's ask: what can we perceive in the double-page spread shown in Figure 1?

As an adult reader, my eye initially skimmed the page until it alighted on the written text. The words, 'I knew I was going to make it', are positioned centrally at the top of the recto page, inside a cream stripe; this forms a kind of banner. The words are written in a serif font called Century Schoolbook, a quite traditional-looking choice.

Below this banner is an image of an underwater scene. Having read the words, my eye returned to the image, moving, as I have been conditioned to do by years of reading, from left to right. The watery background is a matt black. On the verso, Big Fish's head is in view, in profile; the one eye we can see is narrowed, the black pupil (with no iris) is positioned forward. Moving across the spread, we see stems of underwater plants, growing vertically from the bottom of the page to the banner. Initially, the stems are positioned a few centimetres apart. But as we move over the gutter – the middle of the spread where the folded page drops into the book's spine – the stems multiply until they form a kind of underwater forest. Each stem is translucent, having the texture of something like tissue paper. The leaves on the stems are a regular oval shape, although they vary in size and colour. In the midst of the stems, on the recto, we can see Little Fish, again, in profile. His head has disappeared into the foliage. The shape and colour of his body and tail mimic the surrounding leaves. Streaming out behind Little Fish is a series of white dots, indicating bubbles. I have found, in seminars over the years, that asking students to slow down and clearly articulate what they can see on a page is an essential first step before they can analyse what it all might mean.

So, having observed the page closely, we can move to the next concentric circle: structures and their co-constructed meaning. Nikki Gamble (2019:193–6) offers a useful list of structural features to consider when analysing picturebooks, citing the influence of William Moebius and Jane Doonan. Gamble suggests a structural analysis that takes in: colour; light and dark; lines; frames; shape; perspective; position; and size. I will consider each structure in turn and suggest some potential readings based on my own frames of reference. I am only one reader, when all is said and done, and throughout the course of this book, my positionality as a white, British woman, in comfortable middle age, who has spent time working as a writer and in academia, will inevitably affect what I see. There is no such thing as a universal reading of a text or a universal reader, and you may find that you would have picked out different structures and meanings. This is one of the joys of discussing books and is to be welcomed.

Gamble's suggested list of structures begins with colour, and Jon Klassen's choice of colour palette is arguably one of the defining features of his style. Klassen works in earth tones: rock greys and muted browns and greens; he has said that he 'has a fear of colour' and doesn't know what to do with it (Klassen 2023, August 21). On the face of it, Klassen's unwillingness to use bright colours should have been an impediment to his success. As Winner (1982:114, quoted in Coats 2017:161) states, 'children up to age eight or nine tend to prefer fully saturated, high-contrast colours'. So, there is something counterintuitive happening. The colours in Klassen's work are reminiscent of Scandinavian design; homes with pale grey furniture and cream rugs where a dropped juice carton invites permanent stains – spaces, then, in which children might not feel welcome. And yet, Klassen's picturebooks regularly spend months in the *New York Times* bestseller charts. So, what's going on?

Gamble suggests that colour is used to create atmosphere and mood. Here, the black background and the translucent, earthy shades combine to create a sombre, serious atmosphere. It's possible that the novelty of this palette – so different to the primary colours more usually associated with young children – affords a welcome sense of sophistication and maturity to the picturebook. It feels special in its oddness and Klassen is making a virtue of his (self-identified!) shortcomings.

The line-work also references the homely or domestic. The edges of each line have the softness and irregularity of a novice mark-maker – a six-year-old wielding a thick paintbrush, maybe. The texture of the forms has the transparency and variation of something like a potato print. A child might, perhaps, get the false impression that this is simple work. The illustration style leaves me with a delicious impression of work that is both sophisticated and handmade.

This tension between two states continues in Klassen's use of light and dark. The clearest delineation of light and dark in this spread is the sharp border between the banner and the illustration – it severs the page. However, it does so 4–5 centimetres below the horizontal top of the spread. The separation of light and dark leaves us with two distinct 'frames'. The upper frame is a narrow, long rectangle. It has a cream background, with black text on its recto. This thin slice of the page is 'adult's business' – the words to be read aloud. The lower frame is much bigger, taking up the majority of the page with 'children's business' – the images to be enjoyed as the text is read by the adult.

Other layout options would have been available to Klassen. The text might have been overlaid or integrated into the image. Lauren Child, another writer-illustrator, often intersperses image and text in a much more freeform, collaged style, which can be seen in works such as *I Will Not Ever Never Eat a Tomato* (2000). Other options would have been available for the illustration too; it might have entirely filled the frame (a 'full-bleed'), or, at the other extreme, divided up into smaller 'spot' illustrations or a series of vignettes; the illustrations might have been divided into single spreads, rather than one image on a double page. Philip Pullman (2017:145) talks about 'phase space' as a useful metaphor for writers. It is a term borrowed from physics which signifies all the possible consequences of an action. As a writer, it can be a useful exercise to imagine the counterfactuals. Before Klassen arranged all these elements on the page, every alternative action was open to him in the creative 'phase space'. So, we must ask, when reading-as-writers: what consequence does the *actual choice made* have?

By filling the full lower frame of a double-page spread, Klassen slows the pace of the narrative. The audience has to take their time, absorbing the full implications of a single image. The choice to so cleanly delineate image and text is also reminiscent of educational books and beginning readers, where the text is presented separately from the image which it may accurately describe, offering clarity and so helping the child learn to read. The choice Klassen made ultimately gives the narrative a degree of gravitas: we are to take these events very seriously.

We have considered colour, contrast, lines and frames. Next on Gamble's list comes shapes.

The shapes in this spread are dominated by the oval: the fishes, the eye and the leaves. It is a repeating, harmonious shape that evokes the organic rather than the machine-made. It is also a child-friendly shape – a basic drawing of a flower, done by a non-professional, would likely use this shape for the petals and leaves. Again, we are seeing the deceptive simplicity.

However, the shapes aren't just there to create pleasing patterns; they convey meaning. They require that children draw on their mental model of the world, acquired through board books, baby books, and other two-dimensional images, to infer that these are representational shapes imbued with narrative purpose. This is a huge conceptual task demanded of our youngest readers. We are asking them to understand that this stone-coloured oval is intended to be a representation of an actual fish; moreover, that this stone-coloured oval is a fish with emotions and motivations that power it to act, to become a character in a story. It is a leap of wonderful complexity.

The relative size of the ovals adds another dimension of storytelling – there is a big oval (Big Fish) and a little oval (Little Fish). This difference in size reflects a difference in power dynamic. Big Fish is likely to be stronger than Little Fish; size and strength tend to correlate, and size is a handy heuristic for power. This reading, of a powerful big fish, is reinforced by the position of the ovals in the spread – typically objects in the top left of a page are understood to be dominant and objects lower down or further to the right are understood to be subservient (Gamble 2019:195).

So, we have met our characters in a sombre environment and deduced a power imbalance between them. Interpersonal and physical conflict is suggested. Having made the leap to associate the shape with a specific meaning, a child 'reading' the ovals would deduce that Big Fish, with the fixed eye, is chasing Little Fish, who is disappearing into the weeds. Although, of course, the shapes aren't actually moving – this isn't animation. The shape of the page, in landscape orientation, invites us to 'read' movement as Big Fish swims into view. The scatter of white dots invites us to 'read' bubbles as Little Fish hurries to hide. Both of these fish are moving in a linear fashion a short distance apart.

This conflict is, we realize, a hunting scene.

With this realization, the additional ovals – the leaves – now take on added narrative meaning. They are not decorative, they are the stage for the action. They might be a place for the thief to evade justice (if you are rooting for Big Fish), or they might be a place to hide and keep safe (if you are rooting for Little Fish).

A child 'reading' the page would absorb all these structures in a matter of moments: the relationship between line and colour, shape and size, creating a narrative. The adult, reading the text aloud, adds multi-modal complexity to that visual narrative.

So, let us turn to the written words, with the knowledge that they would most likely be spoken aloud – at least the first time the audience meets the picturebook,

I knew I was going to make it.

We will meet an internal narrator many times in the course of the coming chapters; it is a common technique. Gérard Genette (Genette 1980[1976], quoted in Walsh 1997) calls this a homodiegetic narrative, in which the narrator both tells and experiences their own story, moving between these modes of being as the story progresses. This style of narration will use the first-person ('I') point of view.

However, I will stick to the term 'internal narrator', because the mode in which Little Fish narrates his own story is somewhat slippery; he doesn't move between 'tell' and 'experience'. Rather, he uses a dramatic monologue 'speaking' these words. What is less clear is who he is speaking to. It could be that, despite the lack of speech marks, he is speaking the words aloud, and that the child and the adult reading the picturebook are the intended recipients of the speech act. It's possible he is aware of his audience (we will see this more forcefully in Chapter 2). However, the content of the speech leads me to conclude that he is *not* breaking the fourth wall. Little Fish is too desperate for those kind of postmodernist games. He is fleeing for his life, having committed a crime.

The very fact that he insists so strongly – 'I knew' – counterintuitively reveals how weak that certainty is; he is protesting too much. He is either attempting to convince himself or he is delusional. The reader knows this because we can see Big Fish's narrow eye; there is absolutely no certainty of escape here. Little Fish either does not know this or is unwilling to admit it. So, I am not convinced Little Fish is a self-aware internal narrator reporting for the benefit of an audience; rather, he is delivering a feverish, interior dramatic monologue.

I want to return here to the idea of sophistication, which we have already observed in the images and now see in the text.

This dramatic monologue is *ironic*, in that the subtext – what is not said – is the exact opposite of the text – what is said. We, as readers, are able to construct subtext from information provided earlier in the picturebook. We can use context clues to deduce that this is irony. In earlier spreads, Little Fish has followed a syntactic pattern in which he states a fact, then adds that even if that fact isn't true, then that isn't important, because of an additional fact (he then adds that this fact might not be true, and repeat, in a constant cycle of self-undermining). We know from experience that Little Fish lies to himself, and, as we are accessing his internal dramatic monologue, he lies to us. Little Fish is, therefore, an unreliable narrator: he *doesn't* know that he was going to make it, but the horror of that knowledge is too repugnant to contemplate, so it is repressed.

As well as being able to spot the unreliable narrator, the audience is also aware that the journey has always been doomed. We have been able to clearly see what the Little Fish refuses to see – he is being pursued.

To understand that the audience knows more than the narrator requires that the child audience has a 'theory of mind'. Coats (2017:67) tells us, 'Somewhere between ages three and five, children develop an early version of Theory of Mind [… which] is the ability to imagine that other people have intentions, beliefs, desires, and knowledge that may be different from your own.' In order to understand the narrative, the child has to understand that they have knowledge that is different to that held by Little Fish.

This is another kind of irony; this time dramatic irony. The audience is more aware of the truth of a situation than the characters and we, helpless to intervene, can only watch as it plays out.

The structures we have spotted contribute to a sense of menace and doom; we are Cassandras predicting Little Fish's fate.

Now, we can broaden out, away from the page, to reflect on what these observations might tell us about ideology and the final circle suggested by Serafini's discourse framework. By using the word 'ideology', I am not implying any Machiavellian brainwashing on Klassen's part. Rather, that we are all, as writers, shaped by the conscious and unconscious flows of ideas, systems and beliefs generated within the culture(s) we are part of and, in turn, these flows will enter our work. This position is put forcefully by Roland Barthes & Heath (1977:145–8), who suggests that writers 'enunciate' their texts from collages of all the culture that has gone before. However, in the discipline of Creative Writing, the author has to be anything but dead – they are the ones actively selecting between all the options of the 'phase space'. Still, I do admit that, as a writer, often the words that emerge onto the page surprise me; the 'meaning', the 'truth' of what I want to say only becomes clear when the first draft is done, and subsequent drafts are about clarifying that meaning or weeding out anything I didn't mean to say. Ideology will out.

So, ideologically speaking, when reading *This Is Not My Hat*, I am struck by the degree of respect it affords its young audience. Karen Coats (2017:10–11) sets out a range of ideologies for thinking about our ways of conceiving childhood and the art we make for young people. These range from religiously inspired ideas (children are a gift from God) to ideas from the Enlightenment (children are blank slates awaiting instruction) and more. Many of the ways of thinking we have about childhood seem to be rooted in difference – the ways that children are different from adults.

Klassen, though, is emphasizing a conception of childhood that respects the commonalities. His approach suggests a belief that children and adults have more in common than they have dividing them; most crucially, perhaps, that children are *smart*. They have the same capacities for feeling, for understanding, for comprehension and deduction as the adults reading to them – they simply lack time and the experience that time brings (he says more on this in the interview that follows). This conception of childhood has been called the 'kinship model' by Marah Gubar (2016) and posits 'that children and adults are fundamentally akin to one another, even if certain differences or deficiencies routinely attend certain parts of the aging process' (299).

When writing for young people we cannot patronize or condescend to children and expect to make art that will resonate. Klassen demonstrates here just how much a writer can expect of their child audience. The sophistication of the text can be extended to incorporate the sophistication of the audience. He expects a four-year-old (say) not only to be able to move from the concrete to the abstract – to see this brown oval on a dark background and realize this is a story about a fish – but also to intuit that the text, subtext and irony coalesce to create an impressively complex story about a self-aggrandizing fish, doomed from the outset.

This picturebook also implies, to me, that Klassen has an awareness of the role he has as an educator of children. Not, as one might expect, to provide a *moral* education, but rather to offer them a first introduction to their birthright, which is to say *all* of art, literature and culture. He is teaching them to be what Gibson (2010:108) calls a 'knowing reader', someone who is 'drawing on Western notions of "cultural capital"' (Bourdieu 1984, quoted in Gibson 2010:108).

To understand *This Is Not My Hat* the child needs to know how dramatic irony – and a myriad of other literary devices, such as monologue, characterization and suspense – works. This is where Klassen does make concessions to a potential lack of experience of his young audience. As I pointed out earlier, this picturebook is unusually long; it has an extra half-signature. This is because there are five double-page spreads in Act 1 of the book that offer an opportunity to practise comprehension of dramatic irony. In these spreads, Little Fish predicts what Big Fish is doing (sleeping, not noticing his hat is missing, not knowing who took it …) and the images show us that Big Fish is actually doing the exact opposite of Little Fish's predictions. If a child has not encountered dramatic irony before, Klassen takes the time to demonstrate it more than once. In this way, picturebooks can serve as a gateway, opening up access to the wider landscape of literature in years to come (I often say that Booker Prize Winners should thank picturebook writers in their acceptance speeches; it is in childhood that the readers of the future are commonly made).

The adult, reading aloud to our imagined child, can ask questions, or prompt the child, to see whether or not they have understood the literary device and provide more context if it is needed. In this way, the picturebook offers scaffolding to allow adults and children to have a shared cultural experience, perhaps a shared emotional experience if the picturebook is especially funny, or scary or sad.

Although we have the adult mediator in mind, I want to consider the ideological implications of Klassen's choice of genre for a moment. *This Is Not My Hat* bears the genre hallmarks of a horror, or a revenge thriller. We meet the protagonist, after a heist, fleeing the scene with a greater power in pursuit. As Klassen says (see the interview later in the chapter), it is a premise that owes a debt to both Hitchcock's *Psycho* and Poe's *The Tell-Tale Heart*. As I've intimated, readers will bring their own idiosyncratic range of cultural and social expectations to a text. Child readers are unlikely to have experienced Hitchcock or Poe, and so the intertextual allusion (the way in which the meaning of the text is changed because of an awareness of its relationship to another text) will pass them by; whether the adult reader will notice is dependent on how much of a film buff or Gothic-lover they are. But for those who *do* notice, the text will take on an added frisson of pleasure. This picturebook takes the time to offer something to the adults too (a point Swapna Haddow also makes in her interview in Chapter 2).

Whether a specific audience notices the genre roots of this picturebook, it does demonstrate the range of genres available to a picturebook writer: from kitchen-sink drama, to sci-fi and fantasy, to thriller, there is likely a way to interpret the tropes and conventions for our youngest readers and so welcome them into a conception of childhood that acknowledges commonalities, their shared humanity and shared cultural significance.

This won't be the aim of every writer for young people, of course. As Coats suggests, there are many conceptions of childhood. Gibson (2010:104) posits that there will be tension between the role of picturebooks as an artistic endeavour and the perceived needs and competencies of young readers. We have seen how Klassen offers an opportunity to young readers to expand their cultural competencies with the repetition of the more challenging literary devices. However, I also want to consider the question of what might be meant by the 'perceived needs' of young readers. For a long time, the story goes, children's books served a didactic or moralistic purpose before evolving into a form of entertainment (Rudd 2010; Coats 2017). A more recent turn suggests that 'hope' is a new 'perceived need' when writing for young people, a need as identified by the decision-making adults (Lee 2023, and Warga interview in Chapter 5). This linear history risks flattening the complexity of what children's books are 'for' (Rudd 2010; Coats 2017). Different books from the same period might offer moral or social education or entertainment; one author might favour didacticism over entertainment (and vice versa) with different books in their career, publishing houses might curate their list with adult sensibilities in mind (in the UK, for example, Nosy Crow's unique selling point (USP) is that their books are both 'child-friendly' and 'parent-friendly' (Nosy Crow, 2024)).

When we look at *This Is Not My Hat*, the morality offered is ambiguous. Is it saying don't steal? Or, completely conversely, is it asking us to root for thieves? Is it saying the world tends towards justice? Or, completely conversely, is it saying vigilante violence is inevitable? Is it saying we're doomed before we begin? Yes. Yes, to all of those positions; an audience could come to all these conclusions and more about the morality of the text. If the reader keeps turning the page, beyond our spread, they come to a scene where both fish are hidden in the weeds and then only Big Fish emerges, wearing his hat. What happened in the weeds? There is one witness – a crab – but he looks on wordless. The audience is required to come to their own conclusion about the fate of Little Fish.

The fact that Klassen uses animals as his characters contributes to this moral ambiguity. Imagine for a moment a counterfactual visit the 'phase space', where the picturebook is about two children instead, one of whom has stolen a toy and runs into the bushes to hide; then, the victim of the theft emerges from the bushes, holding the toy, and the thief isn't seen again. Suddenly, the vigilante violence is foregrounded in a way which is less entertaining and considerably more uncomfortable. The choice to use anthropomorphic fish allows for more latitude when it comes to deviant behaviour. Which, in turn, allows us to be more open-minded about the rights and wrongs of the whole situation.

With that, let's leave Little Fish swimming into the weeds, his fate, as yet, not a completely foregone conclusion.

Cited Works

Barthes, R. and Heath, S. 1977, *Image, Music, Text*, Fontana, London.
Child, L. 2000, *I Will Not Ever Never Eat a Tomato*, Orchard Books, London.
Coats, K. 2017, *The Bloomsbury Introduction to Children's and Young Adult Literature*, Bloomsbury Publishing, London.
Gamble, N. 2019, *Exploring Children's Literature: Reading for Knowledge, Understanding and Pleasure*, 4th edn, SAGE Publications, London.
Gibson, M. 2010, 'Picturebooks, Comics and Graphic Novels' in *The Routledge Companion to Children's Literature*, ed. D. Rudd, Routledge, Abingdon; New York, pp. 100–11.
Gubar, M. 2016, 'The Hermeneutics of Recuperation: What a Kinship-Model Approach to Children's Agency Could Do for Children's Literature and Childhood Studies', *Jeunesse: Young People, Texts, Cultures*, vol. 8, no. 1, pp. 291–310.
Klassen, J. 2012, *This Is Not My Hat*, Walker Books, London.
Klassen, J. 2023, *Jon Klassen in Conversation with Peter Lord*.

Lee, C. 2023, 'More than Just a Thing with Feathers: The Importance of Hope in Middle Grade Fiction', *Leaf Journal*, vol. 1, no. 1, pp. 1–10.

Lewis, D. 2001, *Reading Contemporary Picturebooks: Picturing Text*, Routledge, London.

Nosy Crow, *Nosy Crow About Us*. Available: https://nosycrow.com/about-us/ [2024, Apr 10].

Pullman, P. 2017, *Daemon Voices*, David Fickling Books, Oxford.

Rudd, D. ed. 2010, *The Routledge Companion to Children's Literature*, Routledge, Abingdon; New York.

Serafini, F. 2010, 'Reading Multimodal Texts: Perceptual, Structural and Ideological Perspectives', *Children's Literature in Education*, vol. 41, no. 2, pp. 85–104.

Walsh, R. 1997, 'Who Is the Narrator?', *Poetics Today*, vol. 18, no. 4, pp. 495–513.

SECTION 2: AN INTERVIEW WITH JON KLASSEN

ELEN: Could you start perhaps by talking a little bit about the Hat trilogy and where this one sits? Did it feel like a middle child?

JON: No, it didn't. Well, that's a nice analogy, because I wonder how many middle children are purposefully middle children, or whether they thought they were the last child? The reason it turned out to be a trilogy was simply because I'd sold three books to Candlewick, my publisher. I thought we were going to make two more books with the same animals and the same kind of setup as *I Want My Hat Back*. I really liked those animals. I was very comfortable with them, and I liked the place that it made in my head.

And I tried ... I think I almost liked that first book too much. I just ended up with copies of it: the rhythm of it; the way the animals interacted; the page turns and everything.

It reached the point where I would send in, you know, versions of those books to my editor and my art director and then take them down [criticize them] in the same email. I'd be sending these roughs [draft artwork], which were pretty involved – I don't like to send things until they're pretty far along – and so, I'd have basically a complete book and I'd send it to them and say, 'This is crap I don't like it.' I had done this enough times that they finally came back to me and said, 'You don't have to make a book with those characters. Don't force it if you're not feeling good about it.' My art director put it like, 'If you want to go somewhere else, you should try to go somewhere else.'

That for some reason made me think I should go somewhere very far away. And for some reason in my mind, underwater is the opposite of above water ... it just made sense that I would do something reversed.

I thought: *we should reverse everything about the book.* If *I Want My Hat Back* is dark characters on a light background, put me somewhere completely different, and let's do light characters on a dark background – a black background, even. I thought of deep underwater. It was all organic like that, you know ...

The first one I gave them was a story about a gang of fish. It was called *Ten Bad Fish*. And they rode into town (which is just them riding through the weeds). The first thing they do in the book is to steal a little fish's hat, just to establish that they are up to no good, but also just to sort of nod to the last book. I thought it was a cute idea. And they terrorize and make fun of sequentially bigger and bigger fish and animals in the book until they wake up a very big fish. They realize right away that they've gone too far. So, they head back and the big fish behind them is silently eating them one by one as they go; so it's six bad fish, five bad fish, four bad fish, until the very last beat of the book is one bad fish with his little blue hat on that he stole at the beginning of the book. And it's a wordless last beat; you turn the page, and the book is over. You know on that beat, he will be eaten. And I sent it to the publisher, and I thought: *you know, there's something in thi*s. But it's feeling pretty mean right now. It's just a bunch of jerks riding into town and being eaten by an even bigger jerk or at least it is, as far as we can tell. The whole thing just paints a picture of a very miserable place. But I thought: *there's something here.*

And the editor said, 'Well, what is your favourite part of the book?'

And I said, 'Honestly, it's at the end, when there's just one little fish and one big fish. It's a very clean premise. And I like it visually. Even when he [big fish] is not on screen, I think it's the most fun when he's just back there and we know he's back there.'

And she said, 'I agree, it's a very heavy book right now. If that's funny to you, if you think there's something in that, then just open up that last beat.'

For some reason, writing is the hardest part for me. What I'd found in the first book was a way in through dialogue. I could write a dialogue, and I didn't have to write narration – I didn't have to write anything. I just had to write what they were saying. And so, I went back to that with this *Ten Bad Fish* thing. At first, they were speaking as a group, in dialogue with these other fish that they were terrorizing. And I thought: *What if we reverse that too? What if it's just a monologue?*

What if it's *The Tell-Tale Heart*, the Edgar Allan Poe story? What if it's just one fish, who's committed a crime at the beginning of the book. And he's just convincing us that there's a reason for it? And the whole time we can feel in this story – and in the Poe story – that this is over, he's finished.

But as soon as I thought of the monologue idea, the whole thing was clear, and I wrote it in the space of like twenty minutes.

It was the same with the first one. It was, like, all this Rubik's-cubing with these disastrous drafts of the book, until something clicks. Then the final version comes out, ready-made, almost, with very few changes.

I sent that twenty-minute draft off at, like, midnight. And I woke up in the morning and I read it again and I thought: *Oh my god, I've sent in* I Want My Hat Back *again*! I've sent in a book about a character who steals a hat and gets potentially eaten for it. I did the same book again. And so, I wrote to the editor before she'd had a chance to answer and I said, 'I'm so sorry. I basically sent you the same book, but with fish. Let me try again.'

And she wrote back again and said, 'Hold on, this might have something. They're very different books, Jon.'

I thought: *Are they?*

And she said, 'Yeah, you know, they're completely different viewpoints on the same action, but that's valid.'

And I didn't know any of this stuff. You know, I was new at writing and very insecure about it. I still am.

And so, it was a kind of organic accident that made it a second book. By then, *I Want My Hat Back* had begun to pick up steam, out in the world, and I think that was making me nervous too.

It's very scary to have a book ... It's one thing to have a book fail, but it's another thing to have a book succeed. And both things make you kind of nervous in different ways.

It was surprising to me, it was a shock to me, that critically it did as well as it did. We got a lot of awards and stuff for it. To me, it just felt like: *Can we land this plane?*

I wanted to land a second one to prove that the first one wasn't a fluke; that was my goal. It was just not to screw it up.

ELEN: Did it feel lighter to you? If *Ten Bad Fish* felt too mean, was this a lighter place?

JON: Yeah, it did. I think it didn't for the … Actually, I say it all came out in one piece, but there was one change that I made after the first draft. The first draft didn't have the crab in it. With the first draft, I finished it, and I roughed it out. And I thought: *This is very lonely; this giant fish is the only one who knows what happens.*

And that made me feel sad … And I have to do this beat a lot with my stories. I have to do it with illustration too where I think: *The audience is the third person here; the audience is the witness.*

If I'm sad because nobody else knows about the little fish potentially disappearing, that's not right; because the audience knows, the audience is our witness. So, I shouldn't feel sad, but for some reason, in the contained universe of the book, it just felt sad.

And so, I wanted to put someone in there mostly for the last bit, when the big fish swims away. We see the crab again watching him leave. And that was what I wanted him for. I wanted him to see, and to know what had happened. And not even to say anything, because he doesn't say anything. There was something about the warmth this brought to it; we have someone there now who – maybe by his silence – doesn't think all was well-handled.

And I don't know why I needed that because, again, I think that the audience is the crab. They see and he sees.

I needed to introduce the crab somehow, and so we get that earlier beat, where he meets the little fish and then sells him out right away. That was his introduction, but it started with that second bit, where he was watching. And he knew. And so, then it didn't feel cold anymore; then it felt okay. And there was some humour in it and there was a witness.

ELEN: Yeah. As you said, it's a monologue, and it could be a monologue spoken out loud and the fourth wall is being broken and audience is hearing; or it could be an internal monologue which would make it a self-contained world.

JON: Yeah. It's strange because I don't formally get excited by breaking the fourth wall very often. At least in books. I like it in theatre very much. I think that it's really exciting as a theatre device.

The monologue, I think that's right ... He's looking at us sometimes – at the beginning he is – but after that, he's in it. He's looking where he's going and he's thinking to himself as much as anything.

I think that my characters ... It's always strange to hear the books read out loud, because I think of them thinking to each other – even if they're in dialogue. I don't hear voices for them. It's more just like these weird ESP thoughts or something.

And so, the monologue fits that, I think very well.

Which is how *The Tell-Tale Heart* feels to me too, right? He's thinking to himself. He's wandering around in the yard outside the house, or something like that, thinking this as much to himself as to anybody else.

Also, there was another big touchstone for me, which was the movie *Psycho*. At the beginning she [the central character, Marion Crane] has done this crime, you know; she's stolen this money and she's driving. She's driving through the night. And there's a very interesting thing that Hitchcock does with that, where she's hearing – or at least we're hearing – what must be going on back home. We hear her boss discovering the loss of the money and asking her co-worker about it and the co-worker saying, 'I don't know where it is, and Marion left.' We're hearing what must be happening back home. And it's not clear whether it's really happening and we're hearing it, or whether it's her thoughts about what must be going on. There's an ambiguity there.

It's just fascinating to me, that you can do that and leave it ambiguous. I don't know. That ambiguity, between whether he's saying it or whether he's thinking it and what he knows and what we know, it just always seemed interesting to leave that open.

ELEN: There are so many techniques in the book that suggest a generous estimation of children's capabilities: dramatic irony; unreliable narrator; ambiguity about the voice; the climax happening off screen. So many inferences have to be made and you trust that children can do it. Could you speak about that?

JON: I think it's pretty relative, those feelings that it describes.

[...]

I remember feeling guilty all the time as a kid. You try to get away with stuff and you're lying all the time. You're experimenting with lying and you can't believe you've figured out how to do it.

When I talk to kids about this, we talk about how to draw characters who are lying. We talk about moving the eyes, so that you're not looking at the person you're lying to, because it's very hard to lie when you're looking at someone. And I say, the next time you lie, try to do it.

When you put it that way, when I say, 'When you lie again, probably this afternoon, because that's what's gonna happen', it doesn't mean that I'm endorsing lying, it just means I'm acknowledging that it happens. It's edgy. It's nice for them to hear and they kind of giggle when you say it. But I also feel like there's a bit of grace there. To be like, 'It's going to happen. We know you're doing it. And it's not because we should, it's just because that's what people do.'

And so, the question of the book isn't whether you should do this or not. It's just what happens sometimes, when you tell the wrong lie to the wrong fish, right?

The dramatic irony, especially, took some training. I think I'm actually most proud of those pages at the beginning of the book, where we're teaching them about dramatic irony. The big fish is looking in those different directions and the little fish's explanation is the exact opposite.

So, 'He's asleep, he will be asleep for a while', and the eye opens. And then, 'I've stolen his hat, but he won't notice that it's missing' and the eye goes up to where the hat should be. Those first five spreads teach them what dramatic irony is, and then we're off on the story. Now the book can begin. But we've had to spend quite a bit of time, in picturebook terms, teaching them what the mechanic of the book is. I had the most fun engineering that, with this big fish just sitting still, but his eye moving and reacting to the opposite of what was going on.

That to me is my favourite stuff to work out. And I think you can teach them if you put it in simple visual terms. You can teach them that. But it's also really fun, because you see that he's wrong and that we've already established he's a liar and a thief and everything else.

And so hopefully you're getting entertained by this too, because you know what's coming – probably by page six. You know the fish is going to get eaten!

The best bit is teaching them about that stuff. I think it's so much fun to condense those complicated dramatic tools into picturebook form. To reduce them to simple language and not, I hope, lose any of their nuance or their power.

ELEN: I've heard you say before that your books are like fables that have forgotten what they're supposed to teach. Which I think is beautiful. I wonder whether there is a connection between that and the fallibility of your characters? Whether it matters that we tell children how flawed people can be?

JON: The crab is an interesting example of that. How I think of him – how I thought of him when I wrote those beats – was that when he promised he'd keep the fish's secret he really did promise. He thought, 'I've got you. There's no way that I'll give this up.' And then he's faced with a giant fish, and he immediately gives it up. But he's scared! He doesn't have the thing he thought he had.

I've run into a lot of kids who, once they know that the crab is about to give up the little fish, they don't give him that generosity. They think he's a bad crab. They think that when he promised, he was planning on selling him out.

So, the book doesn't do the thing I thought. I thought it did the thing you're talking about where there's some mercy there. There are times when you're gonna promise things and you can't do them. That's what I thought the crab was about. But it turns out a lot of kids just want to see him as a straight villain – even though we've already got one in the book already. They are like, 'He's bad! Look at him, he lies!'

And I was like, 'Is it a lie? Because he really thought he was gonna do it.'

I guess it was a lie. But that's an interesting conversation too: What's a lie? Is it a lie when you break your promise, because you just fell apart? Does the sincerity that was there at the beginning count for anything?

All that interesting stuff, right?

[…]

Anyway, I don't think that this book is an introduction to these feelings for these kids though. I really don't feel I'm introducing them to feelings – new ones. I think it's stuff they know already. I have to think so.

ELEN: I think there is a tendency for people to feel like they have to protect, when they're writing children's books.

JON: I think that protection can come in a lot of different ways though. I've hit on this idea recently, that when you talk about darkness for kids or what's appropriate for them, if you show them idealized worlds, I think they would feel left out. Because that's not how life works, and they'd be wondering if they're doing it wrong. They'd ask, 'Here's this book that presents how things ought to go and how come I can't get that? How come I don't have that?'

I remember reading the *Frog and Toad* books [by Arnold Lobel]. And I remember thinking for the first time that I recognized their relationship, because it's not a completely solid relationship. There's an unevenness to it. Toad wants to be around Frog more than Frog wants to be around Toad. There's a desperation in Toad's relationship with Frog that Frog just doesn't have. Frog likes him very much, but there's no desperation. If Toad left, Frog would be fine; and Toad would not be fine.

And he [Arnold Lobel] never resolves that in any of the stories. It's an undercurrent through almost all of them. And I remember reading that and being like: *I know this. I know this relationship. I have friends with whom I am Toad, and I have friends with whom I am Frog.* It felt so exciting and real and rich to me, to see that play out in these very simple stories about eating cookies and losing buttons and stuff. I remember feeling validated by it, for lack of a better term. That's what it meant to me. And so, I don't think you have to resolve it.

And kids have that; kindergarteners have that; everybody has that. Let's show that.

I don't want to write the other [idealized] thing anyway. It's not fun. There's a selfish aspect here too. It's not fun to write. What fun is that to write? I don't have any surprises for myself then. Whereas, if I have a relationship and it's my job to find out where it's headed, that's a much more creative exercise and interesting to me.

And that's one thing I have noticed, even if kids don't quite get what you're doing, they know when you're turned on in the work, they know when you, as the person making it, are excited.

SECTION 3: *THIS IS NOT MY HAT*, WRITING EXERCISES

Exercise A – Multi-Modal Stories

As we have seen, the text is only one element among many in a picturebook. As a writer, rather than a writer-illustrator, it is important to reflect on what you can leave out as much as what you put it.

1. Imagine a four-year-old character exploring a setting you know well. In full prose, write their experience, aim for 200 words to establish the character, setting, mood, atmosphere and genre.
2. Now, cut anything visual – this might include: naming the place; any descriptions of it; naming the characters present, etc.
3. Now, consider whether the shape, colour or linework can convey mood and atmosphere. Again, cut anything that states mood or atmosphere.
4. Now, consider that the character's facial expressions and body language can convey emotion. Cut anything that conveys emotion.
5. Now, consider that size, placement and texture can convey conflict. Can you cut anything that overly states conflict?
6. Finally, reflect on what a writer *uniquely* offers to the multi-modal experience. This includes: the content of dialogue; specific internal thoughts not implied by the images; the dexterity and playfulness of language; elements of rhetoric, and any subversions of the implied truth of the images (to create, for example, an unreliable narrator or dramatic irony). Add anything uniquely yours to the final iteration of the text.

Exercise B – Using Spreads

Spreads are a significant constraint on the picturebook writer. However, many people find that constraints serve to fuel their creativity.

1. Write the numbers 1–12 along the left-hand margin of a page.
2. Take the beginning of the story you wrote for Exercise A and work out a potential plot using these story structures in turn. Next to each number, set out what would happen in each spread.
   a. The Three-Act Structure. Have your character move out into the world (e.g. visit a new place, meet new people, observe a new phenomenon) in spreads 1–4; have the consequences of their movement play out in spreads 5–9; have the finale and return to status quo happen in spreads 10–12.
   b. Rising Tension. Have the character move out into the world, building in intensity in spreads 1–8; experience a crescendo in spreads 9–10 before returning to calm in spreads 11 and 12.
   c. The Refrain. Have your character use a repeated phrase of your choice on spreads 2, 4, 6 and 8. On spread 10 alter the refrain in a significant way. You can decide whether the refrain returns in spread 11.

Chapter Two

SECTION 1: *DAVE PIGEON*, WRITTEN BY SWAPNA HADDOW AND ILLUSTRATED BY SHEENA DEMPSEY, A CRITICAL DISCUSSION

The reading journey doesn't run on a fixed schedule; some children will learn to read at three or four, others not until they are much, much older. As readers, we may return to beloved childhood books when we need comfort, or we may never have stopped reading picturebooks and novels for young people even as we added books for adults to our bookshelves. So, it is somewhat artificial to say that there is a 'next stage' when it comes to children's literature. However, if we were to stand in a library or bookshop and turn from picturebooks to the next display stand it is likely we will see it labelled something like 'Early Readers', 'Chapter Books', '5–8 Years', '6–9 Years' or 'Junior Fiction'. These are all somewhat interchangeable labels for books intended for a newly independent reader; someone who is able to decode the sounds and meanings, but perhaps is learning fluency and confidence.

So, the next extract we're discussing is taken from a book intended for this audience: *Dave Pigeon*, written by Swapna Haddow and illustrated by Sheena Dempsey. It is a book that bears the hallmarks of a compelling Early Reader (which is the label I prefer as it doesn't contain a specific age range, and thus accommodates varied reading experiences).

Typically, books for this readership will look like novels. They will be chunky with a spine wide enough for the title to be visible from a distance, although inside the font size and margins will be generous, disguising a wordcount much lower than is typical for a novel. Early readers can be anything between 1,000 and 20,000 words, depending on the degree of fluency its intended readership might have. *Dave Pigeon* is 10,000 words, putting it in the middle of the range. Images and illustrations are likely to be present, but full-colour illustrations are rarer, and the images are likely to support comprehension of text rather than subvert it (as we saw in Chapter 1 where illustrations were used to construct dramatic irony in *This Is Not My Hat*). An adult might be present while these books are being read (a carer or teacher, perhaps), but it can't be assumed. Overall, therefore, the 'ecology' is more akin to an adult's reading experience than that of a picturebook.

However, there are needs that a newly independent reader has that an adult reader may not. Fluency is a difficult thing to achieve; the journey can be frustrating or disheartening. There is a tendency for Early Readers to reward, with easily accessible pleasure, those who persevere. Early Readers are likely to be plot-driven, which means that there is a clear sequence of actions arising as a consequence of an initial change to the status quo. Early Readers are also likely to be fast-paced and – often – funny. The Scholastic (2019) 'Kids & Family's Reading Report' surveyed the reading preferences of children aged 6–17 – a very broad demographic! – and found that 52 per cent of children wanted books that made them laugh.

Which is, of course, not to say that humour is the only easily accessible pleasure: action, adventure, friendship, pets, magic, wish-fulfilment and more all feature heavily in books for this age group. They also tend to run into series; young readers want 'more of the same' as they build stamina as readers. Coats (2017:70) warns these books can become 'formulaic'. However, Early Readers can also be an opportunity for creative writers to explore the ludic qualities of books, using iteration and re-iteration in playful ways to deliver 'the same, but different'. *Dave Pigeon* is a strong example which delivers plot, parody and postmodernism to excellent effect as its readers develop confidence.

The extract below is taken from the end of 'Chapter 2 – The Human Lady's Home'. The story so far is that we have met Dave, the eponymous pigeon protagonist, and his friend Skipper who serves as the scribe of the story, a Watson to Dave's Holmes – although with a good deal less success in life than those esteemed gentlemen. The pigeons have been taken in by a human lady, because her Mean Cat hurt Dave's wing and he is recuperating in her shed. The text below is accompanied by two black-and-white line illustrations. I will describe the illustrations later on, as part of my discussion. In this scene, Dave and Skipper meet a new bird-character: the canary, Tinkles:

'I'm Tinkles.' She looked around the shed and whistled. 'You've done all right for yourselves.'

Tinkles was so small, she was somewhere between the size of a baby pigeon and a doughnut. She had a pointy pink beak and streaks of gold and white through her yellow feathers.

[illustration]

'Are you from around here?' I asked.

'I live next door.'

Dave looked out of the window, arching his neck. 'I can't see your shed.'

Tinkles chirped a laugh. 'Shed?' She shook her head. 'Not for me, thanks. I live in the house with the Human Man. I've got myself the full works. Private cage, my own bath and an endless supply of top-end bird seed.' She leaned in close. 'I've even got the brand new Super Swing. It has five speed settings and a cup holder.'

Dave grunted. 'We have biscuits and chocolates and pastries in our house.'

'Biscuits, you say?' Tinkles whistled again. 'Nice.' She hopped back up to the window ledge. 'It's a shame you don't live in the house then, isn't it?'

I headbutted the window back open. Tinkles fluttered out. 'Best be off, boys. I can't stay too long with that crazy cat around.'

She took off across the lawn, gliding over the fence back to her home.

Dave watched her go. He cocked his head to the side and looked at the Human Lady's house. 'I don't know what a Super Swing is but I feel like we need one.' He waddled closer to me. 'We have to find a way to move into the Human Lady's house.'

'What about Mean Cat?' I asked.

'We're going to get rid of her.'

[illustration]

Skipper. If you don't mind, I'll do the chapter titles from now on.

What's was wrong with naming Chapter 2 'The Human Lady's Home?' Boooooring!

(Haddow and Dempsey, 2016:32–5)

This short extract is only 300 words long, which takes up three printed pages, and yet what strikes me so clearly is the economy of the writing and the quick pace of the storytelling. We meet the new character, launch a couple of conflicts, establish a new character goal and begin to shape a plan of action in a matter of moments. These are all valuable elements that typically contribute to a fast-paced plot. For the child reader, this efficiency of storytelling rewards their perseverance as they work towards mastery of the skill of reading. Something is *always* happening. Let's take a closer look at exactly what is going on.

> 'I'm Tinkles.' She looked around the shed and whistled. 'You've done all right for yourselves.'

We have – as with *This Is Not My Hat* – an animal cast. This time an array of birds; pigeons and a canary in this extract, but a full cast of international birds by the climax of the book. Rowe Faustino (quoted in You, 2019:25) cautions that anthropomorphism can bring out 'the worst in many aspiring writers – cloying cuteness, dreadful didacticism, sappy sentimentality, awful alliteration'. An unreflective use of any writing technique risks producing lazy and cliched prose. However, here, Haddow's canary is as un-cute and unsentimental as it's possible for a canary to be. She is a cool assessor of the accumulated 'wealth' of the pigeons. The juxtaposition of the cutesy name 'Tinkles' with the wise-guy whistle and wide-boy appraisal create humour. Her name – presumably given to her by a doting human owner – is at variance with her personality as expressed through her dialogue, which uses an adult idiom, 'done all right for yourselves'. Not only are two unexpected elements clashed together, which is often a fundamental building block of a joke, but also Tinkles serves as one of the three types of comic characters identified by Andrew Horton (2000). These three types are: the imposter (who has pretensions), the innocent, and the ironic figure (or the trickster). Tinkles is a trickster 'trying to make things happen on the sly for their own advantage' (Horton 2000:23).

A final element of humour, beyond these surprising contrasts and comic personas, is the sheer absurdity of birds participating in the 'rat-race', amassing status symbols and 'doing alright for themselves'.

The comedy continues,

> Tinkles was so small, she was somewhere between the size of a baby pigeon and a doughnut.

There may be some readers who are familiar with the size of a baby pigeon, but this can't be considered a Standard International unit of measurement. So, again, humour is created through the confluence of two unexpected ideas. Of course, the unlikely metaphor is only unlikely for a human reader; the pigeon narrator, Skipper, knows exactly how big a baby pigeon is. This realization that Haddow is privileging the narrator's frames of reference above the reader's draws our attention to the fact that we are *reading* and is the first hint of postmodernism, which we will see more forcefully expressed later.

> She had a pointy pink beak and streaks of gold and white through her yellow feathers.

It is at this point that we have the first of our two illustrations. The line drawing, done in a sketchy cartoony style, shows Tinkles and a baby pigeon, in front of

FIGURE 2 Dave Pigeon © *Sheena Dempsey 2016.*

a height chart of the type associated with police line-ups. Also joining them in the line-up is a frosted doughnut, dripping crumbs. Both birds are wide-eyed, as though a little surprised to be there with baked goods. Tinkles wears a 1980s workout headband. She is a little bigger than the doughnut. We are offered visual gags as well as wordplay: the wordless presence of a doughnut and the absurdity of a canary in workout clothes. The police line-up invokes parody, one of the thirteen classes of comedy identified by a MasterClass article on the subject (MasterClass 2021). The police line-up has been used as a motif in films such as *The Usual Suspects* and *A Bronx Tale* as well as more child-centred media such as *The Simpsons*. This intertextuality is another hint of the book's postmodernism.

Cinema parody continues through this description of Tinkles; she is coded in a particularly feminine way: pink beak, streaks of gold, yellow feathers. This physical description coupled with her knowing dialogue suggest that Tinkles is a bird version of the femme fatal archetype. Kennedy (2017:30) suggests 'the dangerous woman of the hardboiled tradition is manipulative, deceitful, murderous, and sometimes even psychotic'. Although Tinkles might not be psychotic, she certainly brings dangerous ideas with her and upends the harmony of Human Lady's shed. Tinkles is somewhere between a secondary character and a tertiary character in the novel. She serves a particular role, in service to the protagonist's narrative, and then leaves. However, by leaning on an archetype, Haddow can endow Tinkles with the suggestion of a more complex inner life than might have been the case, which is why she is something more than a two-dimensional tertiary character.

The illustration of the baby pigeon is not anthropomorphic; it wears no clothes, and its surprise is very birdlike. The degree to which an animal character might be an animal or a stand-in human is a spectrum, and it is worth taking a moment to reflect on what animal characters have to offer writers working in picturebooks and Early Readers.

In my interview with Haddow, which follows, she says that she prefers using animal characters because they are afforded a freedom that human children can't exhibit. What could be more independent than a pigeon, after all? It can roam anywhere and get up to mischief in a way that would be impossible for a six-year-old human.

There is also the generally held belief that animal characters are easier to sell internationally than the geographically specific children they serve as an avatar for; it is easier to erase cultural difference when using bears or kittens or puppies and many illustrated books need translation sales to make them economically viable.

I would also argue that there is something celebratory in selecting the humble pigeon as our protagonist. Yes, there may be a whiff of the slapstick about them as they peck at a discarded chip – or croissant, as is Dave's preference. But they are also animals who share our domestic spaces. For those millions of us who live in cities around the world, pigeons are a visible part of the human habitat. Ursula K. Le Guin (2009:105) writes that children have an 'innate, acute interest in animals as fellow beings, friend or enemy or food or playmate, [which] can't be instantly eradicated ... And imagination and literature are there to fill the void and reaffirm the greater community'. The greater community is the wider natural world of which we are a troubled and troublesome part. Dave and Skipper are representative of the pigeons in our 'greater community'. In some crucial ways, Dave and Skipper are very pigeon-y pigeons. They may talk to each other in Standard English, but they discuss the sorts of topics that a pigeon might well fixate upon, if a pigeon could talk: food, cats, where to sleep, food again. Like many urban pigeons living beside humans, Dave and Skipper appear somewhat ramshackle in the illustrations; the wild birds are able to remain more fully bird-like.

Writers choosing to use animals in their fiction might reflect on the degree to which they wish to co-opt the animal as a human avatar versus allowing them to remain animal. Thebo (2023) provocatively explores the ethics of non-human representations at a time of human-induced climate change. She suggests that when the animals in literature are just 'furry puppets' (4) this reduces opportunities for children to understand and connect with Le Guin's 'greater community' within their literature.

It is noteworthy that the two books I have selected here to discuss fiction for younger readers both contain animal protagonists. This is a choice I made consciously, to allow me to discuss these craft and ethical issues, but is also a failing I must acknowledge. By selecting two animal stories, I have to ask myself, what did I leave out? When we get to meet a morally dubious protagonist (Little Fish) or a protagonist with a high degree of independent agency (Dave Pigeon), who are we not meeting? Who am I not introducing you to?

The most obvious answer is stories about children who are minoritized in the Global North. The Centre for Literacy in Primary Education (CLPE) has been tracking the number and quality of books for young people that feature racially minoritized children – the annual Reflecting Realities Report is the result of that work. From a baseline of 4 per cent in 2017 (CLPE 2018), the proportion of picturebooks featuring racially minoritized characters has risen to 30 per cent in 2022 (CLPE 2023:6). In the United States, similar data are collected and published by the Cooperative Children's Book Center (2024), which also show an upward trend from a low baseline.

This inequality of racial representation is a systemic, rather than an individual issue. Responsibility for change is shared among writers, illustrators, agents, editors, sales and marketing, booksellers and librarians and, ultimately, the reading public. It can't fall on the head of any one writer to affect change single-handed (and this assumes, of course, that every writer *wants* to affect change in this area, which isn't the case). So, as writers, we are left to reflect on the questions: when making one choice, which other choices are closed off? As Pullman's 'phase space' narrows, am I confident of the path I am on?

We have strayed far from Dave and Skipper and their encounter with Tinkles with these musings. Let us return to the shed:

'Are you from around here?' I asked.
'I live next door.'
Dave looked out of the window, arching his neck. 'I can't see your shed.'

This is a simple exchange of information between the characters. However, it speaks to one of the fundamental concerns of literature for newly school-age children and consequently their Early Readers: the question of their place in the world. As Coats (2017:70) says, '[school-age children] focus on their peers and how they measure up'. We discussed conceptions of childhood in Chapter 1; another conception of childhood is that it is a period of socialization. The lives of very young children focus on the home, the family, the domestic; as they grow, they become more aware of the society (or societies) beyond. Dave, in this passage, has assumed that all birds are like him, and their situations will be the same as his, namely they live in sheds. It doesn't occur to him that there might be other ways of doing things. As children move out of the domestic (home, family) into society (school, friends' homes and beyond), it becomes apparent, through experience, that there are multitudinous ways to exist in the world. And that they, potentially, may not 'measure up'. Peer pressure is now *A Thing*. Dave's observation reflects this thematic concern.

Tinkles chirped a laugh. 'Shed?' She shook her head. 'Not for me, thanks. I live in the house with the Human Man. I've got myself the full works. Private cage, my own bath and an endless supply of top-end bird seed.' She leaned in close. 'I've even got the brand new Super Swing. It has five speed settings and a cup holder.'

Now Dave's eyes are really being opened. Unknown possibilities begin to crystalize. Tinkles gives a short monologue here that lays bare the differences in their situations. Beginning with amused disbelief ('chirped a laugh'), she goes on to use another adult idiom, 'the full works' before listing the status symbols she owns. She is a sophisticate, or a show-off, depending on how one might feel about consumerism. Certainly, she offers a potential view of bird-life that has been unknown to Dave, the wild pigeon. She is aware of the affect her description is having, she leans 'in close' to deliver the final flourish. Again, her persona recalls the archetypal femme fatal whose morality might waver in the face of temptation. The humour, again, comes from the confluence of two unlikely pairings: the real life of a bird (cage, bath, seed) and the consumerist labels attached to those objects ('private', 'endless', 'top-end'), before reaching absurdist heights with the ridiculous idea of a bird needing a cup holder. However, even the femme fatal canary is closer to the natural world (and Le Guin's 'great community') than she is to people; despite living in close proximity to a person, she doesn't use his given name, instead she uses the proper noun 'Human Man'; he is a provider of all her luxury, but not an intimate. As with many communities of children, the birds live lives that are parallel but distinct from the grown-ups.

Dave, like a child faced with friends who own 'cooler stuff', reacts to Tinkles' boasting,

> Dave grunted. 'We have biscuits and chocolates and pastries in our house.'

His first reaction is to withdraw into himself and simply grunt. His second reaction is to attempt one-upmanship. Still, Dave remains a wild pigeon at heart and the only status symbol he can imagine is food-based.

> 'Biscuits, you say?' Tinkles whistled again. 'Nice.' She hopped back up to the window ledge.

Initially, it appears that perhaps she has been taken in and finds Dave impressive – she repeats what he says, whistles, admires his biscuits. As readers, we experience a pause, a hiatus, as she completes a physical action and hops to the window ledge. For a moment, the delay afforded by the pause allows us to believe poor Dave might triumph. But then, Tinkles delivers her body-blow,

> 'It's a shame you don't live in the house then, isn't it?'

Timing is everything and this joke lands so well because of the enforced pause that preceded it. We understand that Tinkles sees through Dave's bluff. This barbed exchange, with Dave coming to notice difference, to be tempted into bloviation and then be humiliatingly found out, is a painful journey of innocence to experience. No less painful because it is happening to an injured pigeon. Maybe even more so, as Dave is our Everyman (the 'innocent' in Horton's tripartite classification of comic characters and another important archetype). There but for the grace of God ...

> I headbutted the window back open. Tinkles fluttered out. 'Best be off, boys. I can't stay too long with that crazy cat around.'

Skipper, our internal narrator and story scribe, takes the literal blow here, headbutting the window open. It gives us another moment of levity – this time slapstick humour – but it also reminds us of the knock both pigeons have received during Tinkles' short visit. Having set the mechanism of plot in motion, she takes her leave, reiterating for us, before she goes, that the villain of the piece – the antagonist – Mean Cat, is still at large.

> She took off across the lawn, gliding over the fence back to her home.

Once she has sowed the seed of discontent for the pigeons, Tinkles 'glides' home. The verb choice indicates her ease and degree of comfort. She may even have taken pleasure in the extent to which she has discombobulated the pigeons.

Tinkles has served her plot role – she arrived, created conflict and left. Returning to the idea of economy and brevity in storytelling, she served as the 'Act 1 problem'. In screenplay terms, this is the complication in Act 1 that comes after the inciting incident. The inciting incident, the event that disrupted Dave and Skipper's status quo, was the attack by Mean Cat, which saw them move into the shed. Tinkles has added *complication* to life in the shed by introducing an awareness of status where there was no such awareness before. This discovery will be the engine for the rest of the act, and indeed the rest of the book (for more on using screenplay structures, and how they might be used to shape novels, see *Save the Cat!* by Blake Snyder and *Into the Woods* by John Yorke [2013]). So, this short conversation is pivotal to the plot. The pacing here is so economical that Tinkles was able to fulfil this crucial role in a few hundred words. But she isn't just a cipher for plot. She is a character informed by an archetype and this allows for a reading of her that suggests more complicated emotions – ennui, archness, manipulativeness – than simply being a talking plot point would allow.

> Dave watched her go. He cocked his head to the side and looked at the Human Lady's house. 'I don't know what a Super Swing is but I feel like we need one.'

The small physical action, watching Tinkles go, gives us another moment of pause, while the consequences of this exchange are allowed to reverberate. We stay with the physical action, cocking his head and looking, but this time it is not to buy time, it is to indicate that the subject of his attention has shifted. Tinkles has gone but has left a terrible aftermath behind: envy and avarice.

Dave doesn't know what these strange new desires are, but he knows they are compelling and irresistible. The fact that these primordial, hitherto unknown emotions are being felt over something as ridiculous as a canary's Super Swing only deepens the bathos (or pathos, depending on how keenly we feel the interiority of a pigeon unhappy with his lot). Dave's thwarted Everyman stands in a long line of sad clowns, disappointed by the world and what it offers them, from Charlie Chaplin's Tramp, to Basil Fawlty, to David Brent. Again, we see how powerful the use of archetypes can be for a writer. Their use allows us to create more three-dimensional characters, quickly and with broad brush strokes. They come with baggage and, by using them, the writer can use this associated baggage to dress the character without having to waste words. Archetypes are economy in action.

> He waddled closer to me. 'We have to find a way to move into the Human Lady's house.'

From the Act 1 Problem, we see here the emergence of an Act 1 Plan. Dave has to respond to envy with acquisition. He wants what Tinkles has: a place inside a human house. However, even here, at the moment of inception, the plan is already tinged with doubtfulness. The verb choice 'waddled' is not how pigeons walk; it is an action typically more associated with aquatic birds, ducks or penguins, maybe. So, there is slapstick humour here again, but also a sense of a fish-out-of-water; something where it shouldn't be. Additionally, Dave doesn't say the more economical, 'we have to move into … ', he says, 'we have to find a way to move into … '. The action is set at one remove, with success just a little further out of reach than might be desired.

This establishes an interesting moral quandary for the reader. Those familiar with the conventions of tragedy may be able to spot the hamartia here – the fatal flaw in our hero that will inevitably lead to their downfall. Dave has discovered avarice and has succumbed to it. It is unlikely that a child reader will be familiar with the structures of Greek theatre. But it is possible that, from these small seeds of doubt, they may intuit at some level that all will not go well for Dave on this quest. As we saw in Chapter 1, books for young readers can serve as an introduction to the vast edifice of world literature and here, Swapna shows us the inner workings of Greek tragedy through the medium of pigeons.

As I stated in Chapter 1, the question of whether the role of children's fiction is to provide any kind of moral or ethical education has a long and contested history. However, in Haddow's case there *is* a moral education at play, and arguably an authorial ideology in evidence. Haddow associates envy and avarice with tragedy and so provides a traditional ethical framework for her characters. Having said this, the framework is delightfully disguised by the degree of humour that is intimately bound up with the tragedy; the tragedy hides behind a veil of parody, slapstick and well-timed jokes.

This Act 1 problem and plan concludes with another important plot point,

'What about Mean Cat?' I asked.
'We're going to get rid of her.'

We are very nearly at the end of Chapter Two 'The Human Lady's Home' and so this small exchange has an additional job to do. As well as serving as a strong ending, it has to propel the reader on, making them want to read the next chapter. Cliffhangers can be a very effective way to maintain the curiosity of the reader, but here Haddow adopts an alternative strategy, which is to use a statement with reverberating implications. The engine of the plot has been established – Dave feels envy, and this motivates his goal to move into the Human Lady's house. However, there is an impediment, an obstacle to his success: Mean Cat. Skipper's question serves to remind both Dave and the reader of the forces of antagonism that will inevitably stand in the way of Dave's goal. Dave's reply to Skipper is more assured than his goal-setting was. He is not 'trying to find a way' to get rid of Mean Cat. Dave is more certain than that. He and Skipper are '*going* to get rid of her' (my italics). The unfolding tragedy is already in motion as Dave's focus shifts from the goal (moving in) to the mechanism (getting rid of Mean Cat). He is reinforcing Mean Cat's role as his enemy and that battle is more important, perhaps, than the outcome. Dave is already losing sight of success; this is the price of pigeon hamartia.

However, before this chapter ends, there is a tiny epilogue. This is a multi-modal novel, and the mode shifts here from prose to comic book. There is a second illustration, this time of our two pigeon protagonists, speaking in a series of speech bubbles,

Skipper. If you don't mind, I'll do the chapter titles from now on.
What's was wrong with naming Chapter 2 'The Human Lady's Home?'
Boooooring!

This is a fascinating little coda. The shift in narrative mode from prose to comic book has signified a shift into a much more experimental positioning of the text. We have seen hints of postmodernism before this point; here we see it in full effect. Postmodernism is a very broad term often used to indicate an acceptance of the relative (in)stability of reality. Pantaleo (2014:326) offers a number of defining techniques whose presence suggests postmodernism. *Dave Pigeon* uses a great number of these techniques, including: characters who are aware of themselves as characters and comment on the story;

disruption of the time and space relationships of the narrative; typographical experimentation; and elements that make readers aware of the processes by which the narrative is being constructed.

In this coda, Dave and Skipper are arguing about how the book, the very object in the reader's hand, should be written. By having this conversation, they are drawing our attention to the material artefact. They reflect the idea that each chapter title, each sentence, each illustration is a choice made by an active creator and that other choices were possible. They point to the 'phase space' and say 'Look, this is all made up. Someone is making this up.' As well as Greek tragedy, Haddow is introducing young readers to material relativism, social constructionism, even a touch of nihilism. Again, as we saw in Chapter 1, good books for children give them valuable cultural capital.

In *Dave Pigeon*, Haddow delivers easily accessible pleasure in spades.

Cited Works

CLPE 2018, *Reflecting Realities: Survey of Ethnic Representation within UK Children's Literature 2017*, Centre for Literacy in Primary Education, London.

CLPE 2023, *Reflecting Realities: Survey of Ethnic Representation within UK Children's Literature 2022*. Centre for Literacy in Primary Education, London.

Cooperative Childrens Book Center 2024, *Books by and/or about Black, Indigenous and People of Color (All Years)*. Available: https://ccbc.education.wisc.edu/literature-resources/ccbc-diversity-statistics/books-by-about-poc-fnn/ [2024, July 24].

Coats, K. 2017, *The Bloomsbury Introduction to Children's and Young Adult Literature*, Bloomsbury Publishing, London.

Haddow, S. and Dempsey, S. 2016, *Dave Pigeon*, Faber and Faber, London.

Horton, A. 2000, *Laughing Out Loud: Writing the Comedy-Centered Screenplay*, University of California Press, Berkeley.

Kennedy, V. 2017, '"Chick Noir": Shopaholic Meets Double Indemnity', *American, British and Canadian Studies Journal*, vol. 28, no. 1, pp. 19–38.

Lo Guin, U. K. 2009, *Cheek by Jowl*, Aqueduct Press, Seattle.

MasterClass 2021, Oct 26, *13 Types of Comedy: Popular Types of Comedic Performance*. Available: https://www.masterclass.com/articles/types-of-comedy [2024, April 11].

Pantaleo, S. 2014, 'The Metafictive Nature of Postmodern Picturebooks', *The Reading Teacher*, vol. 67, no. 5, pp. 324–32.

Scholastic 2019, *Kids & Family Reading Report*. Available: http://www.scholastic.com/newsroom/online-press-kits/kids-and-family-reading-report.html, [2025, June 17].

Snyder, B. 2005, *Save the Cat!: The Only Book on Screenwriting You'll Ever Need*, Michael Wiese Productions, Los Angeles.

Thebo, M. 2023, 'Thebo, Mimi, "Talking Tigers: Concepts of Representational Ethics Applied to Non-Human Characters in Writing Children's Fiction"', *Leaf Journal*, vol. 1, no. 1, pp. 1–8.

Yorke, J. 2013, *Into the Woods: A Five Act Journey into Story*, Penguin Random House, London.

You, C. 2019, 'Representing Zoo Animals: The Other-than-Anthropocentric in Anthony Browne's Picture Books', *The Lion and the Unicorn*, vol. 43, pp. 22–41.

SECTION 2: AN INTERVIEW WITH SWAPNA HADDOW

ELEN: I'll start by asking where did Dave and Skipper come from?

SWAPNA: Well, where did they come from? How far back do I go? Okay. So, when I found out I was pregnant, I wanted to do something special for my son. [...] I thought I would write him a story, right?

So, I wrote a story for him, and I even illustrated it, even though I'm not the best at drawing. I was working on it during lunch times at work. I was working at the Prince's Drawing School, which is now the Royal Drawing School. One of the other students (Louise Yates), she saw it, and she was like, 'Oh, this is really brilliant! You should send it to my agent!'

I think that was when the penny dropped that: *Oh, my God! People do this as a living!* So, I'd always been writing, but I never shared things. You know, I kept journals and stuff like that. But I'd never shared anything publicly.

I obviously thought: *Oh, okay, I'll send it off.* And they were like, 'This is rubbish.' Which it was, because it was like the first thing I ever wrote. [... But,] even though they weren't gonna take it on, they said some really lovely, helpful things and encouraging things about my writing.

[...] And then, in 2012, I saw this competition with the Greenhouse Funny Prize. At that point, I'd been keeping an eye on agencies and just seeing what kind of things did they want, wish lists and stuff. And I saw this advert for the Greenhouse Funny Prize. And I thought: *Right, I'll enter it.*

And so, I wrote this story about a granny that tells a lot of lies. And it didn't win, but it did get shortlisted. Julia Churchill at the time, was like, 'This is really funny; you should consider writing funny stuff.' At that point, because I didn't win ... I didn't take it personally, but I was like: *I'm definitely not good enough for this. There's definitely other authors out there who can do this better.* So, 2013 was my self-pity year. Then, 2014 came and I thought: *Right, I see this competition's come round again. I'm going to enter it.* So, I started writing this book called *Pat Pigeon*. [...] I started writing this book, and it was such a slog, and it was really boring. It was really rubbish. There was about one week to go to submit my book. And I was like: *I'm gonna scrap this. I'm just gonna start again.* And so that's where Dave came in. I renamed the pigeon Dave. I think the thing with *Pat Pigeon* was, I was trying to think very hard about a story. I was like: *What could happen to this pigeon?* And with Dave, there was no story. The first, original draft of that book, there wasn't a story. It was just Dave and Skipper having a chat. They were just these two really daft pigeons. So, I submitted it, and it won, which was amazing. And then, of course, I then had to write an actual story. So, Dave and Skipper basically started off just as this very conversational set-piece, almost, rather than any sort of story. [...]

ELEN: That seems so wild, given how plotty and how fast-paced the book ended up.

SWAPNA: Yeah, it does seem weird. Because I really don't think there was a plot. And it's amazing that anyone thought there was potential in that. Especially because around that time, I mean 2014, publishers, editors – agents, even – they want a clean script. They don't have the time or the energy to really start nurturing an author from the start. So, the fact that anyone thought there was potential in this, basically a character study of two pigeons, is kind of a bit bonkers. But I'll always appreciate that they did.

ELEN: Were there jokes already present? There must have been.

SWAPNA: Yeah, there were a lot of jokes in there. There were a lot of puns. [...] The hook of the story was that there were these two pigeons, and you didn't really know what they were going to say next. You couldn't, because it was quite outlandish. And bonkers.

ELEN: That does chime with some of the things that I feel about the book. It has a shaggy-dog-story quality and an Odd Couple dynamic.

SWAPNA: See, I really like that dynamic when I'm reading books myself, or even watching movies. That's something that draws me in straight away. [...]

ELEN: Odd Couple, but with animals?

SWAPNA: Animals, yeah (laughs). I'm a bit of a cheat when it comes to young fiction, because I want my characters to do really bonkers things. But in the real world we can't really send a 5-to-8-year-old just disappearing out of the garden. So, I do cheat a little bit and use animals. Then you can sort of break the human-world rules. But I like to keep them in a quite realistic situation, if you know what I mean? Like as realistic as it can be? But yeah, that's my that's my top tip, really. If you're writing for young kids, there's only so many things you can do with a 5-to-8-year-old. So, if you want to break the rules, you're gonna have to give them some sort of talking pet, or just turn them into an animal and let them go nuts.

ELEN: Could you talk a little bit about the way that you get humour into your texts?

SWAPNA: This is a thing that I've not really thought too hard about. I think first off, you can't think too hard about it. The minute you overwork a joke, it's a bit like bread, it's just not gonna work. The fresher the joke ... I actually struggle a lot with this in editing. [...] I'm re-reading it so many times, I ruin the joke for myself. So, I try and keep it as fresh as possible. I think honestly the humour side of things is something in-built in me, because it's definitely something that my family has. We're not a close family, and we're not a particularly functional one. But when bad things happen, it's humour that we go to, and that always binds us. So, I think in general, I've always found, no matter how rubbish your situation, if you can laugh about it or can you find the humour in it, that has always saved me.

So, I think when I write these characters ... And they are just stray pigeons, their lives aren't great. They're lucky that they have the shed, but they're not living the high life. I mean, Dave's not even got two wings. They're constantly being barraged by people who want to eat them or kill them, or something. And so, I think the humour comes from being able to laugh in a dark place. [...]

Honestly, the first book was not a hopeful story for me. I was writing this book as these two pigeons who had suffered a horrible attack. And now, although they had this wonderful place to stay, they really were just relying on someone giving them scraps. And every time they try to better their life, they keep literally hitting a brick wall (because of the human lady's house not being particularly accessible). When they finally get somewhere, they're hijacked by all these other birds that want to eat their biscuits. It was actually quite 'pigeon noir'. But I don't like the idea of giving kids such miserable stuff to read. So, I prefer the vibe of something that feels a bit grimy and dirty but is funny too, in a Roald Dahl-y kind of way. His books are so traumatic if you really break them down. But the humour, the fun and the action mean you can easily read that and be like, 'What a wonderful place the chocolate factory is.' It's a terrible place!

So, I guess I'm coming at it from it from that vibe. Very rarely, a few kids will come up to me, at events, who've picked up on the darkness of some of these things, and they're like, 'When are the pigeons just gonna have a nice time?' But all the other kids are like, 'No, they're having the best time. It's so funny, they're having an adventure, and they're having loads of jokes.' But yeah, every now and then I'll meet a kid and I'm like: *Wow, he gets it.*

ELEN: Can you talk a little bit about the illustrations in the book?

SWAPNA: Yeah, it was interesting, because coming into this, I didn't really know how it all worked with an illustrator. But in the book, Dave and Skipper tell their story and then, in real time, they interrupt the story. From that early point, we struggled with how that would look. So, I actually got to meet Sheena [Dempsey] then. Usually, it's the illustrator dealing with the art director; and the writer dealing with the editor. And it only comes together in-house. But Sheena and I got to meet each other before any illustrations were drawn. And when we met it was brilliant, because we are the same age, we got on, we had the same sort of views on life, we had the same ideas for the book, of the griminess and pigeoniness. I would say she worked independently, but we would communicate over things.

I think when I'm writing, I see it almost like a movie. The very first drafts are almost all dialogue. It's like a film script. And then I go back, and I'm like: *We should describe something here.* And so, I was starting to see it in her style of drawing and illustration. So, as we got to Books 3 and 4, I knew the kind of things that would be amazing for her to illustrate.

[...]

I'm very cautious to tread on an illustrator's toes, because I know what they add to the story, and once you start fiddling, you lose that magic a little bit.

[...]

ELEN: I really love the way that the feathers have those barbs almost like fur.

SWAPNA: Yeah. They're not perfect pigeons, because they're living on the streets, you know, living croissant-crumb to croissant-crumb. They need to feel like that, but without feeling icky, you know, because there's a purity in their friendship. And they're really quite lovely characters.

ELEN: I know that you've written picturebooks, and you've written early readers, and I wondered if you could speak to the difference or similarities?

SWAPNA: I think the one big similarity is, you can't talk down to your audience. They're smart even at 3 years old, very smart. If you're reading a story to them that's talking down to them, you can see them just glaze over. So, that's probably the biggest similarity going from writing for 5-to-8-year-olds, or even like slightly older, and then writing for 3-to-5-year-olds. Overall, you can't condescend to them. They know stuff.

I think the thing with writing young fiction is that these kids are reading the books on their own. I know my books are sometimes used as read-alouds, especially in classrooms. But I think of it as being for an independent reader, and the reader is a child, and they're at the forefront of my mind. When I'm writing picturebooks, at the forefront of my mind is that there's an adult reading this as well. So, on some level, I'm trying to give them things in the book that they would also enjoy, that they'd want to read again and again and again.

With *My Dad is a Grizzly Bear* and with *My Mum is a Lioness*, those books are a sort of tribute to being a parent. I hope every parent that reads it is just like, 'Oh, my God! I am the greatest.' I really hope they are giving themselves a pat on the back, because it's so hard to be a parent. So, I hope those books do that. I hope they sort of talk on a level to parents as well as children. So that's my main thing. When I'm writing a picturebook, I'm thinking about that.

[...]

And then, obviously, you've just got less words to play with. So, every single word needs to be there for a reason and has to be doing something. Not necessarily moving the story on, it just has to be doing *something*. Has to be earning its keep. I think that those are the main differences.

Sometimes, when kids ask me, you know, 'Who are you thinking about when you're writing a book?' I kind of want to say, 'no one', because the minute you start thinking about who might read this book, that expectation alone can really stifle your writing. Because it's really hard to please everyone. So, in a way, if you think you're writing for no one, or just for yourself, it's just easier. But also, in saying that, you have to be realistic. If your book is going to be published, or it's going to be out there in the world, you need to remember that, you know, the under-fives can't read (well, they can't read words, they're certainly reading the pictures). And the people reading the words, they're going to have to read these like maybe 100, 200 times, depending on how much this child likes that book. So, you've got to give them something fun or interesting. Or something that at least at the end, when they shut the book, they can be like, 'God. I am a good mum, aren't I?' You know that they can feel really good about themselves, like, 'Yes, I've nailed it.'

SECTION 3: *DAVE PIGEON*, WRITING EXERCISES

The exercises in this chapter are offered with the intention of encouraging you to reflect on big, bold storytelling. This is the kind of writing we typically see in the 5-to-8-years section of a bookshop. Of course, this doesn't mean it is impossible to write more lyrical, poetic or reflective books for this age group – books like that exist too! However, the exercises I'm suggesting do cleave to the idea that newly confident readers like easily accessible pleasure.

Exercise A – Pacy Plots

Pace can be thought of as the number of words used to deliver a narrative. A word budget, if you like. As we saw with the extract from *Dave Pigeon*, economical narratives deliver a lot of plot using a small word count.

1. Choose a narrative you are familiar with (this might be an anecdote you tell often, a fable or folk tale, or the story of a book/film you know well).
2. Write the narrative using the most economical budget possible – use fewer than 100 words.
3. Ask, what did you have to leave out? Which parts felt anaemic or flat?
4. I am upping your budget by fifty words. Where will you choose to spend them? Will you scatter the extra words throughout, or is there one place that needs them more than the rest? Do you need them for the set-up, or finale, perhaps? Or to round-out the protagonist a little? Rewrite the story, this time with fewer than 150 words.
5. If you choose, you can repeat the task with yet another fifty words.
6. Think of a writing project you might want to work on. What's its likely word budget? Where will you need to spend it most? Where can you cut the word count to free up the budget elsewhere?

Exercise B – Plot Engines: Character Goal, Internal Desire Fuelling Outward Action

In plot-driven narratives, with lots of fast-paced action, characters will have easily understood desires that serve as the 'engine' for the decisions they make, and so the course of the action.

1. Pick an archetype – here are some suggestions: the cheerful sidekick; the wise mentor; the reckless hero; the hapless Everyman (there are many, many lists available online). For the purposes of this exercise, the archetype is going to be the protagonist of the story, regardless of what role they typically play.
2. Give your archetype three interesting details (for example, make them a pigeon!) to put some flesh on the bones.
3. Turn to their internal life; choose an emotional need they have. Perhaps they want to be courageous or brave; perhaps they want to satisfy an envy or jealousy; perhaps they want to feel connected or cared for.
4. Make a list of the potential *action* they might take to meet their emotional need; it can be as sincere or ludicrous as you like.
5. Plot out the steps they might take to attain their goal; try to keep the steps short and direct. You don't have to deliver on the need but try to move quickly to the action that the need generates.
6. Write a scene or two of your character in action. How does the engine power the movement in your piece?

Exercise C – Plot Impediments, the Forces of Antagonism

In order for a vigorous plot to emerge, with lots of distinct story-beats and action, it is wise to create obstacles that will thwart your protagonist from attaining their emotional need. A common way to do this is to establish either an antagonist (a sentient being working in opposition to the protagonist) or a 'force of antagonism' (forces working in opposition to the protagonist; however, they don't need to be a single character, or sentient – Dave's hamartia is an example of such a force).

1. Use the plot you created in Exercise B, above. Now that you have a protagonist with a clear need and defined action, they will need to be thwarted.

2. Make a list of potential antagonists. You might choose to use an archetype again. Select your favourite.
3. As with the protagonist, give your antagonist three interesting details to start to round them out.
4. Your antagonist will need a reason to serve as an obstacle to the protagonist. However, that reason doesn't need to be as emotionally deep as the motivation of the protagonist. They might seek power, or notoriety, or dominance and – as long as it is plausible – that can be enough. Make a list of all the things the antagonist might do that will thwart the protagonist's emotional need. The antagonist might deliberately sabotage the protagonist's goals, or the protagonist might simply be caught in the crossfire of the antagonist's activities.
5. Insert a few obstacles caused by the antagonist into your Exercise B plot. How does that add drama or complicate things in a satisfying way?

Exercise D – Writing Funny Through Unlikely Metaphor

Fast-paced plotting isn't the only way to deliver easily accessible pleasure to young readers. Humour is also beloved when it comes to Early Readers. One way to create humour is to bring together two unlikely pairings – the surprise will often make us laugh.

1. Look around the space you are in and find an everyday object, something like a book, a lamp or a shoe will do nicely.
2. Make a list of the object's qualities – factually note things like its size, colour, shape, dimensions, age, etc.
3. Next imagine a space as unlike the place you are in as possible – perhaps a zoo, an international space station, a Roman amphitheatre …
4. As best as you can manage, without visiting your unlikely destination, make a list of as many of its attributes as you can recall – it's size, colour, dimensions, etc.
5. Look at both lists. Can you find a way to turn two items on the list into a metaphor? For example, your lamp might be roughly the size of an otter; it might be as beautiful as a rusting space station; or the lamp might be as mutinous as a gladiatorial revolt.

Chapter Three

SECTION 1: *THE STRANGEWORLDS TRAVEL AGENCY* BY L.D. LAPINSKI, A CRITICAL DISCUSSION

Note: this chapter contains spoilers for *The Strangeworlds Travel Agency*.

The Strangeworlds Travel Agency by L.D. Lapinski is the first novel in a fantasy sequence aimed at confident readers of around 9–12 years old. This category has been called junior fiction or children's literature, but the term middle grade (MG) is coming to dominate, even in countries that don't use the American Middle School system from which the term gets its name (I suspect because #MG is easier to use on social media than #childrensliterature). Typically, readers at this stage are fluent and can handle all of the writing techniques (flashbacks, dual narratives, polyphonic voices, present tense, etc.) a novelist chooses to throw at them – the writers of picturebooks and Early Readers have laid excellent groundwork. Literature doesn't need to be an entirely 'easily accessible pleasure' anymore, some challenges might be welcome. So, the full gamut of genre is available to the writer (with the exception of romance and erotica; kissing is yucky, for the most part).

Strangeworlds is a fantasy adventure with the premise that interdimensional travel can be achieved by stepping into the right suitcase. The titular Agency holds some 700 suitcases through which travellers might voyage. As such, it is a portal fantasy with a mechanism reminiscent of Diggory's discovery of the Wood Between the Worlds in C.S. Lewis' *The Magician's Nephew* (1955), or Will Parry's discovery of the subtle knife in Philip Pullman's *His Dark Materials* (1995–2000) sequence. However, it owes its greatest debt to the ultimate 'travelling box', Doctor Who's TARDIS, as Lapinski explains (in the subsequent interview). Although the influence of these seminal texts is strong, much of their cozy traditionalism is disrupted by Lapinski's careful reflections on the class and gender in their choice of protagonists and the social milieu from which the characters are drawn.

The extract I'll be looking at comes early in the first book in the series (there are three books in the main trilogy, plus two novellas). The main character, Flick, has recently moved to a new town where she has stumbled across the frontage of The Strangeworlds Travel Agency, discovered the existence of magic, and been invited to become a member of the agency, due to her uncommon skillset. She asks Jonathan, the young custodian, for time to think about it. We join her having made her decision,

'You came back,' Jonathan said as Flick walked into the shop the next day. He looked up from sweeping the floor to give her a wide and slightly self-satisfied smile. He was wearing brown tartan trousers, with a mustard-coloured shirt and a waistcoat that was a bit too big for him. It had an embroidered peacock on the back.

Flick closed the door behind her. It had been easy to come back. Her parents were at work, and Freddie was at day-care. As soon as her mother's bus had vanished down the road she'd almost run through the estate to get into the village. She had *A Study of Particulars* in her backpack, along with a water bottle and a banana. There was a box of plasters in the front zip pocket as well as a change of socks and pants. If she was going to travel today, she wanted to be ready. 'Yes. Is that sand on the floor?' Flick asked as she stepped forward and it crunched under her purple Converse.

'Oh yes,' Jonathan sighed despondently.

'Did you go to a beach or something?'

'Heavens, no. Not so much a beach as a desert. Some people can't even be trusted to give their boots a shake out before they come back.'

Jonathan tapped the dustpan out into a steel waste-bin and put it and the broom to one side. Flick tried to think of what to say.

'I read that book,' she said.

'And?'

There was a beat of silence. The travel agency stirred in the warm summer air and above their heads, the floorboards creaked.

Flick took a deep breath. 'I want to travel.'

(Lapinski 2020:72–3)

Flick has decided that she does want to become a member of the agency and use the suitcase-portals to journey between worlds. Mendlesohn (2008:xix) suggests that the portal fantasy and the quest story are intimately bound. The quest is a very familiar story-shape whose 'mono-myth' is often associated with Joseph Campbell's influential *The Hero with a Thousand Faces* (1949) and the Jungian 'meta-plot' model proposed by Christopher Booker's *The Seven Basic Plots* (2004). There are some important differences between these models, but what they have in common is that a Hero becomes separated from their community, follows a path of adventure, overcoming obstacles in order to find a boon – they embark on a Hero's Journey.

The Strangeworlds Travel Agency is, in some ways, a very traditional Hero's Journey, while at the same time offering some welcome innovations. As I consider this extract, I will be particularly interested in how these interconnected frameworks of Hero's Journey and portal fantasy are upheld in the text and how they are subverted. Let's jump in,

'You came back,' Jonathan said as Flick walked into the shop the next day.

We have our two protagonists, still unsure of each other, reuniting in an evocative setting. A magic shop as the locus for adventure is a common trope in fantasy writing, we see it in Mr Baslam's 'Eggsotick Serplys' shop in Dianna Wynn Jones's *Charmed Life*, Diagon Alley in the *Harry Potter* series and Pinn's in Jonathan Stroud's *Bartimaeus Trilogy*, among many others. The magical shop captures our imaginations. It blends the occult and eldritch with the quotidian and mundane; shops are everywhere, magic is not. The setting for this scene is a microcosm for the wider world-building, a world in which interdimensional travel is made possible by mundane mechanisms. A world in which adventure is within reach of a 12-year-old Hero. She heard the call to adventure and at first refused it, but Flick has now decided that she wants to listen and so has returned to the shop.

In both previous chapters we met an internal narrator. This time there is an external narrator, a persona telling us the story who is not also one of the characters in the piece. It is this external narrator who is reporting on the actions taken by the characters and – as we will see – has a degree of access to their thoughts too.

This has traditionally been the narrator of choice in children's literature and is a particularly fruitful technique to employ in fantasy fiction. A narrator who isn't tied to the experience and awareness of only one character is free to roam across narrative space and time. For plots that are more epic or saga-like the ability to comment on cultural norms and traditions that are unknown to the protagonist might be useful. The external narrator can move between characters across parallel settings in a way that doesn't require the creation of a brand-new idiolect, as would be the case in a polyphonic novel (a novel with multiple first-person, internal narrators). The external narrator is, therefore, a useful companion on a quest.

However, there is an additional feature of the external narrator that is of practical use to writers of portal fantasy. It answers a need, identified by Mendlesohn (2008:7), that 'the authority and reliability of the narrator must be asserted'. Mendelsohn is talking about the 'club-story' here, tales told by an authority figure to an assembled audience. An external narrator is, conventionally, a *reliable* narrator. If they tell you something is so, you believe it is so (at least within the pages of the book). They have the appearance of impartiality and objectivity. Again, a very useful feature for fantasy, where it might be harder for the reader to suspend their disbelief. Therefore, when the external narrator establishes the scene here – Jonathan speaking, Flick returning – it has the same veracity as if we were there in the room, watching it happen ourselves. An external narrator is conventionally a trustworthy eyewitness, with all the power that implies.

> He looked up from sweeping the floor to give her a wide and slightly self-satisfied smile.

Jonathan has been cleaning and Flick has interrupted him. It's an interesting little beat. Perhaps this action reveals something of Jonathan's character: he may be fastidious. Or perhaps it reveals something of the nature of the agency: it is a place that requires vigilant cleaning.

Our narrator might have chosen to tell us exactly what the action signifies through direct exposition, interpreting the meaning of Jonathan's action for our benefit (they are the voice of authority after all), but instead, we are left to make up our own minds.

The second half of the sentence, however, does incorporate interpretation: Jonathan's smile is 'wide and slightly self-satisfied'. What is curious about this sentence is whether the interpretation is authoritative. Is this the narrator exercising their power to tell us something definitely true? Or is it subjective? Is this Flick's slightly dismissive opinion of Jonathan? Because, although the external narrator is structurally separate from the characters, they don't have to remain so at all times, they can shift. The narrator can, as may be the case here, move into 'close third'. This is when the narrator assumes a position so close to one single protagonist that they have access to their subjectivity and even their inner thoughts or interiority. Were the narrator able to access the subjectivity and interiority of *all* the characters then it would be at that point that they would begin to morph into an omniscient narrator. Sometimes 'close third' is termed 'free indirect style' and both terms are commonly used interchangeably. However, I see a subtle distinction between the two. To me, the close third implies a close 'psychic distance' (called 'narrative distance' by Gardner (1991), and 'psychic distance' by Darwin (2010), which is the term I favour as there are already enough 'narratives' about the place), whereas 'free indirect style' to me implies a further psychic distance while still accessing the character's point of view.

To unpick this a little. As Philip Pullman (2017:245) says, 'the narrator is a character invented by the author'. Moreover, this is an 'inhuman' character with the ability not just to flit between the minds of the cast but also to move amid and along time and space. Pullman admires what he calls the 'classical tone' used by such an inhuman creature; a measured, judicial coolness. This narrator is likely to write in the third person and in past tense, an almost invisible, traditional choice that emphasizes the completeness of the account. I contend that, on the one hand, the 'free indirect style' is characterized by the use of an objective, 'cool' perspective coming from a narrator with authority, whether or not they are accessing the character's thoughts.

On the other hand, the 'close third' narrator is one who allows themselves, at times, to be subsumed by the voice of the character they are cleaving to. The coolness might be replaced, temporarily, by the heat of the living, human character. When the narrator is entirely subsumed, we would say that the writer is working in very-close psychic distance. When the narrator returns to their own inhuman coolness, the writer is working in far-out psychic distance. These are subtle distinctions, and it can be tricky to decide where the narrator stands in relation to the characters at any given moment, but it is a wonderful technique to play with, for a writer.

So, back to the magic shop. The cool, judicious narrator in far-out psychic distance tells us that 'He looked up from sweeping the floor.' We believe the narrator, why would we not? However, the second half of the sentence is a bit more slippery. That 'wide and slightly self-satisfied smile' might be the narrator's objective account, or it might be Flick's subjective one. Is it the narrator's thought, or Flick's? Looking to the vocabulary used and the rhetorical sibilance, I find myself concluding that this is *not* Flick's thought. Flick is a young, contemporary girl, and might use more robust, less lyrical language to describe Jonathan. I am forced to conclude, then, that the narrator is telling the truth, and Jonathan genuinely is self-satisfied.

> He was wearing brown tartan trousers, with a mustard-coloured shirt and a waistcoat that was a bit too big for him. It had an embroidered peacock on the back.

The narrator continues to focus on Jonathan, this time by describing his appearance. Anderson (2005) suggests five ways by which an author can reveal character: interpretation, appearance, action, thoughts and observations, and speech. In this instance, Jonathan's appearance is being used to reveal more about his character; each of his clothing items were chosen by him in order to curate a particular presentation (as is the case for most of us, resources permitting). He has decided that this is the right ensemble for an 18-year-old young man to wear to work.

Not only does this choice evoke a glamorous eccentricity (an embroidered peacock!), but it also suggests a certain affinity with the past. There's something of the steampunk cosplay about his choice. On the one hand, his clothes evoke the Edwardian gentleman, someone with a role to play in the machinery of empire; on the other, over the course of the series we come to learn (through subtle clues which are age-appropriate) that Jonathan is a gay trans man. In this context, his choice of presentation takes on a different set of cultural signifiers; his flamboyance can be read as resistance to the heteronormative hegemony.

> Flick closed the door behind her. It had been easy to come back. Her parents were at work, and Freddie was at day-care.

Here we can see the coming-together of the Hero's Journey and the portal fantasy. In this act, Flick is *separating* herself from her regular community; she literally closes the door on it (we will further discuss thresholds in Chapter 5). Then, we have a sentence with a dual meaning: it had been 'easy' for Flick to come back. 'Easy' in the sense that the decision to go on an adventure was an easy one for her to make – we are told in an earlier scene that she is keen to see the world. But also, it was 'easy' for her to come back, because no-one is going to wonder where she is and try to stop her. She comes from a working-class family and, as such, is treated as older than her years. This process of 'adultification', treating minoritized children as though they are less innocent than their peers, is dangerous and, in real life, can lead to harms at the hands of the police and other services. In literature, DasGupta (2024:6–7) suggests a range of narrative strategies a writer might employ to act as 'resistances' to adultification. These include widening the genres and settings within which minoritized children are allowed to play and star. Lapinski adds to these strategies by reclaiming a situation that may have been cast as dangerous to Flick herself and to wider society (an unsupervised, working-class child) and recasting it as an opportunity (an 'easy' route to adventure).

> As soon as her mother's bus had vanished down the road she'd almost run through the estate to get into the village. She had *A Study of Particulars* in her backpack, along with a water bottle and a banana.

Flick's social class has been determined earlier in the book, but the details selected by Lapinski continue to reinforce our understanding here. Flick's family use public transport, earlier in the novel Lapinski tells us they do not live in the picturesque village but rather in the controversial new-build estate. Interestingly, the narrator uses further-out psychic distance to deliver this information, using 'her mother' rather than the closer-in 'Mum'. There is a blend here of Pullman's cool classical tone with the rebellion and resistance represented by working-class joy.

Lapinski offers a welcome a diversification of both the Hero's Journey and portal fantasy in MG literature by having the adventurers be a working-class girl and a gay trans man. However, some of the traditional trappings of the genre remain. Mendlesohn suggests that portal fantasies are, by nature, 'anthropologist'. The protagonist enters a static other world as a curious stranger, a tourist; from there the plot 'relies upon both protagonist and reader gaining experience' (2008:xix). In this sense, there can be a colonial inflection to portal fantasies as they serve up exotic backdrops for stories that foreground the experiences of the traveller. Jonathan's choice of clothes, read as sartorially influenced by the wardrobe of an Edwardian gentlemen, sits within this milieu.

So, although the identities of the cast are more diverse, there are traditional genre patterns present too: this is the Strangeworlds *Travel* Agency, after all; anthropological exploits in unchartered lands comes with the territory. Having said this, Lapinski is well aware of the undertones and by the third book, Jonathan's confident assertion that he has any right to be the custodian of other worlds and is free to travel with impunity will be challenged, but for now, in Book 1, the magic system works inside the conventional tropes of the genre. Crossing borders is not without its dangers, but these two young, white travellers don't need visas, passports or sponsors to attempt the journey.

We can see this play out, on a small scale, as Flick 'packs' for this adventure. She brings the items a young person with a well-developed sense of practicality (a result of her class background) would take on an Edwardian-style globe-trot: the guidebook and easily transportable victuals. But even here, there is a degree of active subversion at play. The book *A Study of Particulars* has only the illusion of rationalist authority. Behind its pompous, self-important title, it is actually a rag-tag collection of somewhat unreliable observations, recorded haphazardly by whoever happened to assign themselves the task. As the series continues, Lapinski challenges the idea that this agency has any 'natural' authority at all.

> There was a box of plasters in the front zip pocket as well as a change of socks and pants. If she was going to travel today, she wanted to be ready.

In the first sentence, the narrator expands on Flick's inventory. Again, it reinforces our perception of Flick as a resourceful, competent young person, well used to taking care of herself and others. We can also see how closely entwined the portal fantasy is with the quest story; this list of items is reminiscent of the character inventory we might expect in a quest videogame with medical supplies added to the food. The final items on the list 'socks and pants' deliver a moment of bathos, of unexpected humour. I choose to view this as another strategy of resistance against the adultification of minoritized children. There is often an association between minoritized children and 'gritty', 'urban' or realist writing that foregrounds pain; moreover, readers from these groups can become alienated from the fantastical (Thomas 2019; Patterson 2022); humour can serve to disrupt that association. Yes, Flick is a child whose childhood contains elements of adulthood – taking care of herself, planning ahead – but she is allowed to remain a child with this moment of levity.

The narrator slips into close-third to report *why* Flick has packed with such care: she wants to be ready. This time, the narrator uses vocabulary that might well have come directly from Flick's internal monologue. Note the grammatical construction 'if she was' rather than 'if she were'; although both are correct, the traditionalist narrator would have used the subjunctive mood; Flick doesn't know what the subjunctive mood is.

> 'Yes. Is that sand on the floor?' Flick asked as she stepped forward and it crunched under her purple Converse.

Here we get our first sense of the other worlds to which the Strangeworlds Travel Agency is connected. Jonathan has been sweeping up sand that has arrived on Earth from another world in the multiverse. Writers of portal fantasy will always have to grapple with the demands of world-building as they determine what exactly is on the other side of the portal. There are some writers who agree with Tolkien that 'labour and thought and [...] a special skill, a kind of Elvish craft' are required in order to create what he terms an immersive 'Secondary world' (Tolkien, Flieger & Anderson 2008:61). This involves giving the impression of a holistically imagined environment in which systems such as habitats, communities, economies, cultures and religions, histories, governance, hierarchies and more are in place. Other writers, such as Brandon Sanderson, fear writers risk becoming 'so enthralled with building the world of your story that you never finish the world-building and never start your story' (quoted in Sangster 2023:324).

Whether the writer curates an encyclopaedia for their world or wings it, Sangster contends that they aren't in total control, 'audiences enjoy the illusion of wholeness, but are prepared to collaborate in that illusion, working to fill in the gaps' (317). We, as readers, are bringing all we know about the real world and the fictive worlds of literature with us. As we read this line and see Flick pre-empting her first journey by treading on interdimensional sand, we are already working to fill the gaps. Is the sand from a realist desert of the sort found on Earth, like *Lawrence of Arabia*? Is it from a sci-fi dystopia, like *Dune*? An orientalist fantasy-land like Narnia's neighbouring Calorman? Something else entirely? We don't know yet, it's just sand. But we are ready to collude in the creation.

Before we move on, I want to notice the shoes Flick wears as she stands on the sand: purple Converse. She too is choosing how to present herself through clothing, and, like Jonathan, has a somewhat flamboyant taste. There is kinship between them here at least. There's also something delicious about the confluence of the magical (interdimensional sand) and the mundane (streetwear); the eldritch and the quotidian sparking off each other again.

> 'Oh yes,' Jonathan sighed despondently.
> 'Did you go to a beach or something?'

'Heavens, no. Not so much a beach as a desert. Some people can't even be trusted to give their boots a shake out before they come back.'

In this section, we see the contrasting idiolects of the three characters present (I am including the narrator as a character). A character's idiolect is the extremely specific way that they would speak in a particular circumstance, as influenced by identity factors such as age, background, class, level of education, and situational factors such as the degree of ease they may be feeing and their current emotional state.

The narrator only has a few words here, 'Jonathan sighed despondently'. The use of the somewhat old-fashioned adjective aligns with the earlier reading of this quite classical narrator as a formal traditionalist.

Flick's idiolect is contemporary and informal; her 'or something' is relaxed and conversational.

Jonathan, on the other hand, is anything but casual. His gentle expletive, 'Heavens, no' sounds archaic to modern ears, perhaps a little prissy. The syntactical arrangement of his next line of dialogue has a formal construction, 'not so much a [...] as a [...]'. Even his admonition of the people who have caused the mess invokes the diction of an Edwardian nursery, 'can't even be trusted [...] give their boots a shake out'. Jonathan's idiolect is steeped in upper middle-class, British whiteness. I would be willing to bet that he attended a fairly expensive private school at some point. Were it not for his trans-ness, he could be a character drawn from the First Golden Age of children's literature.

> Jonathan tapped the dustpan out into a steel waste-bin and put it and the broom to one side.
> Flick tried to think of what to say.

Again, here we see a fascinating elision from the external narrator. As a (usually) classical narrator, they share more in common with Jonathan's upper middle-class idiolect than they do with Flick's working-class one. However, Flick is (usually) the focalizing character, which is the character through whom the events of the narrative are viewed. As we have seen, the narrator is able to move into Flick's mind using both close-third and free indirect style. In these sentences, the narrator uses a 'Jonathan' vocabulary to describe his actions: 'waste-bin' rather than 'bin', 'broom' rather than 'brush', but then shifts to close psychic distance and non-Standard English as they report Flick's thought: she 'tried to think of what to say' rather than the more grammatically correct 'think of something to say'. There's an elegant dance happening here, as the narrator moves gracefully between different degrees of intimacy and different points of view.

'I read that book,' she said.

'And?'

There was a beat of silence. The travel agency stirred in the warm summer air and above their heads, the floorboards creaked.

This is a pivotal moment in the book. It is the point at which Flick, our protagonist, is on the cusp of adventure. It is a liminal moment, between two states of being for Flick, the ordinary and the magical. It is its own 'portal' moment.

As such, Lapinski gives readers 'a beat of silence'. We're invited to pause for a moment to notice and observe time more ritually. As we observe, the magical system 'stirs'. The shop itself is personified. Another writer might have turned inwards, to Flick, who might, for example, have felt her pulse quicken or her breath catch. Lapinski chooses to turn outwards to the setting. This again underscores the significance of setting and world-building in fantasy writing. The travel agency wakes in 'warm summer air', this is a joyful, languid wakening. Readers are invited to draw symbolic connection between the agency and Flick herself. With this line of description, Flick is stirring too. The setting is being used effectively, as an avatar for the character and her state of mind.

Flick took a deep breath. 'I want to travel.'

Here we do switch to Flick's embodied experience of the moment: she takes a deep breath and answers the call to adventure. Her Hero's Journey begins.

Cited Works

Anderson, L. 2005, *Creative Writing: A Workbook with Readings*, 1st edn, Routledge, Abingdon.

Booker, C. 2004, *The Seven Basic Plots: Why We Tell Stories*, Continuum, London.

Campbell, J. 1949, *The Hero with a Thousand Faces*, 2nd edn (1968), Princeton University Press, Princeton.

Darwin, E. 2010, *Psychic Distance: What It Is And How To Use It*. Available: https://emmadarwin.typepad.com/thisitchofwriting/psychic-distance-what-it-is-and-how-to-use-it.html [2024, July 7].

DasGupta, P. 2024, '"All Children, Except One, Grow Up": Adultification in Alex Wheatle's "Crongton Knights" and Jewell Parker Rhodes' "Ghost Boys"', *On Writing for Young People* Bristol, UK, November 2023. *Leaf Journal*, vol. 2, no. 1

Gardner, J. 1991, *The Art of Fiction*, Vintage Books, New York.

Lapinski, L.D. 2020, *The Strangeworlds Travel Agency*, Orion Children's Books, London.

Lewis, C.S. 2023 [1955], *The Magician's Nephew*, HarperCollins, London.
Mendlesohn, F. 2008, *The Rhetorics of Fantasy*, Wesleyan University Press, Connecticut.
Patterson, C.W. 2022, 'Towards a Manumissive Black Fantastic in Fandom, Fantasy, and Literature for Young People, or: A Case for the Black Hermione', *The International Journal of Young Adult Literature*, vol. 3, no. 1, pp. 1–29.
Pullman, P. 2017, *Daemon Voices*, David Fickling Books, Oxford.
Pullman, P. 2018 [1995–2000], *His Dark Materials* (3 vol), Scholastic, London.
Sangster, M. 2023, *An Introduction to Fantasy*, Cambridge University Press, Cambridge.
Thomas, E.E. 2019, *The Dark Fantastic: Race and the Imagination from Harry Potter to the Hunger Games*, New York University Press, New York.
Tolkien, J.R.R., Flieger, V. and Anderson, D.A. 2008, *On Fairy-Stories*, HarperCollins, London.

SECTION 2: AN INTERVIEW WITH L.D. LAPINSKI

ELEN: Could you start just by saying how the how the idea for the agency arrived and perhaps what you did to grow that initial idea?

L.D.: It's such a children's book cliche, the magical portal. But actually, I wasn't thinking of children's books when this idea popped into my head. I was, am, a massive nerd, and it was *Doctor Who* that was the biggest influence.

I remember talking with one of my friends and saying, 'If I was the companion' (who's obviously always the hero, and the Doctor's always the haphazard weirdo being dragged around from world to world, not actually knowing what they're doing, even though they think they know what they're doing) 'I would want to bring the TARDIS with me, because, if the cybermen are gonna start shooting at me, I want an easy way out.'

I remember seeing an interview with Stephen Moffat who said the hardest thing to do when writing for *Doctor Who* is to figure out where to put the TARDIS: if it's too close, there's too much of an easy way out; and if it's too far away, then there's no exit at the end. And I remember thinking: *Well, what if you could pick it up and take it with you?*

And that's where the suitcase thing came from, because I thought: *Okay, it's got to be something small. It's got to be something portable. It's got to be something that people would accept from a traveller.* [...] It came out of wanting a transportable TARDIS.

ELEN: Did it come with Jonathan?

L.D.: Oh, yeah, Jonathan was the first character. He strolled into my head, fully formed. He put his feet up on the desk, and he's never left. He's still there. His story is over, but he's still there, rattling around. He wasn't meant to be such a main character, but he's very loud and very flamboyant and dramatic. [...]

But yeah. He arrived with the Travel Agency. They came as a package. I thought – because I knew that we would need more than one magical portal – they would all be stored together in one place, which is obviously disguising itself as this sort of incognito shop on the High Street. I really liked that. And Jonathan, as the guardian of that place, just arrived with it. He was already in there. He was installed from the word go!

ELEN: Could you talk a bit about the magical system?

L.D.: It was retroactively written. So, *Strangeworlds* was written in the space of about three months, and we sold it three days later in a pre-empt [a pre-emptive offer made to shut down an auction]. It all happened extremely quickly, and it was sold as very much a first draft manuscript; there were bits that said, 'insert description here'. It was very much the bare bones of a book.

So, the editor who bought it was brilliant and had amazing ideas for it. She wanted it to be a huge, enormous series; we're talking like seven books here. She was very much focused on the plot: what exactly are they looking for? How can we big-up this thing with Jonathan's dad? And all the rest of it. She had some massive structural edits, so I got stuck into those, and that took about five months. However, at the end of those five months, the editor who bought the book went on maternity leave and I was given to another editor, Lena McCauley. And she read the book, and she went, 'How does this work?'

Not once had anyone who'd read it up to that point asked, 'How does this work?' I remember sitting on the top floor of the Hachette building, where the cafe is, when she asked that question, and I felt like I'd had a grand piano dropped on me. I thought: *I don't know! A wizard did it??*

And looking back, that was the best thing that could have happened, because we went right back to the drawing board.

It was the idea that Jonathan needed a reason to keep Flick around that was really the catalyst for the magic system. She has to be special to some degree. She has to be able to do things that other people can't do. We already had the magnifying glasses as a way of finding magic, but it was very, very tiny. It was like a little footnote. Collaboratively, we brought that out, made it more of a big deal.

And then – you'll probably hear this lot from writers – it was like everything just fell into place. The magic in the universe is what is driving the schisms, which are inside the suitcases. The suitcases are actually just a McGuffin [a device to drive a plot]. They are a wonderful hook for marketing but, as far as the magic is concerned, they are not very relevant. The schism could be trapped in anything: in a drawer; a jam jar; in the toilet; they could be literally anywhere.

It was the actual magic system that we needed to work on. So, it was an afterthought. It came about after the plot, after the book deal. It came quite late in the game, really. Because Lena had asked that question, 'How does this work?'

[…]

Once we had a system of magic, it meant that the world-building could get a lot more concrete. It gave us something for the thieves to actually want. They want magic. It is currency, something they can exchange. It was something desirable. It was something that could drive the villains for the whole rest of the series.

And it was that [discovery of the magic system] that made us think, 'Okay, this can't be an ongoing chapter book series, where you can have endless adventures. This is an epic fantasy trilogy. This is a big story that's going to have a definite ending.'

[...]

ELEN: You've said in the past that you like to think about the emotion that the worlds they visit evokes in your reader, and I wondered if you could say a little bit about that?

L.D.: So, I am terrible for reading a book, loving a book, and then remembering absolutely nothing about it seventy-two hours later. I remember how it *felt*, though. I won't necessarily remember the names of the places, but I remember the feeling. And so, I always do my world-building backwards. I start with how it's going to make my characters – and therefore, by extension, the readers – feel. Feelings in books are contagious, and if characters feel a certain way, then the reader will as well.

So, I always start with the feeling, whether that's going to be fear, or excitement, or happiness, or whatever it is. It's a lot easier to start with the feeling, then describe it, and then do the suitcase with the clues of what it's gonna look like. If it's the pirates' world, it's going to be all barnacled and salt eaten, and all the rest of it. I'll do that, rather than starting with a suitcase, doing the description of the place, then finding out how the characters feel about it – which is how you read it.

ELEN: There is a line in Book One that I love. It's the line, 'You couldn't pretend to be controlling the electricity with your mind if the plugs didn't crackle.' How did you approach the intersection of class and fantasy?

L.D.: When I was growing up, if you wanted to read a book, it was about kids who lived in London or Oxford. Nobody from the East Midlands had adventures; we didn't exist.

So, I knew as soon as I started writing, that it was going to be set in Nottinghamshire. There's a lot of Nottinghamisms in the language that I didn't have to fight to keep, but I had to explain. I kept them in, because it's how I talk; it's how my parents talk; it's how my friends talk!

It seems like, if there was a character in a book when I was younger and they were poor, or they were working-class, it was always this enormous plot point. It was something they were going to overcome; like it was some sort of obstacle, rather than it just being real life. Where I live, someone who is 12 years old, going to pick up their little brother from nursery, is run-of-the-mill. That's ordinary. And I remember hearing from a teacher once, who seemed very concerned that that Flick was going to pick Freddie up from nursery school, 'She's only in Year 7.' But I know that she will have had her own key for several years at this point. It's not a big deal. That's normal.

[...]

Why isn't it seen more? When you bring up class in children's literature, I often think it turns into a plot point. It turns into a big deal. It's, 'Look! This is representation!' And you know, it's a book, set in a tower block. And everyone is looking at it. Why? There's millions of kids who live in tower blocks. There's millions of kids who live in council houses. This is not a big deal. I should think there's more kids who live in council houses than live in mansions. So why don't we see it?

ELEN: I've noticed that the narrator is very Nottinghamshire when they're focalizing Flick, but more posh when the focus is on Jonathan.

L.D.: It was consciously crafted. Because Jonathan is older than Flick and he is of a different social class – he's quite well off – he is putting on a persona. Even if he's not aware he's doing it, he is putting on an appearance. He wants to be seen as an adult. He wants to be seen as knowing exactly what he's doing. He is very pretentious. He's a very pretentious boy. And that had to come through, even though it's a third-person narrator. Actually, if it was first-person, and his book, he would be insufferable. I would still be writing it now. So yeah, it was consciously crafted.

And I think it kind of tickled me a bit, because they are both from the same city. They live five minutes apart, and yet, because Jonathan has gone to private school and has been brought up in this incredibly sheltered family and thinks himself incredibly important, the way the narrator talks about him is very different to how the narrator talks about Flick.

ELEN: One of the other things that I wanted to pick up on was the kind of incidental queerness in the text. I particularly like that you have a nonbinary villain. I feel like that's jumping forward a few steps in terms of representation. Was there a conversation about that with your publisher?

L.D.: All credit to my editor. Not once did she say that I shouldn't make Swipe [the nonbinary thief] a villain. She was totally on board from the word go. So, all credit to Lena there. But it was something I did on purpose. At that point – I mean this was written about five and a half years ago – I had only just come out myself as being nonbinary. I hadn't seen a single nonbinary character in literature, especially not in children's literature. So, I think you know, reading Judith Butler and things like that, you are aware that [nonbinary] people exist;

however, I had not seen us in children's books at all. I was hyper aware that I was about to put this person in, this character in, and thought: *this is going to go down like a lead balloon, not be noticed at all, or be made into a massive deal.* And it hardly got noticed at all!

I put Swipe in. And obviously Swipe uses they/them pronouns. And I sent it off, and the only comments were that there was a little bit of grammatical confusion, because Swipe is with another person at the time. As you read it, you did sort of trip over 'they', which is perfectly fine. I don't mind editing to make things clearer around that.

It was published, and hardly anybody noticed. And I thought it was great.

Also, Jonathan is transgender as well. And again, it's not explicit in the text. However, it is there, if you are the sort of person who picks up on those things. Like, when he's having his flashback moment, we know that he's wearing school uniform, and the uniform includes a skirt. He gives away a birthday badge, which is pink, and he says that the person who gave it to him thought he was a girl.

And again, almost nothing!

Apart from the people who did pick it up, who went bananas with joy about it, which was just so, so good.

I had one reader who's now become a friend. [...] He was live-tweeting along, as he was reading. I remember him going, 'Is it wrong for me to head-canon Jonathan as trans?' And I didn't reply. I thought: *I cannot possibly reveal this. You're going to have to discover it for yourself.* And the moment that he got to the chapter with the badge, he just exploded in this rainbow-riot of joy on Twitter. So that's exactly why I've done it. There's no coming out [in the novel]. No one ever says, 'I really need to tell you something; my name is ... and these are my pronouns.' No, there's none of that. Jonathan would not have that conversation with anybody.

I have actually written a coming-out scene with him and his dad. It's never been published, but I wanted to write it just for me. But after that I don't think he bothers telling anybody. It's not stealth, because if someone asked him, I don't think he'd deny it. Obviously, when he gets wet in the second book, and he has to get changed, he goes through a lot of body dysmorphia because he has to wear other people's clothes, and he hates that.

It's never a thing. It's never brought up. It just is. There are nonbinary characters or trans characters. There are queer characters of all descriptions and it's just never brought up. Because that's real life.

ELEN: I wanted to ask you about portal fantasy and the Travel Agency. Are they tourists, or, as they call themselves 'custodians'? How did the way they see themselves evolve?

L.D.: I was hyper aware, even when I was writing the first book, that there was this massive sort of colonialist vibe coming through, whether I wanted there to be or not. I've got these two white kids, you know, traveling to these places … naming these places. I mean, my God, the size of your heads! They're claiming to be custodians over these other worlds, because that is what they've been told they must do. Jonathan has been told this from a very young teenager: this is your responsibility; this is what we do in this Society.

By the time the third book comes around, I like to think that Jonathan, in particular, has wised-up to this quite a lot. He's nearly nineteen by that point. And he does come across a section in a book where there is a name of a world […] It has been given a name by the Strangeworlds Travel Society. And then it says, in the description, that the people who live here call it such and such. And he changes it back in the book; he crosses it out and changes the name back to what the people who actually live there call it.

I thought: *I have to include that.* Because for two whole books we've had people taking ownership of places that aren't theirs and claiming to look after places that aren't theirs. I wanted to show: *No, this is not a good thing actually. It does not belong to you.* You don't have to go with something you've come up with, because it's easier to say, or because you thought it's more catchy, you know. Call it by its actual name.

They revisit some of the worlds we've been to before, like Five Lights, who are not keen for these outsiders to come in and tell them how they ought to be doing things. I really liked writing that because I think it really showed how, particularly as white colonialist countries, we are incredibly guilty of sticking our oar in and thinking we are the saviours for coming in to help you. Like, did you think to ask before you weighed in? So yeah, I think the first book, you can very much view it through a colonialist lens.

I think it is possible to write portal fantasy without having this sort of colonialist angle hanging over it. But this doesn't. And it does take three books for the characters to realize that actually, no, this is not a good thing and I'm glad I had the chance to be able to write that.

SECTION 3: *THE STRANGEWORLDS TRAVEL AGENCY*, WRITING EXERCISES

The four exercises in this chapter are intended to help you think about the structure of a classic Hero's Journey and its connection with the portal fantasy. Beyond that, I'm also offering an opportunity to practise specific writing techniques that relate to how you present your characters and worlds to the reader. I'm hoping you might mimic the narrator's elegant dance in *The Strangeworlds Travel Agency*.

Exercise A – Emotional World-building

L.D. Lapinski says that they begin their world-building by thinking of the emotion they want to evoke in the reader. We're going to follow that process in this exercise.

1. Pick an emotion from this list: curiosity; fear; joy; despair; anger; excitement.
2. Write your choice of emotion at the centre of a blank piece of paper. From that central point, build a word-association mind-map. Write down any words, situations, symbols, images, objects, people, etc. that you associate with your chosen emotion.
3. Do this four or five times, so that there are multiple trains of thought spreading from your central point.
4. Now take a look at your mind-map. Connect some of the most evocative or meaningful items with a line drawn between them.
5. Use these selected items as the inspiration for a paragraph of descriptive writing – create a world inspired by these items. Think about its landscape; the flora and fauna; the people who might be there; as well as the sights, add other sensory details such as sounds, scents and textures.
6. Now that you have your world ready, the second exercise will help you create a character to explore it.

Exercise B – Revealing Character (after Anderson)

In my discussion of *The Strangeworlds Travel Agency* I cite Anderson (2005) and her contention that writers are able to reveal their characters by the use of five techniques: interpretation, appearance, action, thoughts and observation, and speech. For the sake of this exercise, think of a 12-year-old of your acquaintance (you can remember yourself – or others – at that age, if no handy 12-year-old comes to mind).

1. Let's begin with their appearance. Note down two things about the way they choose to present themselves (their hair, clothes, etc.) and one thing about their physicality that they can't change (their height, eye colour, etc.).
2. Move on to their speech (or idiolect). Note down three vocabulary words that reflect who they are. For example, how would they say something was good? How would they say something was unpleasant?
3. Next, consider their interiority. If this child were to enter the world you created in Exercise A, what would be the first thing they'd notice? What would be their first thought?
4. How would the external narrator describe your character in one sentence? What qualities would they ascribe to them (interpretation)?
5. We'll save 'action' for the next exercise.

Exercise C – Action!

We're going to combine the two previous exercises now. Imagine your character is situated somewhere regular, maybe even quite mundane; they are going to hear the 'Call to Adventure', which is an early beat in the standard Hero's Journey. They will become aware of the existence of your created world.

1. Write a short scene in which the character discovers the existence of a portal that will take them to your world. Write using an external narrator.
2. As you write the scene, weave in a few of the details you noted in Exercise B. Reveal your character at the same time as they discover the portal.

3. I promised we'd return to 'action'. To end your scene, have your character resolve to take an action that best represents who they are at this point in the story – do they plunge deeper into the world, or do they return (for now) to their mundane life?

Exercise D – Psychic Distance

In this final exercise in the chapter, you are invited to edit the scene you wrote in Exercise C, paying particular attention to the position of the external narrator. When editing, it can be very useful to concentrate on one aspect of technique at a time, rather than everything all at once (which can be overwhelming). So, this is a 'pass' (a focused edit) concentrating on the voice of the narrator. You will need three different coloured highlighters or pencils (if you are working in pen and paper); or you can use the highlight function on your computer.

1. Highlight all the sentences where you think the eternal narrator is very 'far-out' in terms of the degree of psychic distance they are using. These might be sentences where the narrator is providing exposition, sharing facts they know, or providing their own commentary on what's going on; they are speaking with authority, telling us about the scenario.
2. In a different colour, highlight all the sentences where you think the external narrator is 'close-in' in terms of psychic distance. These might be sentences that are closer to the idiolect of your character or use the character's physicality or embodied experiences to tell the story; the content might be more subjective or channelled through the character's thoughts or opinions.
3. In a third colour, highlight any sentence where you would like to change the psychic distance, either to move it 'far-out' or to bring it 'close-in'. These changes are likely to be because you'd like the exposition to be clearer (far-out) or you'd like the reader's emotional engagement to be more intense (close-in).
4. Look at the spread of the colours across the scene. Are you happy with them? Do they all make sense in context?
5. Make any changes you've decided are necessary with the voice of the narrator in mind.

Chapter Four

SECTION 1: *OCTOBER, OCTOBER* BY KATYA BALEN, A CRITICAL DISCUSSION

We're staying with middle grade (MG) fiction in this chapter, but this time leaving the fantastical behind and concentrating on mimetic fiction – mimetic meaning mimicking or imitative – novels that attempt to represent our own world as attentively and closely as possible. In other words, realist fiction (acknowledging the oxymoron therein!).

Katya Balen's *October, October* won the Carnegie Medal for Children's Literature in 2022. It is the story of October, a girl who has been home-schooled, or perhaps more accurately forest-schooled, by her father, until he is hurt in an accident for which October feels responsible and she is forced to go and live in the city with her estranged mother. Like many MG plots, the protagonist is forced to leave the safety of her routine domesticity and has to find her place in wider society – here represented by London. October herself is sometimes read as neurodivergent (although this was not Balen's intent: see the following interview). She is certainly often overwhelmed by her feelings and by the city itself. She feels guilty about her father's accident and yearns to return to the woods and the isolated, simple happiness she has there, where she is free to observe and learn from the natural world and her precious stack of books. October's evolving situation is beautifully expressed in Balen's lyrical prose. In the following extract, October has been taken to the shoreline of the Thames by her mother.

> There's definitely a dog and he's slick with water and covered in sand and mud and he throws himself into the river after floating branches and barks his head off. The dark shapes are bent over and scrambling in the sand and some of them have great long metal rods that beep. When I hear that I feel a scrunch in my chest because that sound is Dad's new heartbeat.
> Mudlarks.
> I look up and she says it again. *They're mudlarks. They search for treasure here.*
> Mudlarks.
> Things from the wild and from nature and from the earth and from the sky. Searching for treasure and scraps of stories washed up and washed away again by the iron-grey tide. Forever changing into something new and offering something different with every pull of the moon. The smog of the city lifts up a tiny little infinitesimal shred of itself because maybe this is where stories can end up. Maybe this is where rings end up. A dizzy rush

is swirling up from my tummy and it tingles in my fingers. It feels fizzy and unusual and like something from long ago but new and exciting at the same time. The buzz of stories and searching and finding the old and making the new. I keep staring at the mudlarks and their buckets and their little spades and their beeping machines, which the woman who is my mother says are *metal detectors*. She turns a stone over in her hand and holds it flat in her palm and shows me how it was once glass that the water has smoothed and shaped into a gem. It looks just like the magic stones I found in the woods and slipped under Dad's pillow in hospital. I start to feel the woods and the water stitching themselves together in my mind, and the story of the stones starts to spin again in my brain.
(Balen 2021:171–2)

Let's begin our discussion with the narrator's voice.

There's definitely a dog and he's slick with water and covered in sand and mud and he throws himself into the river after floating branches and barks his head off.

We can't tell, yet, that this extract is from the point of view of an internal narrator (although, of course, we would know this having read the rest of the novel). But we can tell that whoever it is that's speaking has an idiosyncratic point of view. That word 'definitely' is redundant in terms of the sense of the sentence – 'there's a dog' would work just fine – but the inclusion of the word suggests that there might be some doubt about the ontological truth of this canine. There's a slipperiness here; the speaker doesn't altogether trust the world they are observing. However, once the narrator has judged the dog to reliably be a dog, the sentence continues with exuberance: we see a string of simple nouns bonded together with five 'ands'. As with most rhetorical techniques, the Greeks have a name for this, polysyndeton, where conjunctions are used instead of punctuation to add gravitas or excitement. Anyone who has heard an enthusiastic 11-year-old tell a shaggy dog story will recognize this syntax. The narrator is racing to explain the scene. The choice of nouns is also noteworthy – water, sand, mud, river, branches. It is the natural world that is in the foreground for this narrator, regardless of its actual depth of field, regardless of whatever else is part of the scene. The narrator is also aware of the joy animals – mammals – can have interacting with the natural world; it's the verbs that convey this, 'covered', 'throws', 'floating', 'barks'. The dog is revelling in this habitat, and it may be that the dog is a stand-in for the narrator. The fact that the narrator uses the present tense situates them firmly in the 'now-ness' of the story. They are naturally 'staying in the moment' as a dog might, or as an untroubled child might.

It is noteworthy that the narrator notices the dog before they notice people, but there are people present in this scene. As we craft an internal narrator, the details they select, foreground or omit can reveal much about their character or state of mind. Here, we learn that the natural world is more real, more vibrant, to October than anything artifical.

> The dark shapes are bent over and scrambling in the sand and some of them have great long metal rods that beep.

The people, the humans, are just 'dark shapes'. Compare their verbs with the dog's. Whereas the dog was entirely at home in its habitat, the people 'are bent over' and 'scrambling'. To compound their alienation from the natural world, they also show signs of being not entirely human. They have 'great long metal rods that beep'. Note the verb 'have', not 'hold' or 'carry', as might be more expected. There is a deliberate ambiguity over whether these rods are part of the people or just tools. The image of a Dalek might come to mind for readers who are fans of *Doctor Who*. Again, October's observations unconsciously give her away; people pose an uncomfortable risk as far as she is concerned.

One possible reason for the narrator's discomfort comes with the next line,

> When I hear that I feel a scrunch in my chest because that sound is Dad's new heartbeat.

The beep of the metal rods sounds like the beep of the machines surrounding Dad in hospital. However, again, we have that same idiosyncratic point of view from the narrator, who we can now see – from the pronoun 'I' – is October herself. Heartache is expressed as a 'scrunch', a word that is commonly a verb, but here being used more as a noun – more slipperiness as October has trouble identifying her own emotions. The 'scrunch' is followed by a poignant metaphor, the beep 'is Dad's new heartbeat'. Beyond being an apt metaphor, the reader is also invited to extrapolate out to imagine the beep as part of the wires and machine and hospital paraphernalia keeping Dad alive; in this way the beep is metonymic, another rhetorical device in which one small part is used to invoke a bigger whole. The beep invokes the wider hinterland of a hospital and so October's grief, guilt and loss.

This alienation and grief suggest to me that *October, October* is not a story that follows either the Hero's Journey or a Hollywood Act Structure of the types we've seen in previous chapters. It suggests to me that it follows what Gail Carriger (2020) has identified as the 'Heroine's Journey'. This story shape (which can equally apply to male protagonists as to female ones) sees a heroine whose life is ruptured by loss at the beginning of the story and, rather than overcoming obstacles, has to build a supportive network of connections over the course of the story. At this point, October is still isolated, but the beginning of network is just on the horizon as she sees the possibilities the mudlarkers afford.

> Mudlarks.
> I look up and she says it again. *They're mudlarks. They search for treasure here.*
> Mudlarks.
> Things from the wild and from nature and from the earth and from the sky. Searching for treasure and scraps of stories washed up and washed away again by the iron-grey tide.

The vocabulary in this extract is simple – short words that come from a child's lexicon – but there is dexterousness to the figures of speech, an inventiveness that informs October's idiolect, although arguably this is ultimately Balen's voice or style recognizable across her novels. Balen is a literary writer. She pays keen attention to quite simple vocabulary paired with deft rhetorical devices. This is in harmony with the keen attention her protagonist pays to the natural world; there is a synergy of style and thematic content. October is someone who makes unusual connections as she observes the world; moreover, she delivers those observations using deceptively simple words, most often a vocabulary whose etymology is Old English rather than French or Latinate – a down-to-earth choice of words.

It is October's mother speaking the words in italics (so the French-origin word 'treasure' is hers). This has been a convention established from the beginning of the novel – Balen eschews traditional speech marks for dialogue in italics. This has the effect of filtering every utterance, from every character, through October's point of view. Had the dialogue been enclosed in speech marks, then the interlocutor would fully be given their own voice. Expressed through italics, the separation between October and other speakers is less clear, her awareness of them as distinct people is less certain, her own theory of mind less secure.

October's response to the information her mother gives is to deconstruct the noun into its two constituent parts – mud/larks. She goes on to define mud and larks as 'Things from the wild and from nature and from the earth and from the sky.' Again, Balen uses a repeated 'and' – three repetitions this time – however, the effect is not the same as it was earlier, when it signified an over-enthusiastic child. This time the repetition leans into the other effect of polysyndeton: gravitas. It slows the pace of the sentence, giving it a rolling rhythm, echoing perhaps the pattern of a prayer or an incantation. Both the 'mud' and the 'lark' are things from the wild and things from nature, so they share that essence. However, they are also opposites, the mud a static thing bound to the earth, whereas the lark is full of motion wheeling about the sky. October is struck by the contranymic quality of 'mudlark' – that a word can be two opposite things at once.

October here is aware of the 'betweenness' of things, the liminal and the way that words can capture this tension. The mudlarks are caught between the ground and the sky; the people are caught between the land and the river; and she herself is caught between the woods and the city. This geographical liminality is common in MG books, as the protagonists are typically moving between home and the wider society; we saw this in Chapter 3. However, this passage goes somewhat deeper, suggesting a more elemental connection between childhood and the natural world.

October is 11 years old and has been, throughout her childhood so far, a creature of the woods. In this way, she joins a tradition of young people isolated from the human world, immersed in nature, raised separate from society, from Mowgli to Danny the Champion of the World. She's the next in a long line of children viewed as a 'noble savage'; a character filled with wonder and delight at the natural world while being alienated by the urban. The idea harks back to the Romantic conception of childhood and what Christine Wilkie identifies as a blend of 'a beneficent, asexual, innocent interpretation of nature bedded in Rousseauism and the nineteenth century cult of the child' (1997:74). Rousseau rejected the idea of original sin in humans and suggested that it was civilization and urbane adulthood that corrupted young minds, severing them from their innocent state. Children should, he suggests, be educated at home, guided by their own curiosity and observation of the natural world, only later being introduced to society and its structures. This view went on to inform Romantic ideals of childhood as expressed by writers such as Wordsworth and Blake, before trickling down into some of the foundational texts of children's literature (typified, perhaps, most adeptly by the character Dickon in *The Secret Garden*, who has no formal education but by dint of youth and green fingers ascends to the role of mentor and teacher to the privileged heroes of the novel. Dickon is a 'noble savage' both because of his working-class status and because of his uncomplicated relationship with the natural world).

Claudia Mills expands the conception of the Romantic child, suggesting that the Romantic child also serves as a Redemptive child – one whose goodness and innocence 'transforms unhappy and embittered adults: Heidi, Little Lord Fauntleroy, Anne of Green Gables, Rebecca of Sunnybrook Farm, Pollyanna, to name only a few' (Mills 2012:171). There is a confluence of innocence, the natural world and childhood in these characters that serves as a tonic to adult characters, they bring a wholesome grace to the world. If October were simply a Romantic child, refashioned for twenty-first-century tastes, then her narrative arc might see her love of nature heal the broken adults, perhaps even curing her father. However, this is not the choice Balen makes. October breaks with this particular tradition of the redemptive Romantic child; she is not seeking to redeem adults, she is the one who is in need of redemption. She is the one, she believes, responsible for her father's accident. Over the course of the book, it is she who must be forgiven and healed, something that can only come about if she forges strong enough connections with other people.

Her shift of location, from the woods to the city, is a kind of purgatory for October and we see her, in this scene, in a moment of grace, where the city offers her something of the magic she has been missing.

Or rather, it is the edgelands of the city that provides grace. The Romantics saw the child's natural habitat aligned with the pastoral, and, by extension, the city aligned with corruption and harm. As Owain Jones writes, 'The urban environment is seen, not only for its problems, but also for its sophistication and its complexity, as a hostile environment for the innocence of childhood, and therefore for childhood itself' (2002:24). However, the city can be redeemed in contemporary storytelling – most children, after all, will be part of the urban population. More recent writers for young people have co-opted the wastegrounds, the brownfield sites, the canal towpaths and abandoned buildings of the city. These are places where city children can play, somewhat unsupervised, where they can create imaginative landscapes for themselves, away from prying eyes. Writers such as David Almond, Phil Earle and Alex Wheatle have made use of this alignment in their work, offering their child characters freedom by giving them access to edgelands. The children who play in the city's edgelands might be 'wild' in a Romantic sense or, less flatteringly, might be 'feral'.

It is this, more thorny, contemporary tradition where we might situate October – between the land and the water, the woods and the city, the wild and the feral, the child and the adolescent, needing to be afforded grace. As October undertakes her Heroine's Journey, forging connections in this edgeland, the city is redeemed too. This outcome is particularly welcome at a time when children are aware of the climate crises and writers for young people are desperately concerned to find ways in which literature for young people might respond constructively. The need for realistic hope in fiction is often suggested as a constructive way to discuss climate change with young people (Thebo 2023; Barrington 2024) and this redemption of the city is, to me, realistic hope.

The next sentence reflects the grace that the tides of the river represent, and there is a subtle shift in the language which speaks to these more abstract ideas,

> Forever changing into something new and offering something different with every pull of the moon.

October's idiolect moves into the lyrical here. Compare this sentence with the child-like idiolect describing the dog earlier. Gone is the breathlessness. This sentence uses poetic devices more liberally – the tide 'offering something different' is a personified, mercurial being. It is given the abstract epithet the 'pull of the moon'. There is the merest hint of agency to the river, that it might be deliberately placing offerings on the shore. It is very subtle personification, but the device brings poetry to the prose.

This sentence can also be read as an allusion to October's situation. She too is changing over the course of the book, and this passage is a particular moment of epiphany. The link between tides, phases of the moon, menstruation and impending puberty for October is also implicit in the imagery.

Any change in October's current situation, where she is miserable and feeling lost, represents hope. We see this more explicitly in the next sentence,

> The smog of the city lifts up a tiny little infinitesimal shred of itself because maybe this is where stories can end up.

Smog in London is a very Dickensian image (as well as being associated with the immediate post-war years, of course). However, these days, the coal-burning power stations of Battersea and Bankside are now expensive homes, shops and art galleries. So, by invoking the 'smog of the city' with this archaic image, Balen is drawing on the Romantic conception of the city as polluted and polluting. Smog here is used as more metonymy, it is a stand-in for everything awful in the city: the overwhelm, the noise, the grime, the loneliness, the isolation and more.

The hope and grace offered by the tide has shifted the smog 'a tiny little infinitesimal shred'. Balen here uses a little hyperbole, a rhetorical device that is associated with exaggeration, perhaps even with playfulness. The shift in rhetoric creates a shift in tone and so a shift in atmosphere, the idiolect of the child re-settles.

> Maybe this is where rings end up. A dizzy rush is swirling up from my tummy and it tingles in my fingers. It feels fizzy and unusual and like something from long ago but new and exciting at the same time. The buzz of stories and searching and finding the old and making the new.

The ring is an important symbol in the plot; October has found one of a pair of eternity rings and hopes to find its lost partner (the theme of reuniting being a significant one for a character on a Heroine's Journey). As she watches the mudlarks search through the gifts of the fresh tide, October wonders if the lost ring might be found. This idea is electrifying for her, and we can hear the zap of that electricity in the repeated 'z' sounds in this sentence: 'ring-z', 'dizzy', 'tingle-z', 'finger-z', 'fizzy', 'buzz' and 'stori-z'. Balen is using the repeated sound in the words, the parechesis, to support the meaning. October's tantalizing hope is the idea that it might be possible to find something old and make it anew – in short, redemption.

> I keep staring at the mudlarks and their buckets and their little spades and their beeping machines, which the woman who is my mother says are *metal detectors*.

This sentence again repeats the word 'and' – a device we're now familiar with. Here the idiolect has returned more firmly to that of a child. The repetition of 'and' here is more like the shaggy dog structure of the first instance rather than the spell-casting, prayer-like structure of the second instance. This is the voice of a young girl attempting to understand and make sense of the myriad details she is observing that were outside of her experience until only moments before. The zenith of her epiphany is over and the language reflects the return to the quotidian.

In this attempt at understanding, we can also see October's slippery relationship with nouns – the part of speech which allows us to name and classify. Notably, it is 'the woman who is my mother' who provides the missing noun 'metal detectors'. Again, the italics are being used to indicate speech. October's mother is aligned with the urban, the rational, in opposition to her father who is the Wild. October's mother is attempting to impose an unwelcome order on October and, in fact, rejected life in the woods, leaving when October was very young. By offering nouns to October, her mother is offering taxonomy with its implied reason and fixed boundaries, the clean, straight lines of the city, in direct opposition to October's desires. The pain of this rupture, their different worldviews and the rejection October felt and still feels, means that October refuses to reward her mother with any of the softer, gentler names we might expect a young girl to use; no 'Mum', 'Mam', or even 'Mother'. Most writers for young people have to consider what to call the parents in their novels – the choice will be closely aligned with the choice of narrator: first-person, close-third, omniscient or some other variation. Balen has selected the most distant naming convention that seems possible, to reflect October's distress at being in her mother's presence, 'the woman who is my mother'.

October's distress in this urban environment may come from another source too. Although Balen is clear (see interview) that October was not written as neurodivergent, it is perfectly possible to justify a reading of her as an autistic child. As Balen acknowledges, she, as the author, is 'dead' and readers do and will 'head-canon' (an informal term for non-official interpretations common in fandoms). October is often overwhelmed by stimulation and can slip into rages when the emotions are too difficult to process; she can hyperfixate. Of course, as someone raised away from people, overwhelm in the city would affect October whether she was neurotypical or neurodivergent. So, without diagnosing her at all, there is still room to consider what Melanie Yergeau (Heilker and Yergeau 2011:488) characterizes as 'autism as a rhetoric', which is a style of communication seen as a response or argument to a discrete set of circumstances. By thinking deeply and carefully about October's communication response in a particularly challenging set of circumstances, Balen has alighted on a rhetoric that includes not just the devices we might expect from a literary writer (symbolism, metonymy, etc.) but also physical rhetorics, mannerisms, ways of seeing the world, naming conventions and so on that coalesce to create October's unique communication style.

In the next line, we can see how October's communication style serves to hold her mother at arm's length, even as they share a sympathetic moment,

> She turns a stone over in her hand and holds it flat in her palm and shows me how it was once glass that the water has smoothed and shaped into a gem.

This small plot point, of a mother showing an interesting object to a child and explaining its provenance, is conveyed to us in reported speech. This is typically a device a writer uses when they want to convey something quickly as it would be too dull to represent in full dialogue form; it's commonly seen in phrases like, 'he told us how to use the machine' or 'we got him up to speed'. Even the fact it is reported speech is somewhat obscured by the use of the verb 'shows', which is a *visual* rather than an *oral* act. Mum's voice is repressed in October's storytelling. And yet, this is also a symbol – the stone was once a shard of glass, spiky and dangerous, yet time and tide have turned it into something smooth and precious. We are, of course, invited to draw parallel conclusions about the effect time and tide might have on October. Balen is making use of one of the creative joys of using a first-person narrator, the possibilities it offers for rendering an unreliable narrator. This is a narrator who tells the reader one thing – perhaps even believes it themselves – which the reader realizes is wrong or misconstrued (we have already met one unreliable narrator in Little Fish, Chapter 1).

October is an unreliable narrator because she believes her mother to be so different from herself, having chosen an urban life above a life in the woods.

And yet, the reader is shown a different side to October's mother, one who notices and cherishes the little treasures of life. She is not so different from October, even if October can't yet see it.

> It looks just like the magic stones I found in the woods and slipped under Dad's pillow in hospital.

Here, October herself is drawing parallels between a gem associated with her mother and 'magic stones' associated with her father. The symbol is being broadened to draw October's whole family into its orbit. The stone has shifted from being a symbol of transformation to being something that can effect change, a charm or amulet. This scene contains a moment of epiphany and the change it causes is felt almost immediately.

> I start to feel the woods and the water stitching themselves together in my mind, and the story of the stones starts to spin again in my brain.

The lyrical voice returns for this moment of insight from October – again she is slightly older than her years. We can hear it in the rhythm of 'the woods and the water stitching themselves together' as the stress falls on the 'w' sound. There's a hint of a rhyme in 'water' and 'together'. Alliteration returns, this time with the 'st/sp' sound in 'story of the stones starts to spin', which transitions to parechesis with the repeated 'in' sound with 'spin again in my brain'. This final sentence of the extract revels in the power of words to create musicality. This internal harmony reflects the content and meaning of the sentence – that she can feel disparate parts coming together to create a new story. This is the hope for redemption that she was seeking, hope that the two locations which have represented two sundered parts of herself – the woods and the Thames – should be able to be stitched together, like the edges of a wound, like torn cloth, to make something newly whole. The liminal space of the edgelands, when combined with Rousseau's wilderness and the spell of a story, should lead to healing. Crucially, October is finding this healing path for herself and unlike older texts – *Heidi*, *What Katy Did* – it is not October's disability that needs healing (should a reader choose to read her sensory overwhelm as a disability). Rather, October needs to forgive herself and allow the two parts of her life – the woods and the city – to co-exist. And here we have seen the scene structure and language demonstrate the first step to allowing those confluences and connections to take place.

Cited Works

Balen, K. 2021, *October, October*, Bloomsbury Publishing, London.

Barrington, R. 2024, 'Writing Hopeful Climate Fiction for Middle Grade Readers', *Leaf Journal*, vol. 2, no. 1, pp. 1–15.

Carriger, G. 2020, *The Heroine's Journey*, Gail Carriger, Milton Keynes.

Heilker, P. and Yergeau, M. 2011, 'Autism and Rhetoric', *College English*, vol. 73, no. 5, pp. 485–97.

Jones, O. 2002, 'Naturally Not! Childhood, the Urban and Romanticism', *Human Ecology Review*, vol. 9, no. 2, pp. 17–30.

Mills, C. 2012, 'Rousseau Redux: Romantic Re-Visions of Nature and Freedom in Recent Children's Literature about Homeschooling', in *Time of Beauty, Time of Fear: The Romantic Legacy in the Literature of Childhood*, ed. James Holt McGavran, University of Iowa Press, Iowa City, pp. 169–83.

Wilkie, C. 1997, 'Digging Up "The Secret Garden": Noble Innocents or Little Savages?', *Children's Literature in Education*, vol. 28, no. 2, pp. 73–83.

SECTION 2: AN INTERVIEW WITH KATYA BALEN

ELEN: Could you start by talking about the genesis of the book and the sorts of things you were thinking as you were settling down to write?

KATYA: So, I never plan books, and that can have various outcomes. I can have a very vague idea, or I can have no idea at all. With this [*October, October*] I had a vague idea, which is nice.

So, my father-in-law, about ten years ago, sold his quite normal house in Buckingham and bought forty acres of woodland. He built a house and went off-grid. [...] When I went there for the first time I was like: *Well, this is quite an incredible place.* My partner obviously didn't grow up there. But I thought: *What if you did? What if you grew up here?* And not only that, what if you didn't really leave; what if you didn't go to school? And then, one day – you know, something's got to happen – what if you had to leave?

And that was it; that was all I had. I really struggled at first to know what to do about the mother. I was like: *I don't want it to be a two-parent family.* One, I think that's slightly too neat, and it could be a bit too twee or cozy, you know, mama-bear and papa-bear and baby-bear in the woods. And two, when October leaves, she's got to go somewhere. And so, I was like: *What should I do? How do I work this? Should her mother be dead?* Actually, figuring out what to do with the mother became, I guess, the hinge of the story. And that was quite good, because I was already about 8,000 words in at this point.

[...]

I think that the dynamic between October and her mother, that was an interesting thing for me to explore. I think that we're quite used to fathers being absent in literature – and in the world – and a mother being absent is a richer seam. I didn't want it to be blaming a woman for not being the right sort of mother, because I think that we get a lot of that. I just thought: *Well. Could we show someone who's trying their very best, but not willing to sacrifice everything on the altar of motherhood?* i.e. living in a wood, with, you know, dodgy electricity and no friends.

[...]

ELEN: I wondered if you could talk about the connection between October and the woodland?

KATYA: I grew up in Peckham. But I loved nature. I wanted to live in the countryside. I always begged to live in the countryside, and my parents are like, 'No, we have jobs in London.' [...] So, running around the countryside, that's what I think children want. I think they want to feel wild and feel free, and I think it is trickier in a city. I think about all the things that I was able to access, you know, all the museums, all the free things, all the culture, all the art, which I'm sure has put me in great stead. But you know, when you're seven, you're not like, 'Oh, yeah, we're going to Georgia O'Keeffe at the National Gallery again.' You're like, 'I wanna be climbing a tree.' So, it's a balance.

But I do think it's important that children should be able to experience all of the country they live in. Essentially, they should be able to go and see the sea and climb trees in a forest and also go to art galleries. It's impossible, but that's the dream.

ELEN: And you do find the wildness in London as well, in the book. I wondered how that came about?

KATYA: So, my parents live in Central London on the river. When I went to see the house they were gonna buy, I thought: *This is so peaceful, this is so quiet. It's amazing.* It was so quiet and lovely and gentle. And it's not always like that, there's some alcoholics now and again, but, you know. And then I saw the mudlarks, and I was like: *What are those weird old men in anoraks doing?* And I just started to see all these different layers to the city that I've lived in my entire life, and that was really pleasing, I think. You don't really notice the tiny details, the little beautiful bits. And I think that happens with London as well, or anywhere that you live. So, it was nice to see a new side to it and discover the world while I was writing.

I was already 20,000 words in by the time I decided to put them [mudlarks] in, because I saw the men.

When I went mudlarking for the first time, it reminded me of being a child. I think all children are little magpies, and you know they find a stone that they have to put in their pocket, or a feather that they're gonna keep forever. Mudlarking is basically that. You're finding all these cool objects and putting them in your pocket. When I do school visits, I take a load of mudlarked stuff, which is essentially crap, like, it's bits of bone and shells and glass and clay pipe – it's not gold coins, or anything! They love it! And they nick them! I don't blame them because it's this really cool, tangible thing – they believe it might be a portal to another world. There is something about mudlarking. I know it's not for everyone. But that's what I feel like. You could just find anything. And I think that that links really nicely to childhood, where there are so many possibilities that the adult mind gets closed off to.

ELEN: I know that you're careful not to ascribe any particular neurodivergence to October. I wondered if you could say something about that?

KATYA: I think this is something that's very much evolved since the book was published. I think partly that is because I have worked with autistic children. People make a natural assumption that those are characters that I will write about. But I didn't write her as autistic, if I'm honest with you. I didn't. Because I was trying to write a child who had not had the experiences that most children have had – neurotypical or not. Therefore, her reactions to them [the experiences] probably do, I suppose, mirror sensory overload. There is sensory overload! But how do you disentangle what would be organic neurodivergence from what has become environmental?

I think you can say she's completely overwhelmed in exactly the same way as autistic kids are. And I'm like: *Yeah, fine*. But what would she be like if she'd just gone to school at 4 years old? I would say she's not autistic in the woods. So where does that leave you?

I don't know. I'm dead. I'm the author!

ELEN: How would you characterize your writing? Do you have a sense of the style?

KATYA: I do have quite a strong internal sense that I want my writing to be beautiful. I think that would be my main aim. Really, I mean, I don't do plot very well. I don't plot, as I said prior. I'm not good at thinking about what should happen in a book. As a result, very little usually happens. And so, I know I need to put some sort of flesh on the bones. And I want that flesh to be really nice. So, I do have that thought in my head. And that's as far as I can analyse my own style, because that's how I go into it.

ELEN: What does the process look like to get there?

KATYA: I'm quite strict. I am quite ordered with my writing. I work out how many words it needs to be, which for a middle grade book is about 40,000 words. And I look at my calendar, and I work out: *if I write 1,000 words a day, when am I gonna finish?* But you know, I'm really disciplined. I will just write, and quite often, because I don't really know what's gonna happen next, I go back. And I, sort of, add and add, and I pile more stuff on. And then that generally causes some sort of catalyst, and I can move forward, but I will quite often be in the same third of a book for a week. I'm adding to the work every day, but I'm just fleshing out, fleshing out, fleshing it out.

I think one of the ways in which my writing works for me, and ends up the way that it does on the page, is because I'm quite free. I think that's probably the nub of it. I don't know what I'm going to write next. I can go anywhere. I can do anything.

ELEN: Does that mean you need tough structural edits?

KATYA: Somehow it always ends up okay. So, this book I handed in yesterday is 38,000 words. And at about 30,000 words, I thought: *This is coming together.* And that can happen at 20,000 or 35,000 or sometimes right at the end. And you just think: *Oh, thank God!* All of the themes that I was throwing at it have finally –

I don't know how it happens! But it's really nice. A lot of it must just be some subconscious thing [laughing]. I put a load of crap in this about feelings and stuff, and then, you know, you start to work out exactly what it is you want to say. So, my edits are very rarely structural. It's usually things like: *What does this character really want? Let's pull that closer to the surface, and maybe prune back some of the other stuff.* So, it's basically, this is the one thing that needs to be pulled up and polished, and the rest is the window dressing.

ELEN: And is it to do with the kind of motor of the book, would you say?

KATYA: I think that works! My motor is always a character. It's always what this character wants, it's their arc, it's their development. It is very rarely anything plotty, because I can't do it. How I feel about plot is that it just starts to feel really creaking and awkward, because I know I need to get this group to go here to do that. And it's like, 'So we walked along the road … '. I find it really hard!

ELEN: It feels mechanical?

KATYA: Yeah, exactly. It's mechanical. It doesn't feel natural. So, I'd rather have a character pulling that all along, rather than car chases and stuff – but children would probably really like that!

ELEN: Oh, I think that there are children who like both, we need both. I wonder, could you say something about your publishing journey?

KATYA: I mean, I've been relatively lucky, and my publishing story is really boring! I was working in social care with autistic children and their families, doing early intervention. My department was being shut down. And so, I was like: *I'm going to get a job, but I've probably got enough savings to do a couple of months of …* I wanted to get into publishing. I did an internship at RCW [Rogers, Coleridge and White Literary Agency]. And I was so impressed by the slush pile. Because even though a lot of it was not good, these people had actually sat down and written a book! I was like: *How can I sit here and say this isn't good enough?* Some of it was laughable, but I didn't laugh! Because I was like: *It doesn't matter; you've written a book! That's incredible.* Yeah. And I thought, if they all did it, maybe I could have a whack at this too. It was something I'd always wanted to do. I make it sound flippant, but it's always a bit embarrassing, I think, for me to declare, 'I want to be a writer.' Especially because I was about 24 and everyone thought I should get a proper job. Which, you know, I guess is what people think. They wait until you've achieved something, and then they go, 'Well done.' Whereas anyone who has this sort of creative ambition, until they prove themselves, people can be really dismissive. I was quite afraid of that.

Anyway. I sat down and wrote a book, and I sold it. I mean, I got an agent for it and sold it. It was all quite smooth. I said, 'If this doesn't work out, at least I tried; just like those people on the slush pile.' I think it's sort of an act of bravery. I don't think I would have been one of those people that keep going and keep going. I was ready to say, 'Well, you need to get a proper job again, so we can't be obsessing over a manuscript for the next few years.' I know that's not what people do; they tend to fit it around work. But I had this opportunity, and I was determined to make the absolute most of it.

ELEN: I do want to ask about dialogue in the book. You've chosen to do the dialogue as reported speech, or it has no speech marks throughout. Can you talk a little bit about that?

KATYA: I think when you read my books you are so – or I try and make it so – in the head of the character that you're pulling that apart to go into open dialogue, as I think of it. [Dialogue that's] being spoken to everyone; I feel like speech marks make it speech to everyone. Whereas italics make it direct to her. It's directly into October's brain. I think that makes it more intimate and keeps up the interior monologue type thing that I like writing.

But the other reason is about aesthetics and confidence. I don't think that I'm very good at writing dialogue; it can sound quite unnatural. This was a way of getting around that, a little bit, you know, just giving those fragments of speech.

ELEN: It's really interesting what you say about being intimidated by dialogue. Jon Klassen has said in the past that he's scared of colour, he doesn't know how to use colour, so his books have that muted palette. Maybe there's something to be said for leaning into your fears and trying to adapt into them and see what that does to your creative output?

KATYA: I mean, fear is part of it, of you, isn't it? And therefore, I think, if you lean into that, you end up with something that is more original and specific to you rather than becoming generic. I risk making myself sound grandiose. But you know, everybody's using colour, and everybody is using speech marks. If you develop something, you become known for something. [...] You know, you could pick out a Jon Klassen image just like that, couldn't you? Because of the colour palette. And you could say the same thing about someone like David McKee or Quentin Blake. Perhaps Quentin Blake was scared of not scribbling!

ELEN: I wouldn't be surprised!

KATYA: Rather than saying, 'I can't do it, so I won't do it' or 'I try to do it and feel really uncomfortable', just embrace the fear. Do what you want! I like that!

SECTION 3: *OCTOBER, OCTOBER,* WRITING EXERCISES

The exercises in this chapter are an invitation to play with style. We all have a natural writing style, a 'voice' that is recognizable from book to book. However, some stories might want you to find a different voice, and knowing how to play with the elements of style might encourage evolutions in your voice.

Exercise A – Rhetorical Devices

We saw many devices used in this extract: metonymy, anaphora, polysyndeton, personification, hyperbole, parechesis, symbolism and alliteration. Many, many more exist and are worth having in your writerly toolbox. However, we will practise using the ones we've just observed.

1. Look around the space in which you are reading. It will provide the material for your writing. Notice, for the time being, things like the source and quality of the light, the size and dimensions of the space, the dominant colours and textures. Can you hear anything? Can you smell anything? How comfortable or uncomfortable is it? What makes it so?
2. Pick one element of the space, describe it in a sentence or two using alliteration (so many of the words begin with the same sound).
3. Add another sentence or two to your description, this time play with parechesis (any repetition of sounds, which may be internal rhymes or part-rhymes too). Take your time with this – one sentence that nails the task is better than three or four that don't quite manage it.
4. Polysyndeton can have two quite contradictory effects (as we saw in the extracts) – it can slow the pace and add gravitas, or it can be a breathless rush to the end. Decide whether you want sobriety or effervescence. Add another sentence to your description, this time make it long, with limited punctuation. Instead use conjunctions ('and', 'but', 'because', etc.).

Exercise B – Symbolism

1. Pick one object in the space you are in. This is going to serve as a symbol. The intention in this exercise is that you do not name any emotion in your writing; rather, the object will serve as a symbol for that emotion.
2. Imagine a character (you can use one from a previous exercise, or a version of yourself). That character is noticing the object as they take the room in. They are also feeling lonely.
3. Write a sentence or two of description, it should take in the room in general and the object. Without using the words 'lonely', 'alone', 'loneliness' (or any other variation!), convey a sense of the character's loneliness.
4. Imagine that you are skipping forwards in the story. The character has experienced a sequence of events that means that they are no longer feeling so alone. They return to this space. Write a second set of sentences, taking in the room and the object, this time, without using words like 'happy' or 'joyful' convey a sense of the character's happiness.

Exercise C – Word Archaeology

You will need a thesaurus for this exercise (a physical copy or a digital one are both fine). The extract we just looked at played with the constituent parts of vocabulary, the roots of words. Mudlark is divided into 'mud', which is of Proto-Indo-European (PIE) origin, and 'lark', which is from a Proto-Germanic origin. These sorts of words have been used, with only small variation in sound and meaning, for millennia. They are part of the earliest building blocks of English. Other words come from other sources and bring with them the cultural echoes of their history. The English word-horde comes from PIE, Germanic, Norse, French, Latin (both classical and medieval), Greek, the myriad languages of the British Empire and more. Writers can play with these language families in order to create an idiolect for their characters or narrator.

1. Think of a common verb, one that has been around for a long time (for example, to eat, to run, to cook, to sleep, etc.). Find that verb in the thesaurus.
2. Do the synonyms group in any way? For example, I looked up 'to cook' and there are a preponderance of words beginning with

'b' (boil, bake, burn) and words beginning with 's' (stew, steam); there were also words that sounded quite 'fancy' (fricassee, sauté) and words that sounded very 'un-fancy', perhaps because of their recency and association with convenience (microwave, nuke).

3. Imagine a character who might use one of your groups. Write a short stream-of-consciousness, first-person piece and have them use one or two of the words.
4. Imagine the same character, this time meeting another set of words, perhaps because they are in a new situation where those words would be commonly used. How would the character feel, would they adapt their language? Write a second stream-of-consciousness piece introducing one or two of these more novel words.
5. If you are interested, look up your groups of words in a comprehensive dictionary like the Oxford English Dictionary (a public library card will often give you free access) or an etymology website such as etymonline. Do your groups of words have a similar origin? How old are they? Do they sound like they are from the historical period in question, or are their origins surprising? Are they redolent of the time in which they emerged?

Chapter Five

SECTION 1: *OTHER WORDS FOR HOME* BY JASMINE WARGA, A CRITICAL DISCUSSION

Note: this chapter contains discussion of a life disrupted by war and displacement.

With our next extract, we step into a different form, the verse novel. *Other Words for Home* by Jasmine Warga is a middle grade (MG) novel, told in verse. It charts a year in Jude's life, from her initially comfortable home in Syria, which is soon affected by war, to America, where Jude and her mother are sent for safety to live with relatives. Bush (2019:456) says of the book, '[it is situated] at a sweet spot for middle-graders – with bloodshed and complex politicking at a safe remove, but with the obstacles of relocation and sense of family danger fully in place'. We will join Jude and her mother at a key moment of relocation with this extract. I should note that this is not the complete poem, it continues beyond the lines quoted.

> We arrive,
> in a city that I cannot pronounce,
> a city called Cincinnati.
>
> When the plane lands,
> Mama and I are quickly directed to a long line
> for people like us,
> people who are not from America,
> but who are trying to enter.
>
> The line moves slowly.
> My eyelids feel heavy
> and my body does not have any idea what time it is.
>
> It is finally our turn.
> We are called up to talk with a man
> sitting in a booth
> under a sign that says
> *Immigration.*
>
> The man beckons for us to step up closer.
> He has kind blue eyes that seem tired.

Everyone in this airport seems
tired.

He starts talking and I know some of the words
that are coming out of his mouth,
but my mind feels sticky
and I can't quite catch the meaning.

Back home,
I was always good at English.
I was one of the best in my class
at having pretend conversations.
I think of practicing simple phrases with Fatima
right before I left.
I think of how easy they came to me then –
How are you?
Good. Thank you.

Are you hungry? Would you like to go to lunch?
I would like a sandwich, please.

But this man is not asking me
simple things like
if I am hungry or what I would like to order.
He is asking real questions that
I can barely understand like
Why are you here?
And how long do you plan on staying?
(Warga 2019:62–4)

Let's begin our closer look.

We arrive,
in a city that I cannot pronounce,
a city called Cincinnati.

The first thing that strikes me is the nature of the poetic persona. In common with many verse novels written for young people, Jasmine Warga allows the protagonist to speak – or, perhaps more accurately, think – in the poetic voice. Jude is delivering a dramatic monologue, which should not be perceived as a piece of written poetry; Jude is not, herself, the poet, recording these poems in her writing journal. Rather, her interiority is served in poetic sequences. Many verse novels for young people adopt this style of persona, from *The Crazy Man* by Pamela Porter, *The Weight of Water* by Sarah Crossan, to *Activist* by Louisa Reid and many more. The affect is to create distilled vignettes, moments of time in the character's life that the author selects as worthy of attention and allows the character to assume the poetic persona in order to present them. The connective tissue of prose – getting the characters from A to B, scene transitions, chapter structures, are deliberately absent, creating what Imogen Russell Williams (2019), when reviewing Sarah Crossan's *Toffee*, describes as an experience 'as satisfying as a smoothed piece of seaglass, strung together'. The implication of this metaphor is that the poems in a verse novel are units of irregular but similar size and shape. It has been my experience, working with student verse novelists, that the selection of which vignettes to include is crucial to building the forward momentum of plot – stasis is a siren song, unless the verse novelist is watchful. In this extract, Warga has chosen a powerful moment, with movement implicit within it – the moment of arrival in America.

The next thing I notice is, like many other verse novels, *Other Words for Home* is written in free verse. This is emerging as a characteristic of this fairly new form (the first verse novel for young people is generally thought to be *Make Lemonade* by Virginia Euwer Wolff in 1993 (Fisher 2023:4)). Free verse is verse that doesn't follow any set rhyme scheme or rhythm; it is the manipulation of the layout on the page: the line return, with or without enjambment (a line return mid-sentence); the use of stanza and white space, coupled with the poet's intent and use of poetic language which establishes the 'verse' part of the 'verse novel'.

The 'novel' part of a 'verse novel' is established by the narrative. Each poem contributes to an over-arching plot or story, the vignettes accumulating to form the cohesive whole. As Fisher says, 'The verse novel is a performance between end papers' (2023:6) and it is the poetic persona of a central hero who delivers that performance and creates a story.

In this poem, we are at a crucial moment in Jude's story; she is arriving in her new home. As might be expected (and, indeed, is common in verse novels), this vignette in her life, this moment worthy of attention, is relayed in present tense by our internal narrator. We have seen the power of a present-tense delivery before, with October in Chapter 4. In this instance, the use of the present tense underscores the unpredictability of Jude's future. It is a path being made as she steps onto it; her previous life-path has been ruptured by war.

In this beat, we are looking at a single sentence, split over three lines. This division of the sentence allows each line to take on its own resonance, the words are given separate weight.

The first two words state the cataclysm, with the enjambment allowing them their own line, almost as if they were the title of the poem. 'We arrive'; it is the action from which all subsequent consequences arise. Even though this is a vignette, it is threaded with movement.

Jude's alienation from the place of her arrival is the next note-worthy part of this experience. This is the thing that matters to our protagonist. She cannot pronounce the name of her new home; her outsider status is already becoming established. However, there's a delicacy to this confession, a beauty: there is the formal language 'cannot' and the sibilance of 'city' and 'Cincinnati'. There is poetry here and it doesn't take second place to narrative. Additionally – and try this aloud – 'the city of Cincinnati' is something of a tongue-twister for those (like me) unused to saying the name (or producing the sibilants, to borrow from Linguistics!) very often.

> When the plane lands,
> Mama and I are quickly directed to a long line
> for people like us,
> people who are not from America,
> but who are trying to enter.

The fourth line of the poem establishes the precise setting; Jude is at the airport. As each poem in a verse novel is a discrete entity (a bead of 'seaglass'), their spacial and temporal positions, relative to each other, might vary considerably. So, this serves to establish location. The description of the airport is sparse – it has 'a long line' and that's all we get. As Fisher says (2023:5), 'a verse novel demands the skill of inference'. It is up to the reader to conjure the surroundings from their own knowledge of an airport. Descriptive passages are eschewed in favour of a tight, emotional core. Typically, the word count of a verse novel is considerably less than a prose novel for the same readership would be (*Other Words for Home* is 30,000 words long). What matters is not the details of this particular airport, but rather that Jude and her mother are there and being funnelled with haste into a long line (or queue in British English). This line in the poem is the longest we've been given so far, echoing the physical space it takes up in the 'real' world. Then, the enjambment makes it clear why this queue carries such emotional weight; 'for people like us' is given its own line, its own space to resonate.

Jude in this moment, is acquiring a new understanding of herself, a new label. She and Mama are in the process of being defined by difference. They are 'not from America'. Again, this is a formative moment as her 'outsider' status takes shape in her own imagination.

This 'revision', re-seeing of herself, will go on to be an important generator of plot/story. We have looked at conflict as a plot generator in previous chapters. Here, it is the internal conflict, of realigning her own identity in the face of external identity markers, which shapes the story. It is in this moment that that process begins.

> The line moves slowly.
> My eyelids feel heavy
> and my body does not have any idea what time it is.

The next two sentences, over three lines, have an internal rhythm shaped by the repeated syntax. The first two lines follow the pattern 'subject; verb; adjective'. The adjectives, 'slowly' and 'heavy' suggest something lumbering and large. Jude is perceiving herself as sinking into a mass; losing herself to some degree. The conclusion of the sentence re-enforces this sense of disembodiment. She has lost sense of time, disconnected from the quotidian rhythms of her previous life and now, traveling across time zones, is untethered. The phrasing is interesting, it is Jude's 'body' that is untethered, not the 'I' self. Again, this suggests a loss of definition of the physical edges of herself. The airport is a place of change and transformation, and Jude is experiencing that here.

> It is finally our turn.
> We are called up to talk with a man
> sitting in a booth
> under a sign that says
> *Immigration.*

The site of transformation is given a locus in these lines, the Immigration booth. It is an official gateway, and a legal transformation will happen when they pass through it. However, the structure of this stanza humanizes this locus to a degree, softening the officialdom. Because the stanza is delivered from the perspective of the child narrator, the booth is seen through the eyes of a child. Jude notices the person first, the man, then the booth, then the official designation of the booth. The verb choices also humanize the official; Jude and her mother are 'called' to 'talk with' him; the 'man' is 'sitting'. There is a conversational slant to this experience, rather than the coldness of officialdom. The enjambment ensures the word 'man' – the person – has prominence. It may be that this is Jude's experience, or it may be that Warga is deliberately softening this experience with an awareness of her middle-grade readership (we discuss this issue in the following interview).

However, the fact the word 'Immigration' is given its own line, and italicized, does afford it weight and power. It is arresting, with all the significance of that verb. Retno Yuliati (2021) offers a study of *Other Words for Home* using an intersectional lens and Patricia Hill Collins' 'matrix of domination' paradigm (an interconnected mesh of structural, disciplinary, hegemonic and interpersonal oppressions). In the study Yuliati considers how Jude moves from a state of oppression to empowerment; moreover that the oppression comes as a result of her age, race, gender, religion and social status. These intersecting identities are at play here as the female, Arab, Muslim child approaches the white, adult, American man.

As she walks up to him, Jude is crossing a legal and cultural boundary. *Other Words for Home* is a transnational verse novel, which is not an uncommon association of theme and form. Friesner (2016) identifies a range of transnational verse novels on themes such as: 'the journey to the United States; the home and families left behind; adapting to a new climate and learning a new language; healing from traumas endured; and participating in new customs that seem alien' (81). Of course, the arrival country does not have to be the United States, as we've seen with verse novels such as *The Crossing* by Manjeet Mann and *The Red Pencil* by Andrea Davis Pinkney and Shane Evans and more, which explore internal and international displacement beyond the USA.

Friesner's list of transnational tropes suggests loss and pain – which, of course, is likely to be present even in the most happy circumstances of relocation. But there is also a case to see transnational writing as having a more positive dimension too. Bambo Soyinka puts it like this, 'When reframed as a threshold, the transnational border is a site for making meaning: it is an imaginative space through which we can move back and forth from the known to the unknown; and from safe to surprising forms of expression' (2015).

As Jude moves through this border, she is experiencing dislocation and dissociation, but it also opens up the possibilities of surprising forms of expression – new and other words for home.

Mikhail Bakhtin suggests that situations like these have a special significance in literature, what he calls a 'chronotope' ('space-time', borrowing a metaphor from physics). He says, 'spatial and temporal indicators are fused into one carefully thought-out, concrete whole. Time, as it were, thickens, takes on flesh, becomes artistically visible; likewise, space becomes charged and responsive to the movements of time, plot and history' (Bakhtin and Holquist 1981:84). The novel, Bakhtin contends, is a series of chronotopes, interrogating particular moments in particular settings in the lives of the characters. He contends: 'They are the organizing centres for the fundamental narrative events of the novel. The chronotope is the place where the knots of narrative are tied and untied' (250).

The relevant Bakhtian chronotope here is that of the 'threshold', 'the chronotope of crisis and break in a life [...] the falls, resurrections, renewals, epiphanies, decisions that determine the whole life of a man [*sic*!]' (248).

Jude is crossing a literal threshold, but it also represents a crisis and break with the life she had before. Going through this threshold will lead to a new life, a resurrection of sorts.

Using this lens of the threshold chronotope recasts the man in the immigration booth as a threshold guardian. We have met the Hero's Journey in previous chapters and, as we have seen, the first stage of the Hero's Journey – separation – requires the hero to depart from their everyday life and move into the realm of adventure. The way is protected by a 'threshold guardian' 'standing for the limits of the hero's present sphere, or life horizon. Beyond them is darkness, the unknown, and danger' (Campbell 1949:64). Suddenly, the significance of Jude's encounter is clear, in narrative terms. This is a trial.

> The man beckons for us to step up closer.
> He has kind blue eyes that seem tired.
> Everyone in this airport seems
> tired.

And yet, although the man has a mythic and symbolic role, Warga maintains Jude's very humanist and child's-eye perception of him. The official in the immigration booth is, above all, a *person*, as far as Jude is concerned. His verb 'beckons' has an old-fashioned warmth to it that an alternative choice such as 'gestures' or 'summons' would not. Jude, her formality giving her the air of a reliable narrator (borrowing perhaps some of the 'classical tone' we saw in Chapter 3), says without doubt that his eyes are 'kind'. So, there is welcome here. There is a solidarity of emotion too, the man seems as tired as everyone else at the airport – they are all just people together. The enjambment places the second 'tired' on a line of its own; this is the overwhelming emotion in this place. Everyone – travellers, staff, officials – need rest and yet are unable to get it. There is unity in collective misery. However, there is also disunity: Jude notices his eyes are blue, an image of racial difference.

> He starts talking and I know some of the words
> that are coming out of his mouth,
> but my mind feels sticky
> and I can't quite catch the meaning.

This is a formative moment for Jude in this transnational text. She is in the process of coming to notice her foreignness in her new home, Friesner's 'alien'-ness. This is explored slowly and deliberately in the verse. He '*starts* talking' (my emphasis), the communication delayed a little by the extra verb. Another extra verb follows soon after, 'that *are* coming' (my emphasis). This creates a sense of stuttering, log-jammed sentences, with more words than are strictly needed. Jude reports that she knows 'some of the words' the man uses, without telling us what those words are – she stands between us and the man as an inadequate mediator. She uses the metaphor 'sticky' to describe her mind; this has connotations of jam or honey, but also, given the airport setting, of griminess and sweat. Her phrase 'catch the meaning' also suggests traps and the stickiness of fly paper. Overall, the poetics create a sense of grubbiness and miscommunication. Jude is undergoing a transformation from her previous middle-class, educated self to something unfamiliar to her, an immigrant.

The transnational narrative can have great appeal to writers for young people because of the symbolic alignment with young characters as liminal beings – they are between or amid countries, traversing borders, while at the same time expanding and contracting into new developmental stages as children, teens and young adults. We will see a fuller discussion of coming-of-age as a genre in Chapter 7, but here we can see how symbiotic the themes of movement and growth can be. In crossing this 'man'-made border, Jude is seeing new possibilities within herself, possibilities which are, for the time being, uncomfortable and unwelcome.

It is worth commenting, at this point, that Jude's interiority, this dramatic monologue that we are reading, is in English only from the most practical and literal point of view. Jude-the-character, rather than Jude-the-narrator, does not yet speak confident English, she speaks Syrian. So, these verses should perhaps be seen as an avatar for a Syrian dramatic monologue. This recasts the formal language we saw earlier ('cannot', 'does not') as perhaps not formal English, but a suggestion that there is another language, with different grammar and registers, here in palimpsest, hiding in plain sight.

> Back home,
> I was always good at English.
> I was one of the best in my class
> at having pretend conversations.

Faced with this evolving identity, Jude retreats into the past (borders can be crossed and recrossed in transnational writing, just as adolescence can be a cycle of growth and regression). 'Back home' is given the prominence of its own line, establishing a temporal and spacial shift into flashback. Jude recalls a continuous past ('always') where she was a gifted student. However, there is pathos to this memory. Although she was one of the best, she realizes now the futility of the task at which she excelled – the enjambment creates almost a 'punchline' effect. The conversations she was so good at were 'pretend'. They were, she realizes, childish.

> I think of practicing simple phrases with Fatima
> right before I left.
> I think of how easy they came to me then –
> *How are you?*
> *Good. Thank you.*
> *Are you hungry? Would you like to go to lunch?*
> *I would like a sandwich, please.*

Jude stays in this bittersweet memory for an extended moment. The man in the booth temporarily forgotten as she returns to a time, only days ago, where she had the confidence of innocence. In the present tense 'I think', she can take solace in this memory. There's a soothing, melodic quality to the sibilance 'practicing simple phrases'. However, the regular rhythm of the line is disrupted by enjambment and the curdling thought 'right before I left' is given the prominence of its own line. Throughout this sequence there are two poles in tension, Jude as a child, familiar to herself and comfortable, and Jude as an immigrant, unfamiliar and discomforted. The next line swings the pendulum again, back to the memory and the specific phrases she and Fatima practiced. Other than the word 'immigration' written on a sign, these are our first words in English; they are presented in italics to indicate the shift in language.

They are the schoolroom phrases of tourist English: greetings; pleasantries and simple purchases. They are the kind of phrases one might learn with the idea of taking a family holiday in the US, or in a tourist hot-spot where English is the lingua franca. The language register is quite formal, 'How are you?' rather than 'How you doing?' or 'How's it going?' They suggest a middle-class lifestyle, where vacations abroad and meals out are commonplace. This is the English of the mobile, easy traveller, someone whose passport is waved through without fuss. But in crossing this border, this threshold, Jude is becoming a different kind of traveller.

> But this man is not asking me
> simple things like
> if I am hungry or what I would like to order.

She returns to the present moment, coming back from the flashback by re-acknowledging her current circumstance. 'But this man' re-establishes the setting by re-establishing the most note-worthy thing in it. This use of the physical setting is an effective way to end a flashback and return the reader to the present narrative time. The observation that these are 'simple' questions are metonymy – they are one small part of her past life and so serve as stand in for the whole edifice of her simple, comfortable childhood.

> He is asking real questions that
> I can barely understand like
> Why are you here?
> And how long do you plan on staying?

The extract concludes with Jude observing that the man's questions are 'real'. It is interesting that she doesn't contrast the man's questions with the 'simple' tourist-style questions by choosing an antonym such as 'difficult' or 'hard'. Instead, Jude opts for an antonym of 'pretend' – perhaps those tourist questions were never going to be real, even if she had stayed in Syria. It casts doubt on her own understanding of this past self; maybe she was never destined to be a simple tourist. Jude is losing her former home, the family she has left behind, and she's also losing her understanding of who she is – perhaps she wasn't the scholar she believed herself to be, after all.

Her statement that she can 'barely understand' his questions is poignant. It can refer, of course, to her unfamiliarity with English – these weren't the sort of questions she and Fatima practiced so she doesn't understand them. Her physical condition, feeling tired and sad, will also make comprehension harder. But, of course, her inability to understand the questions also speak to the sudden and precipitous alteration to her life that has happened because of the war in Syria. The war and its effect on her family is incomprehensible to her. Any answer to the question 'Why are you here?' must incorporate political history, personal circumstance, grief, fear and more. There is no easy answer. And so, Jude's exhausted mind rejects the question.

In our earlier instances of conflict creating plot (Chapters 1 and 2) the conflict came from interpersonal and internal sources. In this instance, we see a combination of systemic conflict and internal conflict serving to progress the narrative. The man is a representative of the state with the legal capacity to determine their futures. He represents a system of international treaties and domestic law. In this sense, he embodies systemic conflict. But he is also a threshold guardian, potentially barring the way to our hero's self-actualization beyond.

On this threshold, standing between two countries, two lives, Jude begins to appreciate that she is no longer the Jude she thought she knew, and the future is just as unknowable. It's awful to leave her here, feeling so discombobulated, so, if you haven't read the rest of the book, I urge you do so, to find out what lies beyond.

Cited Works

Bakhtin, M.M. and Holquist, M. 1981, *The Dialogic Imagination: Four Essays*, University of Texas Press, Austin.

Bush, E. 2019, '*Other Words for Home* by Jasmine Warga', *Bulletin of the Center for Children's Books*, vol. 72, no. 10, pp. 455–65.

Campbell, J. 1949, *The Hero with a Thousand Faces*, 2nd edn (1968) Princeton University Press, Princeton.

Fisher, T. 2023, 'Under the Hood of the Verse Novel: A Consideration of Variation in Form and Technique in the Contemporary Verse Novel for Young Adults', *Leaf Journal*, vol. 1, no. 2, pp. 1–29.

Friesner, B. 2016, *The Verse Novel in Young Adult Literature*, Rowman & Littlefield Publishers, Incorporated, Lanham.

Russell Williams, I. 2019, May 9, '*Toffee*' by Sarah Crossan review – a profoundly moving YA novel in verse. Available: https://www.theguardian.com/books/2019/may/09/toffee-sarah-crossan-review [2024, May 31].

Soyinka, B. 2015, *Presentation to Stockholm Symposium on Transnational Creativity*.

Warga, J. 2019, *Other Words for Home*, Balzer + Bray, New York.

Yuliati, R. 2021, 'Oppression to Empowerment: Syrian Refugee Women in Warga's *Other Words for Home*', *CaLLs: Journal of Culture, Arts, Literature, and Linguistics*, vol. 7, no. 1, pp. 28–38.

SECTION 2: AN INTERVIEW WITH JASMINE WARGA

ELEN: You've said in the past that the book was inspired by your family, and that it started as a piece from the American cousin's point of view, from Sarah's point of view. I wondered if you could just talk about that?

JASMINE: Yeah, so actually, my own family is Palestinian American. But, growing up in Cincinnati, the Middle Eastern community is rather small. And so, our really close family friends are Syrian American. I was not living in Cincinnati anymore, but I came back to visit my parents. We went to dinner at my family friend's house, and at that dinner I was introduced to all these relatives who I had never met before. They had just come over because of the growing conflict in Syria. At this point – this was August 2013 – in America, what was happening in Syria was not really being covered. You know, you didn't turn on CNN and hear about it. It wasn't getting front page coverage in the *New York Times*; it hadn't yet reached that level. But what got me interested in writing the book was not really the geopolitical situation in Syria. It was more the relationship that I was observing between the cousins who'd been born in Syria, and the cousins who were born in America.

And I was thinking: *what would it have been like for me, when I was an eighth grader, if my cousins from Jordan had come to live with me?* At that age, I had such a negative relationship with my identity. I really felt like I was trying to shed my Arabness, my Middle Easternness – because I was in eighth grade when 9/11 happened and I was absorbing all this anti-Arab, anti-Muslim rhetoric. I really thought that I had to pick between, like, my Arab identity or my American identity. And so, I was thinking: *Oh, it would be so interesting to write this book from this American perspective.* I was envisioning Sarah as this character – kind of the way she is in the book – sort of prickly and insecure, and maybe by the end of the book has come to embrace her identity. But, as I was working on the book, the climate in the US started to change. Trump's [2016] campaign was really kicking off. And there was just a lot of rising xenophobia, that I think was always there in America. It's a lazy take to think that these problems started with Donald Trump; I think more that he brought them to the surface. But I was noticing – I was actually really struck by the fact – I lived in a very diverse neighbourhood, with lots of academics, and even the people that I was talking to there, there was a lot of fear and resentment about the idea of welcoming people from Syria to the US. And I was wondering why this was. I was starting to think about the way we cover the Middle East in the US, and our news coverage, and how we only ever see the Middle East as a place of conflict and war. Then that leads people to think that the people from there are inherently violent. And then, of course, Americans will have that fear and might not want to welcome them.

I was also getting frustrated by the way the news covered [the conflict in Syria], I feel like it was so dehumanizing. We see this all the time when we cover global conflicts; we hear these mind-boggling numbers and forget that every single one of those is a person with specificity, and friends that they've lost, and family that they've lost, and hopes and dreams. I think that's what literature is so great at doing; in the telling of a really specific, singular story, it can give the human aspect.

I was really frustrated; I felt kids like Jude were just being sort of washed into this one horde, a voiceless horde. And I ... I'm hesitant ... I never want to say I'm giving them a voice. I think they *have* a voice. Obviously, they have a voice! It just felt like it wasn't being heard. And so, I started to realize that the story I really wanted to tell is Jude's story. But I was nervous about it, because that's so different from my own life experience.

ELEN: So, in your original writing, Jude was presumably quite a big character, but it was Sarah's point of view?

JASMINE: So, initially, Jude was not Jude. Jude was a boy-cousin named Omar, who I kind of repurposed in the ELL [English Language Learners] class. He wanted to play soccer; that was the dream. But then, when I started to really get into the book and realized I wanted to write from this perspective, Jude came to me. I realized: *Okay, I need this character, this is going to be my narrative companion.*

ELEN: That's so interesting, because it feels like a book with so many great female characters of all different sorts, and so to throw a boy into the middle of that is ...

JASMINE: Yeah! I think sometimes you write from not the correct impulse when you first start. I think, I was thinking of the marketability of the book; there was a lot of buzziness around this idea that we need more books with boys in. And I was like: *Oh, if it's a boy, but with a girl cousin, I'll have the girl and the boy, and that'll round it out.* And then, I started to realize that just wasn't the book. I wanted to write a book about Muslim and Arab identity through the lens of lots of female characters who all have a different relationship with it, I think, from Jude to Layla to Sarah. I think sometimes I get frustrated by the broad brush we use when we talk about diversity in children's literature; I wanted to show the diversity within diversity. Groups are not monolith, right? And I think also, I kind of wanted to push back on this idea that Jude – at least in the way we talk about it in America – is a diverse character, right? Diverse is oftentimes like a stand-in for non-white. But really, Jude is coming from an environment that was not particularly diverse. Most of the other people she interacted with in Syria were also Arab; the majority of them are Muslim. And then, she comes to the United States and suddenly she's meeting people from all different kinds of races and religions. I wanted to play with that idea of like: what is diversity? And, kind of, flip that on its head.

ELEN: You have said that, in your mind, each character is asking an interesting question. I wonder if you can just expand on that a little bit? What do you mean by characters are asking a question?

JASMINE: So, for me, I think of stories basically as vehicles to ask questions. I think that when I was first starting off writing, I had this false sense that writing was about knowing things and telling other people. And I realized that, really, what I think storytelling is about is providing an experience that allows the reader to wonder, to think about these questions and then draw their own conclusions. That's really what creates the most rewarding reading experience. I structure my books around this idea, that all of my characters are going on a journey that starts with a question. And I think the novel's job is to complicate that question. From a craft perspective, you might call that plot.

I feel like plot is a weakness of mine, and so I use narrative questions as my way to chart that. The enemy of story is stasis, right? So, you don't want your character's question at the beginning to be the same as your character's question at the end. And so, the writer's task is to work out how is the question going to change? And how's it going to be complicated? And how is your character's question going to change because of the things they learn about the world and the ways that they're challenged?

I used to hear this idea that at the beginning of the book your character has a question and by the end of the book they can answer it, or not answer it, based on what they've learned throughout the book. But I don't see it that way anymore. I see it as that Jude's question has evolved into a different question.

ELEN: Yeah. And I suppose that in their own way Sarah and Layla are asking parallel questions; it's almost as if the questions are circling the theme, coming at a particular issue from different perspectives.

JASMINE: Yeah. I definitely think that narrative question is also a way to think about theme, like you're talking about. I mean, if I were to sum up theme, I would use my narrative questions for that too.

ELEN: I have a question about the big themes in the book. There are some enormous themes in there and yet it feels so solidly middle grade. I wondered if you'd been very conscious of maintaining that balance?

JASMINE: So, first off, I think that you never want to underestimate your reader. I think that actually this age of reader, in some ways, has a more expandable mind in being willing to think about these ideas more than an adult reader. I think that the trick of middle grade is that you have to honour their perspective. For me, it was always about writing through the lens of a 12-year-old, and how she sees the world.

[…]

Because I think the way that I wondered about racism at twelve is very different than the way that I think about it now. Which is not to say that I'm so much smarter, or, you know, learned. Obviously, I have life experience that makes it different and the vocabulary that I would use, and the way that I would see it, would be different. I think being authentic to that is what's important for me when it comes to tackling those issues. There's like a gentleness to middle grade. But I don't think that that's because you're worried about the sensitivity of your reader. I think kids can tell when something is inauthentic, when something is a false adult perspective projected onto a child.

The other thing I'll say is that Katherine Paterson, who wrote *Bridge to Terabithia*, she has a famous quote that when you write for children, you're duty bound to write with hope. I do think that's important. And so, when I think about these themes, even dark, harder themes, I always am thinking about that. I want the book to feel like an invitation to children to make the world a better place, to think about the way that they can use their voice as opposed to flattening them in despair.

[…]

ELEN: I want to ask about the role that class plays in in the book and the decision to have them be quite middle-class.

JASMINE: I think for me, because I knew I was going to be writing so far out of my own experience with Jude, I needed to write about the type of refugee that I had access to, which is my own community. They are people who already had relatives in America who could afford to bring them to the United States. […] I chose for Jude's family to be pretty well-off, because I actually really wanted to show the vibrancy of Syria. Again, getting back to that point I was talking about earlier that it was really important for me, for the young reader in America or the UK, [...] I wanted them to recognize certain markers of Jude's life. She goes to school, she has dinner at home, there's a hotel, these things that are markers of a wealthier, stable place. Because I think there's this idea ... We only ever see these like bombed-out photos of Aleppo, right? And then we think that that's what the country always was like. And I think that that also leads to a lack of empathy for the people who are coming, because we don't understand how dramatically kids like Jude's lives changed.

But for me, honestly, the real reason that Jude's uncle's family is in the situation that they're in, is because I knew that I couldn't tell the type of refugee story that we see in the news. Stories that are so heartbreaking of children getting into unstable boats ... I didn't have access to talk to anyone who had had that experience. I feel that from my comfortable life in America, the way that I would write that story would be very sensationalized and dramatic and just, not authentic. I felt really nervous about wanting to be able to write a really authentic story. And so, Jude's type of refugee story was the type that I had access to. It's my father's own story; his uncle paid for his plane ticket. [...] I was trying to really narrow the lens; that can help you with authenticity. Because you tell yourself: *I'm telling this specific type of refugee story.*

ELEN: People who are somewhat between cultures can find quite creative spaces there. Was that something you found?

JASMINE: My Arabic is not strong by any means, but I did – I do – love the poetry. That holds possibility. Even though you're writing in English, you can stretch the language to capture certain cadence and lyricality, and the way that you place words. And so, in certain points in the book, I was trying to mimic what I felt would be the cadence of an Arabic language speaker, even though the book is told in English.

I like to talk to educators about how I think poetry can be a place for their multilingual students to be able to exalt both of their literacies, because you remove the grammatical rules of English; you can invent your own language and toy with it.
[...]

ELEN: Could you say something about the shift to verse writing, because I don't think you'd done it before?

JASMINE: No, no, I hadn't. And actually, the book initially was not written in verse; I'd written several different drafts of the book in prose. We were actually getting really close to the book being finished. And I think there's always a gap, as a creator, between what you have in your mind, and what you're able to get on the page. And some of writing is learning to swallow that, right? But, for me, on this book the gap just felt too wide. I was like: *It doesn't sound the way I want it to sound*.

And then, I was travelling for work, and I was jet-lagged. In the Los Angeles airport, I just started hearing Jude's voice in verse. I was like: *This is it!*

[…] And then, I just completely rewrote the whole book from scratch. Because what makes the verse novel is obviously not what's in a prose book. You can't just add line breaks; you have to rewrite the whole thing.

But the nice thing was, I had the plot points. I had characters. I always get asked, 'Are you gonna write another verse novel?' And I'm like: *I don't actually know how to start by writing a verse novel*. Because I think the tricky thing about verse novels is the economy of language. You have to distil characters down to their very essence. But I think that was easier for me to do, coming from like the 60,000-word prose novel where I'd explored them and figured out things about them. […]. I think I backed into the verse novel!

I feel like it's very in vogue now to kind of like bash publishers. But I've had the experience that my team, at least my editor and my agent, are very like art-forward, which I really appreciate. They really wanted the best book from me.

SECTION 3: *OTHER WORDS FOR HOME*, WRITING EXERCISES

With these exercises we will explore some of the ideas of tension and liminality that we saw in a concrete way in *Other Words for Home* but are also an intrinsic part of writing for young people in general. Our audience is in flux, growing-up and retreating to safety in stops-and-starts.

Exercise A – Narrative Verse

The concept of 'narrative verse' holds some interesting and creative, tensions. Arguably, it is one of our oldest cultural forms (think of *The Iliad*, for example), and yet it is seen as an emerging form when written for a middle-grade or YA audience. It is a form that privileges vignettes over scenes, with each poem contributing one moment or observation – as a film reel is made up of individual static shots arranged to create the illusion of motion. A writer has to decide which moments to show in order to create narrative structure and momentum.

1. Pick a novel you've read recently, or a film you've watched.
2. If you were going to adapt the story into narrative verse, which moments would be crucial to include? Make a list of three or four *essential* moments.
3. Pick one moment from your list. Make a list of everything you can recall from this moment – the details of setting, the characters present, the emotional timbre, what was said or done and by whom. Allow the list to be impressionistic; don't try to recall everything exactly.
4. From your list of details, underline any that are particularly evocative of the moment.
5. Using an internal narrator turn your list into a short free-verse poem. Aim to distil the moment to its essence by recounting the actions and evoking the feelings, rather than describing surroundings or offering interpretation.
6. Edit the verse, paying particular attention to enjambment – where will you break the lines, add white space, and give key words their own lines?
7. Should you wish, edit the verse again; with this pass, pay attention to some of the rhetorical devices we discussed in Chapter 5.

Exercise B – The Character's Questions

Jasmine Warga discussed her use of questions as a way to manage plotting. The concept of a character arc is well-established, where a character undergoes a significant change or personal epiphany across the course of a novel due to the experiences they undergo. The use of character questions is an interesting tool for managing that development.

1. Using the same story you selected for Exercise A, think of the protagonist at the beginning of the story.
2. Ask yourself:
   - What question do they have about themself?
   - What question do they have about a close relationship they are part of?
   - What question do they have about the wider world or society they are part of?
3. Skip forwards to a central point in the story. Repeat point 2.
4. Skip forwards to the end of the story. Repeat point 2.
5. Have the questions changed? Have they created what might be considered a 'character arc'? Do they intersect with the action in the story in some interesting or generative ways?

Exercise C – The Eyes of a Child

In this exercise we will combine two concepts already explored elsewhere in the chapter: the chronotope of the threshold and the grace afforded by using the perspective of a child.

1. Imagine a doorway of significance to a young person. Whatever popped into your head when you read that phrase will work, but, if you need some suggestions here are a few: the entrance to a bowling alley on a first date; the entrance to High School on the first day of the academic year; the entrance to the kitchen where your parents wait because they need to talk to you; the entrance to a hospital where someone you care about is sick; the entrance to a magical otherworld, etc.
2. By stepping through the doorway, a child (or teen) will be changed in some way. Decide on the age your young person will be as they approach the doorway.

3. Make a short list of the things your young person might notice on the *outside* of the doorway; include a few thoughts and worries as well as a physical description.
4. Imagine the young person crosses the threshold. Make a second list of the sorts of things your young person might notice on the other side of the doorway – again, include thoughts and emotions as well as physical descriptions. Be as aware as possible of their age. What are their frames of reference? What seems notable or interesting to them?
5. Using the two lists, write a scene in which a young person crosses the threshold. Be aware of any slight changes that might happen because of the action. Be aware of their age as you write from their point of view (whether you use an internal or external narrator is up to you).

Exercise D – Transnational Creativity

The degree to which you can engage with this exercise will depend on your own situation and awareness of the degree to which you live between cultures. But we will all have transnational cultural lives to some degree or another – we might watch films made in another country (Hollywood, Bollywood or Nollywood, for example); we might read books in translation, eat food originally associated with other countries, listen to music by international artists, etc.

1. Write your own name at the centre of a piece of paper.
2. You are going to draw circles around your name, indicating your positionality in regard to transnational culture(s). It might end up looking like lots of overlapping coffee cup rings, or maybe bubbles in a bath which have conjoined.
3. Closest to your name, draw any circles to represent cultures closest to you. For example, if I were to do this for myself, I would have two overlapping circles, with my name in the overlapping point for 'Wales' and 'England' as this is where I was born and live now. Further out, I'd put 'Scotland', 'France' and 'Australia' as I've spent a significant amount of time in each.
4. Go further out, add circles to represent cultures which have influenced you in some way. For example, for me, I would add circles for 'India' and 'Pakistan' because communities from those nations shaped the food and music in the city where I went to

university (Birmingham, UK) and 'America' because the cultural hegemony of the US has shaped the TV and films I've watched.
5. Keep going, with the circles getting further away, and maybe smaller, as your connection gets more dissipated.
6. Everyone will have a different pattern of circles and different connections. But, before I move on to the writing task, I'd encourage you to think about the flow of influence, does it travel both ways; are the people able to move as freely as the ideas and cultures, are they as valued? What is the balance of power? (We'll revisit these ideas in Chapter 6.)
7. Pick a section of your diagram where you feel the balance of power is fairly even (for example, on my diagram, I'd put England and France fairly even in terms of the influence they have had on each other). Imagine a child living between those cultures – what might their idiolect be? Their frames of reference? Which idioms and turns of phrase would they use? Write a short character sketch of your transnational child, allowing elements from both cultures to shape the writing.

Chapter Six

SECTION 1: *WHEN THE WORLD WAS OURS* BY LIZ KESSLER, A CRITICAL DISCUSSION

Note: this chapter contains spoilers for *When the World Was Ours* and discussion of the Holocaust.

In this chapter, we meet our first novel for young adults (YA). A definition of YA is a slippery thing, but a reasonable heuristic is that they are often works labelled by publishers for readers aged 11+ or 14+. They will typically contain stories that are thematically relevant to young people, told in a style appropriate for young people – although, of course, the idea of what might be 'appropriate' for any given 14-year-old is debatable; a point I will return to.

Simon & Schuster (2024) lists *When the World Was Ours* as a novel suitable for readers ages 14+. It is, in my view, a heartbreaking–heartwarming historical novel.

A reader, picking it up for the first time, would first see the cover: three children are silhouetted behind barbed wire, one wearing a red swastika on his arm. Opening the book, this imagined reader would see 'A Note from the Author', telling them that the story was inspired by Kessler's father, who escaped Nazi-occupied Czechoslovakia in 1939, and by Kessler's great-aunt Elsa, who was murdered at Auschwitz. Following the Author's Note is a Content Warning for violence related to the Holocaust. Then, with the image of a swastika and the name Auschwitz still fresh in the reader's mind, the novel itself begins,

1936
Leo

I could see the whole world! Or at least the whole of Vienna, and that was my world.

My two best friends, Max and Elsa, stood beside me, their faces pressed to the glass next to mine.

'Look at the tiny people!' Max exclaimed, pointing down below us as we rose higher and higher into the sky.

'The buildings look like a toy town!' Elsa said.

I couldn't even speak. I was too afraid that if I opened my mouth some of the joy inside me might slip out, and I didn't want to lose a single bit of it.

It was my ninth birthday and the best day of my life, bar none.

> When my parents had asked me last week what I wanted to do for my birthday, there was no contest. I wanted to ride on Vienna's Ferris wheel: the Riesenrad. We had lived in Vienna almost my whole life but I'd never been on it. Whenever I asked, Mama would always say I was too young and that I'd be afraid to be so high up. But I wasn't scared at all. I think Mama was afraid herself, really, which is why she decided she wouldn't come with us.
>
> (Kessler 2021:3)

I introduced the peritextual elements alongside this opening passage very consciously, because they influence how this opening will land for the reader. Peritextual elements are all the things that make up a book beyond the words of the manuscript: the cover; the blurb; Dedication; Author's Note and so on. They are elements that the author may have some say in but are ultimately agreed and designed by the wider team at a publishing house: the Art Director, the cover illustrator, the editorial team, Sales and Marketing and so on. In discussing the peritext, I'm pleased to have the opportunity to acknowledge that books are not made entirely by their writers, there is a network of professionals who contribute towards the reader's experience.

The voice in this opening passage might easily be mistaken for middle grade (compare with Chapters 3–5 for some hallmarks of middle grade writing). However, this is deceptive and the peritextual elements are instrumental in preparing us for the darker direction the book will take from this very carefree beginning. So, as my discussion proceeds, I will be touching on what makes this novel 'heartbreaking–heartwarming' and how Kessler crafts the bonds between characters and reader which make it so.

Here on this first page, we meet all the focalizing characters; Leo, Max and Elsa will all be given their own chapters in the novel, and it is through each of their perspectives that the events of the narrative are viewed, thus making this a polyphonic novel. But readers with a good memory will remember that this is the *second* Elsa we have met. The first was Kessler's great-aunt Elsa who was murdered in Auschwitz, as stated in the Author's Note. So, there is a shadow Elsa – a real Elsa – trailing Elsa-the-character. Let's take a closer look at the joy and the darkness here.

1936
Leo

The novel opens with a date and a name. If I were to guess, I suspect that most 14-year-olds would know that the Second World War began in the first half of the twentieth century, but that they might struggle to name the exact year. Our imagined reader might wonder: *Were there Nazis in 1936?* With the cover, the

Author's Note and the Content Warning, they might conclude: *Probably*, and be, therefore, primed to expect brutality and cruelty from this story. But Kessler doesn't deliver misery, instead she delivers its polar opposite,

> I could see the whole world! Or at least the whole of Vienna, and that was my world.

We do not yet know much about our narrator; we've only just learned his name. However, we learn so much about his world-view – his expansiveness, his awe-struck enthusiasm – from the fact that the first line of the book ends with an exclamation mark. Leo's voice is the antithesis of the novel's peritext. We don't know where he is, or what he's doing, but whatever it is, he is doing it with unbridled happiness. This is the only first page I'll be discussing in this book, so it behoves me to stay on this point for a while. The first paragraphs of any chapter are so often concerned with orienting the reader – where are we, who's there, what's at stake? The first paragraph of a first chapter has to do more than that, it has to *hook* a reader, promising them a reading experience they will cherish. A familiar metaphor, the hook suggests that the first page is bait, and the reader is prey. Kessler is pairing the expansive enthusiasm of this boy with the peritext and date and inviting the reader to wonder: *where is this going? Where are you taking me?* We will have an inkling of the abyss ahead, but, if we care for the characters, we will want to go into the darkness with them.

The book as a physical object has created tension immediately, despite Leo's positivity, even *because* of Leo's positivity. Leo is on top of the world – literally in this case, as he is on a Ferris wheel – so the only way is down.

We've seen dramatic irony before, in Chapter 1, where the reader knew more about Little Fish's situation than Little Fish knew himself. We are seeing another version of dramatic irony here, one created not by the words on the page but by the confluence of text and peritext. We know more than Leo and the more we get to know him, the more devastating that knowledge becomes.

> My two best friends, Max and Elsa stood beside me, their faces pressed to the glass next to mine.

Leo is not alone in this first scene; his friends are there with him. We've met many internal narrators and Leo is another. His first line established a close-in degree of psychic distance (see Chapter 3 for a fuller definition of psychic distance). This second line demonstrates that an internal narrator can operate equally well at a far-out psychic distance. For a moment, Leo slips into his role as narrator, with exposition taking precedence over the feeling, experiencing character 'showing' emotion, in order to 'tell' us the facts. Although, even here, the body language of the characters indicates joy, with their faces close together and striving to take in the view.

> 'Look at the tiny people!' Max exclaimed, pointing down below us as we rose higher and higher into the sky.
> 'The buildings look like a toy town!' Elsa said.

From Leo's point of view, as the focalizing character and the narrator of this chapter, these are his best friends. They stand side by side at the same eye level, sharing the same stance. They all follow the same enthusiastic pattern of ending their statements with an exclamation mark. As far as Leo is concerned, they are three peas in a pod.

But how reliable is Leo as a narrator? He believes that these are his 'two best friends' – he isn't lying – but how much can we trust the beliefs of an optimistic 9-year-old? Especially when dramatic irony has already been established.

In answer, Kessler allows Leo's friends to speak for themselves, unmediated by Leo's narration. Anderson (2005) suggests five ways by which an author can reveal character: interpretation; appearance; action; thoughts and observation; and speech. We saw in Chapter 3 how appearance contributes to characterization.

Here we have Leo's interpretation ('My two best friends') and move quickly to Max's speech. Do Max's words align with Leo's generous conception of him? Is Leo right? Or do Max's words betray some darker quality? Is there something to be read into the fact that Max considers the people 'tiny'? Is there something a little disquieting about that choice of adjective? Is Max belittling the townspeople, or is he making a simple, literal observation? Those with a good memory will recall the boy in a swastika armband on the cover.

We aren't invited to dwell on this idea, as Elsa quickly leaps in with her own observation – Vienna is like a 'toy town'. With this image, safe, innocuous, child-friendly, we are returned to more joyful ground.

Throughout this passage, on the one hand, Kessler presents a happy birthday outing, which we could take entirely at face value. But, on the other hand, for attuned readers there will be disturbing currents eddying beneath that surface.

> I couldn't even speak. I was too afraid that if I opened my mouth some of the joy inside me might slip out, and I didn't want to lose a single bit of it.
> It was my ninth birthday and the best day of my life, bar none.

Consider Leo's response to his friends' dialogue: 'I couldn't even speak. I was too afraid ... '. This is a sentence that leads us in one emotional direction, suggesting fear, before flipping 180 degrees to continue in the exact opposite direction: 'that if I opened my mouth some of the joy inside me might slip out'. It is a bait and switch. This opening scene is, as any opening scene should, toying with the reader; manipulating them to care about what happens next.

It is, I would suggest, Kessler's use of a reader's general knowledge to foreshadow the plot of the book which makes this a text for older children. Despite the age of the characters, which breaks much of the advice often given to writers for young people to 'age up' their protagonists in order to create an aspirational reading experience (see, for example, Kole 2012:8), this is a book for teenagers. Kessler presents us with an innocent, prelapsarian world, with our characters literally on top of the world; teen readers will be anticipating the fall. We can see here how text, peritext and readers come together to co-create meaning. Good writers will trust their readers to do at least some of the work – readers like to be trusted.

> When my parents had asked me last week what I wanted to do for my birthday, there was no contest. I wanted to ride on Vienna's Ferris wheel: the Riesenrad. We had lived in Vienna almost my whole life but I'd never been on it.

Leo uses this beat to act as a narrator and contextualize the situation for us. This information serves an expositional function for the reader, but it is nicely disguised exposition. It feels natural, coming from the position of a 9-year-old boy. Kessler gives him a perfectly believable dream, to ride the Ferris wheel, and so allows the book to begin at this high point (the real story – Kessler's father's story – began on a ferry not on a Ferris wheel; see interview).

The Riesenrad Ferris wheel still exists and is a well-known and loved landmark in Vienna. It has been there since 1897. I can only imagine the delight Kessler felt when she realized that this symbolic landmark was legitimately available for her to use. It was a gem thrown up by her meticulous research. As she states in the following interview, it was imperative, she felt, to travel to and know her settings. In this, she follows in a long tradition of historical novelists. T.H. White (quoted in Brayfield and Sprott 2014:49) says, 'you've got to do everything you write about – every bloody thing. [...] ride a horse, wear a suit of armour.' The writer J.A. Thom (2017:34) suggests that 'one of the most important words in the historical fiction business [is] verisimilitude'; which is to say giving the appearance of truth. Painstaking care paid to the chronology of events, the material culture (when was something invented), the idiolect of the characters (for example, their frames of reference) and their ideological positions (can you be Marxist before Marx?) will all contribute to verisimilitude.

However, historical novels are not history. As Philippa Gregory explains, 'I apologise that it's rather obvious; but it speaks to me – Historical fiction – the definition is in the title. It is historical and it is fiction. It's both. [...] it has become essential to me that my work should have the form, shape, language and pace of a good novel, and equally be rooted on the accuracy, complexity and thoughtfulness of good history' (quoted in Brayfield and Sprott 2014:129).

This implies that a historical novelist is seeking balance between evidence-based facts and the drama and beauty of fiction. Kessler has done this here by moving the opening scene to a symbolically significant location, rather than the location evidenced by her father's factual account of events. Yet, because the Ferris wheel *was* in Vienna, at the right time, it remains *plausible.*

I would contend that it is *plausibility* that is the business of historical fiction. Some degree of compromise will be required with, for example, the language and social attitudes of the time in order to make it palatable for contemporary readers. Hilary Mantel says of her compromise, 'I use modern English, but shift it sideways a little, so that there are some unusual words, some Tudor rhythms, a suggestion of otherness' (quoted in Brayfield and Sprott 2014:136).

The degree of compromise with historical accuracy should be given particular thought when writing for young people. Writers should ask: *to what extent will readers be familiar with the historical period in which I'm writing? Will they be able to identify my deviation from the historical record and will that matter?* Sometimes, it won't matter at all (if a character wears a mauve dress at a time before synthetic dyes were available, it probably isn't the end of the world). At other times, it will matter, as was the case with the publication of John Boyne's *The Boy in the Striped Pyjamas.* Its deviation from the historical record caused the Auschwitz Museum (2022) to advise the book should be avoided when teaching or studying the Holocaust. Of course, they are not saying it is not a good novel, not good *fiction.* They are saying it is not good *history* and shouldn't be taught as such. Writers can't control how their books are used – this particular case is a failure of pedagogy. But we can, as writers, think about what compromises we are willing to make with history and why. We can also use peritext (e.g. an Author's Note) to contextualize any of our compromises, if we think it merited, especially when writing for young people whose experience of the world and prior knowledge base is likely to be more restricted than an adult readership.

There are wider issues of responsibility to consider too, not only historical accuracy, but also an ethical engagement with the material in terms of power. As Kessler says in the following interview, 'Being Jewish was part of why it felt important to make sure that I was as accurate as I could be, and I researched it as well as I could.' The events of the Holocaust are objectively horrific, but they are also deeply personal for the families still feeling the repercussions.

The term #ownvoices was coined by Corinne Duyvis (2015) to describe books written about marginalized groups by members of those marginalized groups.

Such works would be written from the 'expert' perspective of an insider and so deliver verisimilitude. There are other potential benefits to #ownvoices writing too; such books would: challenge dominant stereotypes about the marginalized group, work to financially support a wider range of creators within the publishing industry, and – following Rudine Sims Bishop (1990)'s very influential concept of 'mirrors, windows and sliding glass doors' – allow young people from all walks of life to see themselves in literature, to see people unlike themselves and to experience transportative stories. The term has since been criticized for the way in which it has been weaponized in online spaces, leading to writers feeling pressure to reveal personal details about themselves in order to establish their membership of marginalized groups (Lavoie 2021). It was by no means the first call, however, that identified the need for communities with less power to represent themselves in the cultural sphere – it was just the first to get a hashtag. Rudine Sims Bishop, speaking about Black writers in 1982, says,

> As long as people in positions of relative power in the world of children's literature – publishers, librarians, educators – insist that the background of the author does not matter, the opportunities for Black writers will remain limited since they will have to compete with established non-Black writers whose perspective on the Afro-American experience may be more consistent with that of the editors and publishers and whose opportunities to develop their talents as writers have been greater. (13–14)

The same impetus to curate the telling of Black stories with a white readership in mind has been identified in the UK by Karen Sands O'Connor (2024) in her historical survey of the British publishing industry.

Kessler's deeply personal relationship with the subject matter – the novel is in a sense a *Sliding Doors* version of what might have befallen her own father – created an additional weight of responsibility (see interview) and so a strong commitment to getting the details right. I am not suggesting that non-Jewish writers should not write Jewish stories, or that they would have any less of a commitment to good research. I am saying that Kessler's personal relationship with the characters will have acutely activated an ethical lens that a non-Jewish writer might have to work harder to engage, particularly when it came to which compromises she was willing to make. Her writing will be particularly *attentive* as a result, which is a quality Janelle Adsit considers foundational to the practice of creative writing (2017).

There are a range of tools available to help authors consider their personal relationship to the material they are working with. Sunny Singh offers a list of questions:

> Why do you want to write this? What is your personal investment in writing it? Can someone else tell this story better? What does your telling of the

story do? What is your power balance/imbalance as a writer to the subject matter? Finally, should you write/publish this at all?
(Based on Singh 2022)

There can't be definitive answers to these questions (whether someone else can tell it better is unknowable, for example), but they serve as useful prompts to engage an acute ethical lens.

Another useful framework was established by Sims Bishop (1982) for African-American literature and has since been adapted for LGBTQ literature by Cart and Jenkins (2006, cited in Owen 2023:4) which set out three stages for the representation of minoritized characters in literature. These stages are: visibility; assimilation and consciousness. The visibility stage is the inclusion of a minoritized character in literature, but at the risk of such depictions being negative or stereotyped; the assimilation stage is literature which include minoritized characters but assume or impose a cultural homogeneity with the dominant culture; the consciousness stage assumes that the readership includes members of the minoritized group and that the work is, in fact, *for them*, with all that entails. Asking at which stage the wider cultural representation of a group might be at, will, again, engage an acute ethical lens. Are you assuming the people you are writing *about* are also the *readers* for your work? What will they think? Do you need to find out? If you consider that the cultural impact of that group is sufficiently robust (for example, in the case of a man wanting to write from the point of view of a woman, women are sufficiently active in literature that this will be one book among many) then all that remains is to do it well. As Katja Lange-Muller puts it, 'The question for me as a writer is not "May I do this?" but "Can I do this?"' (quoted in Adsit 2019:204). Which, we may note, is the opposite question to the final one posed by Singh: 'Should you write this?' The issue of whether the group you are writing about has cultural capital is complicated for writers for young people. Only a tiny fraction of the work read by children and teens is actually written by children and teens. We adults are, regardless of our heritage, writing for a community we are not part of.

Ultimately, as with all ethical questions, there can be no easy, definitive answer and each writer will have to come to their own place of peace with their choices.

I have wandered far from the three children gazing down from a Ferris wheel at prelapsarian Vienna. Let's return to Leo and his final thoughts in our extract,

> Whenever I asked, Mama would always say I was too young and that I'd be afraid to be so high up. But I wasn't scared at all. I think Mama was afraid herself, really, which is why she decided she wouldn't come with us.

Leo uses a modal verb to indicate an ongoing habit, 'Mama *would always say*'. This gives an air of reliability, of predictability to the past. His mother has traditionally been stalwart in protecting him and worrying about him. We discussed the names characters might use for their parents in Chapter 4, where October used the most distant term 'the woman who is my mother'. Kessler lets Leo call his mother 'Mama', a term which sounds both old fashioned and warm. We are catching a glimpse of Leo's childhood: ordered, predictable, caring.

There is a conception of childhood here that is rose-tinted, it is a place of innocence. Which is not to say that Kessler herself views childhood in a rose-tinted way, but rather that – emotionally speaking – Leo begins this story in the best possible place: loved and cared for. This isn't the Romantic conception of childhood, in which children are untamed, free creatures who are civilized by the adult world and society. Rather it is the position that, in Coats's terms, 'Children are born naturally and innocently good, with an innate sense of justice and compassion, and should be protected from negative influences' (2017:10). Outside of literature, this conception of childhood is very powerful as it has led to politicized and angry debates over whether individual books can be 'harmful' or 'corrupting', ultimately ending in book-banning activities (an idea I revisit in Chapter 7). The flip side of this conception of childhood is that 'good' literature can have a positive effect on its readers. I think there are few of us who write without the hope that our words might influence our readers, but there are researchers who go even further, for example, Kidd and Castano (2013) who posit a causal link between reading literary fiction and the ability to feel empathy.

But we are inside literature and in this instance, 'innocent' childhood is being used as a literary device. It, alongside Leo's enthusiastic voice and the love he feels for his friends, is one of the ways in which Kessler creates a 'heartwarming' novel. The extremes of contentment Leo feels mimic what we saw earlier with the use of the symbolic Ferris wheel to put Leo 'on top of the world'. It is as though we are meeting Leo at the peak of a rollercoaster, ratcheting up to its highest point; again, we are invited to anticipate the fall. This is one reason, among many, that the book is also heartbreaking.

Leo himself 'isn't scared at all'. He has the confidence of youth and a boyhood that has known only comfort. The extract ends with Leo offering a different interpretation of his mother's statements. Perhaps it was not concern for him at all, perhaps she was hiding behind these excuses because of her own fear. This possibility creates a small crack in the facade of innocent childhood: perhaps, sometimes, parents are scared, perhaps they lie or act in bad faith. This is certainly a theme common to YA fiction, the idea that the adult world is messy and complicated. Resonantly, given the trajectory of the novel, Mama has chosen not to come along on this trip. On the best day of his life so far, his family are separated. In this sense, this opening scene serves as a promise of what is to come, the themes of loss and displacement are already present; Leo's inevitable path is already set out before him. So, let's leave him here, where he can still enjoy the moment, for now on top of the world.

Cited Works

Adsit, J. 2017, *Toward an Inclusive Creative Writing: Threshold Concepts to Guide the Literary Curriculum*, Bloomsbury Academic, London.
Adsit, J. (ed.) 2019, *Critical Creative Writing*, Bloomsbury Academic, London.
Anderson, L. 2005, *Creative Writing: A Workbook with Readings*, 1st edn, Routledge, Abingdon.
Auschwitz Museum 2022, *The Boy in the Striped Pyjamas*. Available: https://x.com/AuschwitzMuseum/status/1487017362675093506?lang=en [2023, June 6].
Brayfield, C. and Sprott, D. 2014, *Writing Historical Fiction: A Writers' and Artists' Companion*, 1st edn, Bloomsbury, London.
Coats, K. 2017, *The Bloomsbury Introduction to Children's and Young Adult Literature*, Bloomsbury Publishing, London.
Duyvis, C. 2015, *#ownvoices*. Available: https://twitter.com/corinneduyvis/status/640584099208503296 [2024, July 19].
Kessler, L. 2021, *When the World Was Ours*, Simon & Schuster, London.
Kidd, D.C. and Castano, E. 2013, 'Reading Literary Fiction Improves Theory of Mind', *Science (American Association for the Advancement of Science)*, vol. 342, no. 6156, pp. 377–80.
Kole, M. 2012, *Writing Irresistible Kidlit: The Ultimate Guide to Crafting Fiction for Young Adult and Middle Grade Readers*, Penguin Publishing Group, Cincinnati.
Lavoie, F. 2021, *Why We Need Diverse Books Is No Longer Using the Term #OwnVoices*. Available: https://diversebooks.org/why-we-need-diverse-books-is-no-longer-using-the-term-ownvoices/ [2024, July 19].
Owen, G. 2023, 'Impossible Relations, Ethical Relations: The Stakes of #OwnVoices Representation in LGBTQ Young Adult Fiction', *International Journal of Young Adult Literature*, vol. 4, no. 1, pp. 1–21.
Sands-O'Connor, K. 2024, *'The Repeating Island?' Racial Diversity in Young Adult Publishing*, Goldsmiths University, London.
Simon & Schuster 2024, *When The World Was Ours*. Available: https://www.simonandschuster.co.uk/books/When-The-World-Was-Ours/Liz-Kessler/9781471196812 [2024, July 18].
Sims Bishop, R. 1982, *Shadow and Substance: Afro-American Experience in Contemporary Children's Fiction*, National Council of Teachers of English, Urbana, Illinois.
Sims Bishop, R. 1990, *Mirrors, Windows and Sliding Glass Doors*. Available: https://scenicregional.org/wp-content/uploads/2017/08/Mirrors-Windows-and-Sliding-Glass-Doors.pdf [2024, July 17].
Singh, S. 2022, Jan 6, *Sunny Singh On Writing*. Available: https://x.com/profsunnysingh/status/1479043500691841025?s=12&t=NMasUqVrBkKscUhC08VH1w [2024, July 19].
Thom, J. A. 2017, *Once Upon a Time It Was Now: The Art and Craft of Writing Historical Fiction*, Blue River Press, Indianapolis.

SECTION 2: AN INTERVIEW WITH LIZ KESSLER

Note from Elen: the original idea for the novel is based on a real-life event, which took place in Vienna. Liz's father, as a young boy out with his father, bumped into a British couple – the Joneses. They fell into conversation and ended up spending the day together. The Joneses sent a thank you note with a return address. It was this note, a few years later, that allowed Liz's father to escape Nazi-occupied Austria, as the Kesslers were able to contact the Joneses to ask for help, which they supplied.

Note: this interview contains spoilers for *When the World Was Ours* and discussion of the Holocaust.

ELEN: I might start by asking, *When the World Was Ours* feels like quite a step-change in your career. Did you think that?

LIZ: So yeah [...] there'd been quite a long time that I'd been wanting to write a book that was inspired by what happened in my dad's childhood – the moment that his dad met the Joneses. This tiny moment of good fortune led to a conversation, which led to a letter, which then led to them getting away from the Nazis [...] I've always known that that's why our family is alive. And so, you know, as a writer, for years I had had it in my mind. I just I never really knew exactly how I wanted to write it.

I'd written two time-slip books (*A Year Without Autumn* and *North of Nowhere*) and there was quite a long time where I thought this was going to be the third one of those. Because it was going to be about a girl going back in time and finding herself on the boat where this thing happened originally, with my dad. And she realizes she's gone back in time, and she calls out to the boy, because she knows it's her grandfather. And he looks up. And because that happens, he doesn't scuff Mrs Jones' dress; they don't get into conversation. And there were going to be these two threads running. [...] I was aware that it felt a bit heavier. But at that point, I kind of thought: I don't really wanna write about Nazis. [...] It was going to be another *Sliding Doors*-type book.

And then, I came to talk about it with my agent, Catherine. And she just said (she has these moments of genius, well, she is a genius), she said, 'I wonder what would happen if you took the time-slip element out of it?' And I said, 'Well that's the backbone of it, isn't it?' And she said, 'Well, just have a think about it. I think that takes us away from the heart of the story.'

We got off the phone, and almost immediately the idea came into my head of the way to write it ... Because, although I always wanted to write my dad's story, it's *not* my dad's story that interests me; it's the other side: *What if my dad's story hadn't happened.* The time-slip was a way of doing that.

As soon as I got off the phone, I thought: *I know the way to do it.* There's another character who *doesn't* have that moment. And then I thought: *I need a third character.* It just felt right. I want three friends. Because the other 'what-if' is: *What if he hadn't been Jewish?*

[...] It was a really, really, really tough book to research. Obviously. You know, for *Emily Windsnap* [Liz's internationally bestselling series], we've gone on cruises in Norway, and I'd gone to Bermuda sitting on beaches and snorkelling. And this was three hardcore weeks of concentration camps and walking tours.

ELEN: Could you talk a little bit about what research you did?

LIZ: One of the things that was of absolute, no compromise, importance to me was that this would be a book that was researched. That was honest. That didn't fudge the facts. [...] It was very important to me that this would be a book where no one would be able to say, 'She's not done her homework.' [...] It scared me to be honest. And my way of dealing with that was: *I'm gonna research.*

So, I read every book I could get my hands on about the Holocaust. It was hard going. Then, I knew that I had to do a trip. We had a little van. So, me and Laura, my wife, [...] we took three weeks, and we travelled across Europe. We went through Germany, Austria, Poland, former-Czechoslovakia, back to Germany, Holland. We went to Dachau, Mauthausen, Auschwitz-Birkenau. We were going to go to Theresienstadt as well. But it was the last concentration camp that we were going to, and I was a wreck by that point, and I couldn't face putting myself in front of it again. And that was really sad, because my great-grandmother had been at Theresienstadt. My grandfather – my dad's dad – at the end of the war had gone in with the liberating forces, and he'd found her. She was still alive. She was blind in one eye, and she was very, very poorly. But he found her, and he brought her back to England. She lived a few more years. Theresienstadt was also where my great-aunt Elsa, her daughter, went with her, and she was transported to Auschwitz where she was murdered straight away. [...] So, I was really sad not to go there from a personal point of view. But I couldn't do it.

[...]

Looking back on it, I think it broke me a bit. [...] But when I came back from it, I wrote the first draft of this book in five or six weeks. It was like I couldn't stop. I'd been plotting it. You know I'm a plotter.

ELEN: Maybe this is a good place for me to interject the question: What is your process?

LIZ: So, I am at the far end of the extreme plotters. I always have to plot out. I'll start with an idea. And I have my idea and then I build up, build up, build up. Usually, it's about writing things down in a notebook, lots of hand, pen and notebook stuff at the beginning. So, there was a lot of that. [...] Then, what I do is at some point I think: *Right. It needs organizing a bit better.* So, I type up everything I've got. It doesn't matter in what order. It doesn't matter if there's things repeated or anything. I type it all up and print it out. Then, I cut up what I've printed out into all separate thoughts. Then, I'll place it on my desk and kind of work it out. You know, these bits go together, and these bits go together. These bits have to come before that. So, this goes here and that goes there. And these bits I'm not sure of, so I'll put them in a separate pile. I'll stick all that down and retype it, and scribble on it. I'll do that a few times. [...] And at some point, in a normal book, I'll put chapter numbers on it. I think: *Let's see if I've got about the right number of chapters so it feels like a book.* Anything between sixteen and twenty chapters, or something. Then I'll be, like: *Oh, this feels like it might be about right.*

But with this [*When the World Was Ours*] I had the added things that it's determined by – the dates and by the facts of the background of the war. So, in a way that was easy. There was loads and loads of plotting, loads and loads of research, probably about nine months by this point. By the time I came to write it, I felt like I just had to get it out of me, and I couldn't stop until it was out. I felt like Auschwitz had burrowed under my skin like a cockroach. I had to get it out of me, and I just wrote and wrote and cried, and cried, and wrote and cried, and wrote and cried for six weeks, and then it was done. Next question.

ELEN: I might circle back to that to the idea of split time. What I see in your body of work is a real interest in the consequences of small actions. I wondered about that, and particularly with writing for children, whether that idea of small things being powerful is something that you're conscious of in writing?
[...]

LIZ: When *A Year Without Autumn* came out, I wrote an article for *You* magazine. And it was only then that I realized. Because in this article, I wrote that I was here because of this tiny moment. My dad, you know, had been alive because of this tiny moment. I realized that I feel this tiny moment – this thing – is like this generational, I don't even know what you'd call it, consciousness? I don't even know, because it's not conscious. I don't know what you'd call it ...

ELEN: Precariousness?

LIZ: I mean. Yeah. It's what you said. It's this sense that our lives turn on the tiniest things. It's also about how kindness can have reverberating effects that a lot of time we don't know about. [...] It's a really big thing for me, this sense that we're all one world, that we can affect each other's lives. That if only that moment could have been different, that if you could do that again, that if you just chose to be kind in that moment, you've no idea what difference it could have made. That's my driving force.

ELEN: I also want to give you an opportunity to say something as a Jewish writer of Jewish stories. Did that feel important to you?

LIZ: Yeah. So ... My Jewish identity has always felt quite complicated. There's a very lovely Rabbi locally who I've had conversations with, on and off. I've said to him that I really struggle with things, because I feel like I go against Jewish mainstream thought in many different ways. And he said, 'But this is the essence of your Jewishness! Part of being Jewish, so much so often, is about the questioning and the discussing and the analysing of things. The very nature of what you're saying is inherently part of your Jewishness!' [...] And part of writing *When the World Was Ours*, I suppose, was about the fact that even though I'm not religious, my being Jewish is important to me. And always has been. I guess it was partly a search, a personal search for the grounding of my own identity, and the connection with my heritage. It felt important. Being Jewish was part of why it felt important to make sure that I was as accurate as I could be, and I researched it as well as I could.

There was one thing in the book that was inaccurate. Which I *know* was inaccurate and I left it anyway. I worked closely with a Holocaust expert and made sure that I got everything as accurate as I could. And the one thing that I left in was that when – spoiler alert – when Elsa's shot, she would have been naked. I made the decision that I didn't fucking care about accuracy in that moment, because it was really important to me that she owned that moment with as much dignity as she could have. And it's the most heartbreaking scene I've ever written, and it was important to me that I gave her dignity in the end. So, I wasn't doing that to her.

[...]

ELEN: You said earlier that it felt important that the three characters represent three different sets of 'what ifs', which led to stylistic choices in terms of how they're presented on the page. Can you say something about that?

LIZ: Someone once said that if you've got different characters telling the story of a book you should feel like you can open it on any page and know whose point of view you're in – they should be distinctive enough.

You don't have to use different narrative viewpoints to do different characters; you know, like telling it from first-person and third-person, past, present, etc. You don't have to do that. But it felt like a really good way of separating the voices. Also, it felt like each story led into that quite naturally.

So, Leo is the character whose story was […] inspired by my dad's childhood moment. And there's a sense of him telling his story. By the end – spoiler alert – he's still alive […]. He's an old man. And there's this sense of him telling his story, because that's what it circles back to at the end. So, we're in his viewpoint in the first-person, and he's telling it in the past tense, almost like we're looking back on his story.

Elsa is told in the first person also. And I feel like I've never wanted to be as close, I've never wanted to hold a character as close, to protect a character and have them know that I'm there with them, as much as I did with writing Elsa. So, it had to be the first-person. And there's a sense of urgency and immediacy with Elsa. She only has the present day. […] And so, first-person present was the right choice for her.

And then it came to thinking about Max, and I kind of thought: *Well, I'm not gonna do first-person future, that wouldn't make sense. What do I do?* And I also thought: *Do you know what, I feel like I want a little bit of distance.* I felt like I didn't want to be right in there with him. I don't want to give the world of the Hitler youth the opportunity to be that close to the readers. I want a tiny, tiny little veil. So, this was a very close third-person; this was the way to go with him – and it *is* close. We do feel like we're […] close to his mind almost as we are with the others. But that third-person point of view is just a tiny little bit of a boundary, to keep him at a slight distance.

ELEN: So, you've already talked a bit about your relationship with your agent. Could you say a little about how you got started?

LIZ: Okay. So, I was working as a teacher. And I went away with my mum, to Ambleside [in the Lake District in the UK]. And we were playing a game from *The Artist's Way*. We did this thing called Fantasy Lives, where you write down five lives that you would have if you didn't have the one that you have. […] Mine were basically: writer, writer, writer, writer, writer. It was genuinely an epiphany. […] I started writing a book which was about a year in the life of a girl, and her emerging sexuality. I enrolled on the MA in Novel Writing at Manchester Met. I got on that and had the most amazing time. Well, I got thyroid cancer pretty much almost straight away, which put a spanner in the works. So, I had quite a few challenges along the way. But I'd made this decision that I was going to be a published author within, I think, two years. I wrote the book which at the time I called *Year Out*. And that was the book I wrote on my MA. [...]

At the same time as this, I was living on a boat. One day, for fun, I wrote this poem [...] called *The Ballad of Mary Penelope's Boat*. It's about a woman who lives on a boat with her daughter; her daughter has this big secret, which is at night she goes out to play with the mermaids. I sent the poem to my friend, Lee Weatherly, who was a published children's author. She showed it to her editor and publisher, David Fickling, who said, 'I think Liz has got a good idea here, but she should try writing it as a novel instead of a poem.' So, I thought: *Oh, okay, I'll give it a go*. So, I tried doing that. I started writing it. [...] I just kept on working and got more excited about it. The other book went on hold. I was working with Helen Corner, running the kids' corner part of Cornerstones. She was having lunch with an agent who'd recently started taking on children's authors, called Catherine Clarke. She phoned me on a Friday, and she said, 'I love the sound of this book. Would you send it to me?' And I said, 'No, I'm scared.' She said, 'Send it!' So, I sent it. And then she called me on Monday and said, 'I want to take you on.' We worked on it a little bit, she sent it out to publishers, and I got a book deal with Orion. You know that's made it sound really smooth, and that in a way –

ELEN: No, I don't think you have, actually. Because, those are five or six new beginnings with a little bit of encouragement, but not a firm yes, along the way.

[...]

LIZ: So yeah. That was my story of getting published. Catherine's been with me all these years. She's the best agent in the business. She's amazing, and she's obviously a very dear friend. [...] And one last word on that to people who are at the beginning; people quite often see these big six-figure deals and think that's what they want. Catherine does talks on MAs and stuff, and when she does, she often uses my situation as an example of a good way to have your career: which is that it wasn't any kind of outstanding advance at the beginning, it was about building it gradually. Publishing's changed since then, and you get a much smaller window, I think, to be successful nowadays. But for me it built up gradually, and she's been with me every step of the way, and she's the best.

ELEN: What did your dad make of the book?

LIZ: So, my dad is very proud. He is really glad I've done it. He loved all the publicity that we did at the beginning and the opportunity to talk about the issues. He still goes into schools now – he's 93. He still does talks with the Holocaust Educational Trust. It's really important to him to keep these stories alive. He's very proud of me, and he loves the book. When *Codename Kingfisher* [Liz's subsequent book] came out, he read it, and he said, 'I cried. I thought it was wonderful.' He said, 'It was *almost* my favourite book, but *When the World Was Ours* will always be my favourite.'

SECTION 3: *WHEN THE WORLD WAS OURS*, WRITING EXERCISES

The exercises in this chapter are concerned with positionality – the relationship between the author, the readership and the characters or material of the novel. They are intended to encourage reflection on whose stories are told, how and by whom.

Exercise A – Whose Story?

With every story we tell, we have to decide which characters to focalize and how we are going to do it. Kessler decided to focalize three characters in *When the World Was Ours* – Leo, Elsa and Max – and she gave them all a different narrative voice to reflect their role in the narrative (see interview). This makes it a polyphonic novel; a story told by multiple voices. Another way to think about focalization is to ask who has the most interesting perspective on the events, or whose story might not have been told; some writers retell stories from the point of view of minor characters in the original, for example.

1. Pick a story you've worked on recently – it could be a work in progress or a piece written in response to earlier exercises in this book. Ask, who is the focalizing character or characters?
2. Choose a different character to focalize. What might the action of the plot look like from their point of view? Would they be an observer? If so, how significant or tangential would the action be to them? If they are involved, how might they think about their role?
3. Write a scene from the point of view of this new focalizing character. Use an internal narrator.
4. How does the story change with the new focalizing character? Do they have a different interpretation of the events, perhaps? Make a few notes on what you observe.

Exercise B – The Author's Positionality

As we saw in the discussion, the term #ownvoices is contested for many reasons, but I believe that all writers have an ethical relationship with their writing and should consider the circumstances in which it is made. One part of that might be positionality – to what extent do you and your readers (as identified by the sales and marketing strategies used to reach them) share the frames of reference of your characters? What extra work will need to be done to learn more about your character's frames of reference?

1. Think of the last novel you read. If it's close at hand, flick through it to remind yourself of the content.
2. Write down one of the settings in the novel. Add a few details about it – its location and point in time. If it is a fictional setting, add any settings (real or fictional) that might have inspired it.
3. Make some notes about your own familiarity with this setting. If you were the author of the book, what research would you need to do in order to include the right degree of convincing detail (Liz Kessler, for example, travels to the settings of her work and fills notebooks with observations. Other alternatives include reading guide books or watching travel vlogs).
4. Write down one of the characters from the novel. Add a few details about them – age, ethnicity, social class, sex, gender, sexuality, etc.
5. Make some notes about your own familiarity with these characteristics – are you able to draw on personal experience or memory? If you were the author of the book, what research would you need to do in order to include the right degree of convincing detail (for example, conducting interviews, reading memoirs and biographies, other novels, watching documentaries, films, etc.). Would you want someone with life experience closer to that of the character than yourself to read the book to double-check your verisimilitude/plausibility?
6. Repeat points 4 and 5 using another one or two characters from the novel.
7. Reflect on the power dynamics at play here. Do you have more or less social clout than the characters you are writing about? Do you come from a place with more or less economic strength than the characters? How might that change the way you approach the story? Professor Singh's questions (see discussion earlier in this chapter) might be useful here. Finally, think about your readers – are the people you are writing about the audience for your work? If not, how does that change the way you approach the story?

Exercise C – History and Peritext

In the discussion of *When the World Was Ours*, I reflected on how important the peritextual elements were in our reading of the opening scene. Of course, if you have a work in progress then you can't yet know what your cover might look like. However, it is still interesting to observe how the context can shape our reception of a text.

1. For this exercise, browse the internet for an iconic image from the past – perhaps something like Elisabeth Louise Vigée Le Brun's painting of Marie Antoinette in a (scandalous) chemise dress, Tommie Smith and John Carlos's raised fists at the 1968 Olympics or Grant Wood's painting 'American Gothic'. If you know a little bit about the context of the image, all the better.
2. Imagine that this image is the cover of a book. Make a list of the sort of themes, situations or content you might expect from the book.
3. Add to your list, what emotions might you expect in the opening scene? What atmosphere does the cover image promise?
4. Write a short scene, imagining that this is the first scene in the book. Can you deliver a surprising emotion to the reader, an unexpected atmosphere? Can you write the opposite of whatever appeared on your point 3 list?
5. Finally, make a note of how you achieved the contrast. Do you think the contrast would serve as a hook, or would it be off-putting for the reader? Do you prefer text and peritext to be in alignment or in subversion?

Chapter Seven

SECTION 1: *THE KNIFE OF NEVER LETTING GO* BY PATRICK NESS, A CRITICAL DISCUSSION

Note: this chapter contains spoilers for *The Knife of Never Letting Go* and discussion of gender-based violence.

We stay with YA in this chapter, this time looking more closely at a coming-of-age novel. *The Knife of Never Letting Go* is the first in the Chaos Walking trilogy by Patrick Ness (there are also associated shorter stories set in the same world). It is a fantasy YA, with strong themes around gender, mass communication, privacy, control, ecology and violence. In it we meet, on New World, an adolescent boy called Todd Hewitt. He is being raised in a community of men after a germ killed all the women. The same germ caused men's thoughts to be broadcast aloud. At least, this is the story Todd has been raised to believe. At the start of the novel, Todd and his dog, Manchee, come across an off-worlder, Viola, whose scout ship crashed, killing her parents and leaving Viola alone and traumatized. It becomes clear that the story Todd has known about the fate of women on New World is not true and he, Viola and Manchee are forced to flee the men of Prentisstown. This extract comes near the beginning of their journey together. In this scene, Todd is looking at a book that was hand-written for him by his lost mother. The Mayor of Prentisstown, an authoritarian leader, has forbidden reading; Todd is illiterate,

> I look at the book again, flip through the pages. Dozens of them, dozens upon dozens, all with more words in every corner, all saying nothing to me at all, no answers of any kind.
> Stupid effing book.
> I shove the map back inside, slam the cover shut and throw the book on the ground.
> You *idiot*.
> 'Stupid effing book!' I say, out loud this time, kicking it into some ferns. I turn back to the girl. She's still just rocking back and forth, back and forth, and I know, I know, okay, I *know*, but it starts to piss me off. Cuz if this is a dead end, I got nothing more to offer and she ain't offering nothing neither.
> My Noise starts to crackle.
> 'I didn't ask for this, you know,' I say. She don't even look. 'Hey! I'm talking to you!'
> But nothing. Nothing, nothing, nothing.

> 'I DON'T KNOW WHAT TO DO!' I yell and stand and start stomping around, shouting till my voice scratches. 'I DON'T KNOW WHAT TO DO! I DON'T KNOW WHAT TO DO!' I turn back to the girl. 'I'm SORRY! I'm sorry this happened to you but I don't know what to do about it AND STOP EFFING ROCKING!'
> 'Yelling, Todd,' Manchee barks.
> 'Awwghh!' I shout, putting my hands over my face. I take them away and nothing's changed. That's the thing I'm learning about being thrown out on yer own. Nobody does *nothing* for you. If you don't change it it don't get changed.
> 'We gotta keep going,' I say, picking up my rucksack all angry-like. 'You ain't caught it yet, so maybe just keep yer distance from me and you'll be okay. I don't know but that's all there is so that's what we gotta do.'
> (Ness 2008:109–10)

We can see immediately some of the themes I mentioned earlier, especially communication, gender and violence. Todd, looking at a book written by his own mother, is unable to decipher her words to him. Let's unpack the scene,

> I look at the book again, flip through the pages. Dozens of them, dozens upon dozens, all with more words in every corner, all saying nothing to me at all, no answers of any kind.

This handwritten book is a compelling symbol in this coming-of-age novel. It is an object Todd will return to again and again throughout the trilogy, and as his character evolves so too will his relationship with the object. Each encounter will mark a further stage in his coming of age.

The coming-of-age novel has its roots in the *bildungsroman* ('education' or 'formation' novel), which is a genre concerning the formation of a (typically) white, male, middle-class protagonist (Šnircová 2017) as they move out of childhood and see more of the world. The coming-of-age genre has acquired a range of tropes and conventions over time. We would typically expect to see a combination of these elements: a young person on the cusp of adulthood separating painfully from childhood; a physical journey may take place with the trials of that journey serving to challenge the protagonist; the protagonist may separate temporarily from their home or community in order to undertake that journey; they may come to understand their original community in a new light; that understanding might be hard won; ultimately they may become reconciled to their community and their place in it or they may rebel entirely, unable to accept the compromise that reconciliation entails. These tropes may be present to a greater or lesser degree and the coming-of-age label can be applied to a very wide range of work from Louisa May Alcott's *Little Women* to Alex Wheatle's *Cane Warriors*, via classics of the genre like *The Catcher in the Rye* by J.D. Salinger.

Todd, here, is in the early stages of his coming of age. He is separated from his original community but has not yet gone through the painful experiences that will lead to his maturation. His mother's book serves a symbolic function here. He has brought the book with him, at the start of his separation, but its meaning is frustratingly unknowable to him. He looks through it in a cursory way 'flip[ping] through the pages'. His illiteracy has been imposed upon him by Mayor Prentiss as a way to maintain control – to be able to mould him into the man Mayor Prentiss wants. At the beginning of the novel Todd was in a state of innocence, unaware of his community's secrets. Now he can see 'dozens of them, dozens upon dozens', 'more words in every corner' and each written word is a confounding secret. At this stage of his evolution, Todd is coming to see the 'known unknowns' – he has become aware that the secrets exist even if he does not yet understand their nature.

There is powerful repetition of 'dozens' and 'all' that gives a sense of clamouring, the words trying – and failing – to reach him. The internal narrator delivers this in an unmediated present tense; the failures of communication are ever present, noted and noticed in the relentless moment. We have seen this kind of relentless present before, with October in Chapter 4. Living in the now, unable to understand the flows of communication that forge a shared consensus, Todd is crushed. We see his despair in the negatives repeated at the end of this sentence 'nothing', 'no answers'.

Stupid effing book.

This short, punchy sentence offers Todd's current judgement on the knowledge he has been offered but can't access. He rejects it, bitterly. The community he has come from is a conservative, patriarchal one and here he displays his learned understanding of gendered, masculine behaviour: when confronted by the unknown, shut it down; when confronted by failure, lash out. Todd expresses his shame and vulnerability as anger, blaming the book and, by extension, the woman who wrote it. The ideology he has been raised with is revealed by this flash of interiority – it illuminates a hinterland of world-building.

It is notable that while Ness suggests that Todd curses, there is ambiguity here; is it Todd who says 'effing', or does he say 'fucking' and Ness has pulled a veil over the profanity? I suspect it is Todd himself using the euphemism, as elsewhere in the book he clarifies when he doesn't say 'effing' (40). Either way, the text here is following the common writing advice not to include 'bad language' when writing for young people unless it is entirely necessary (for example, Kole 2012).

This common piece of writing advice offers an interesting perspective on the extent to which novels for young people are themselves perceived by gatekeepers as enablers of 'coming of age'. Do books help young people learn to be adults, or do they hasten their corruption? There are currently splenetic and divisive campaigns running in the United States and, to a lesser extent, the UK on 'book banning' (Corbett and Phillips 2023). For many, on both sides of the debate, literature is seen as a powerful force, able to shape the thinking and even actions of the child reading it. This belief in the power of literature finds positive expression in the suggestion that reading might encourage the development of empathy (Chiaet 2013), and negative expression in fears that books cause harm by exposing children to damaging content which do not reflect 'the values of the community' from which the child comes (Shalvey 2021). In this context those who write, publish and distribute literature for children might find themselves cast (willingly or not) in a role as *loco parentis*. Or, worse, in *loco* for all possible permutation of *parentis*, trying to keep happy progressive and conservative parents both, for fear of garnering negative PR which would harm their bottom line. We should remain cognizant of the fact that all the culture being produced for young people is produced in the context of the marketplace, after all. Such a broad responsibility explains the advice to limit 'shocking' content such as bad language. Here, the euphemism 'effing' would satisfy all but the most puritan gatekeeper.

> I shove the map back inside, slam the cover shut and throw the book on the ground.

Todd's verb choice is striking in this tripartite sentence: 'shove', 'slam', 'throw'.
    They are actions suggestive of violence, of wrestling with the object, and so the symbolism continues. It is almost as though, in his anger and pain, Todd is pushing his mother away. He is also turning his back on the knowledge that he is not yet equipped to access, reminding us that this is a coming-of-age novel, and he has a long way to go yet.

> You *idiot*.
> 'Stupid effing book!' I say, out loud this time, kicking it into some ferns.

In Chapters 3 and 6, I featured the five ways Anderson (2005) suggests an author might use to reveal character (interpretation; appearance; action; thoughts and observation; and speech) and we see these principles again here. Ness reveals so much about Todd in these few lines. First, his self-loathing thought, calling himself an idiot. Then the repetition of the earlier thought 'stupid effing book!' but this time given additional force with the exclamation mark and the fact that it is almost involuntarily spoken aloud. Finally, in frustration, he acts, kicking the book. This short run of interiority>speech act>physical act shows us his state of mind. There is no need at all for Todd, as the internal narrator, to name any of his emotions. In fact, given his upbringing, it is probably beyond Todd's capacities to name his emotions. As a narrator, having to interpret himself, he would be at a loss. But, as readers, we are able to deduce. Todd, we might think, is having to repress his perfectly legitimate emotions – grief, loss, hurt – and sublimate them into something much more socially acceptable in the community he is part of – anger. Unsurprisingly, the sublimation sours the emotions, turning them toxic. Penfold (2023:4) says that through story beats like this, Ness is 'exposing the damaging effects of binary approaches and narrow interpretations of gendered identity'. In character terms, Todd has been raised with clearly delineated boundaries and binaries. These don't just apply in terms of gender, but also in terms of age: before his thirteenth he is a boy, upon turning thirteen, he is a man. It is that simple. There is no messy adolescence in Prentisstown. However, as he journeys away from home, he comes to question these 'narrow interpretations' and it is the pain of this questioning that leads to the fractured, souring self here.

> I turn back to the girl. She's still just rocking back and forth, back and forth, and I know, I know, okay, I *know*, but it starts to piss me off.

Todd isn't alone in this scene. But he had temporarily forgotten the presence of Viola. Our attention is realigned by his physical motion, his 'turning back' which is both literal and metaphorical. Todd 'turns back' to the plot. Such a moment of embodiment can be a useful transitional phrase and we see the technique commonly used to draw a memory or flashback to a close (as we saw previously in Chapter 5). The person Todd finds, as he is brought back to attention, is just as distraught as he is himself. 'The girl', not yet a named person, not yet endowed with full personhood, is rocking. Todd is confronted with something that he believes is impossible – a living girl – and yet she is real. His mind, lacking as it is in plasticity because of his upbringing, cannot comfortably accommodate new information. The syntax and word stress show us the pressure Todd is feeling. The repetition of 'I know' and the interjection of the pacifier 'okay' mirror her compulsive rocking. The two characters might be feeling similar emotions, but Todd is unable to allow himself to empathize with Viola, and instead the emotion turns to irritation. Again, this rejection of vulnerability reveals his character and something of the world that shaped his character. He does swear for real this time, with 'piss me off'; language which is one reason among many why this is classified as Young Adult, rather than middle grade.

> Cuz if this is a dead end, I got nothing more to offer and she ain't offering nothing neither.

This sentence demonstrates the degree to which Ness has created a specific idiolect for Todd that reveals his character and something about his world and worldview through diction. His idiolect is a way of speaking – and thinking, this is interiority, after all – informed by working-class, rural Americana. Todd lives beside a swamp, on a farm, and his idiolect could be that of Louisiana or Mississippi; Tom Sawyer hovers as a shadow somewhere in his literary heritage. The 'cuz', 'ain't' 'nothing neither' are a non-Standard English that situates Todd as an uneducated, unread boy, not given to social niceties. These are signifiers, of course, borrowed from our Earth and transposed to New World; as Sangster suggests, 'in practice, [...] fantasies always rely to some extent on existing resources of language and understanding. They work towards qualified originality through iteration and extrapolation, rather than by creating worlds out of the void' (2023:300).

Todd is telling his own story in his own words – partly because he has no access to any other kind of language; he cannot code switch, even if he wanted to. And Ness is borrowing an idiolect from Earth (from Americana) to supply the necessary signifiers. Todd's idiolect speaks to the degree to which his world has been kept artificially narrow by the community raising him.

> My Noise starts to crackle.

It is with 'Noise' that the high-concept nature of this novel becomes clear. A 'high-concept' book is one in which the premise can be simply stated and yet the implications of that premise are powerful enough that the audience is excited at the prospect. The premise of *The Knife of Never Letting Go* is, 'what if all the unfiltered thoughts of men were broadcast out loud?' Elsewhere in the book, Ness writes, 'without a filter, a man is just chaos walking' (42), which gives the trilogy its title. Todd cannot control his Noise, a concept of such profound significance that it is represented as a proper noun. His interiority is displayed as sensory images and sound, a multi-modal telepathy with those around him. In this story beat, we are reminded of this fact, the 'crackle' reminiscent of radio static, suggesting a faulty communication. The detail chosen here is drawn from a palette of imagery that reflects the central theme of mass communication. In order to pull off the central conceit, Ness must construct and maintain a fully convincing world. We have already seen how Todd's character and idiolect are one symbiotic element of that construction, but even the choice of imagery is working to reinforce the construction.

> 'I didn't ask for this, you know,' I say. She don't even look. 'Hey! I'm talking to you!'
> But nothing. Nothing, nothing, nothing.

Todd's statement here echoes a familiar teenage refrain, 'I didn't ask to be born.' It is a childish worldview, where, we may hope to think, the world tends towards justice, and we get what we deserve. There is a petulance to it, but an innocence too. At this point in the story, Todd is a boy.

His attempt to communicate is rebuffed, Viola gives him not even a look. And then, his anger returns, again in language that might sound familiar: 'I'm talking to you!' Todd is attempting to communicate here, but is doing so in stock phrases, in cliches, and the subsequent impoverishment of the connection means Viola isn't prompted to respond.

The result of this failed communication is more frustration for Tod and a return to the repeating negatives we saw earlier. We're given a single instance followed by a tricolon (a rhetorical triple repetition), to give us four repetitions, hammering home the nullification: 'nothing. Nothing, nothing, nothing.' It is not just silence that that the word conjures, but also destruction. The silence of women is dangerous here – in a world where men are exposed, but women can keep their own council, the power imbalance is intolerable to the men of Prentisstown. Todd reacts to this power imbalance in the way that the men of Prentisstown do; he loses his temper,

> 'I DON'T KNOW WHAT TO DO!' I yell and stand and start stomping around, shouting till my voice scratches. 'I DON'T KNOW WHAT TO DO! I DON'T KNOW WHAT TO DO!'

Todd's frustration and anger reaches a crescendo and this is demonstrated by the typography. Throughout the book the formal typeface gives way in places to handwritten script in varying font sizes, to give the impression of Noise. It is not uncommon to see YA texts employ some of the multi-modal narrative techniques we saw very commonly employed in picturebooks and Early Readers. Here, the typeface moves to capital letters – the shouting font. Again, the phrase is somewhat cliche and repeated in another tricolon. Todd has no range of communication styles available to him at this early stage of his journey. The short sentences are a feature of Todd's idiolect; they are the terse sentences of a boy with a limited education and a limited number of conversational partners to practice with. All he can do is get louder.

His physicality also reflects this restricted, masculinized mode of communicating, he 'yells', 'stomping' and 'shouting'. These verbs embody his frustration. There is a tightly wrought feedback loop here, where actions and dialogue reveal character, characterization reveals world-building and world-building dictates the action and dialogue. It is a closed system that renders the unlikely New World convincing. It allows the reader to suspend their disbelief so we can accept gendered telepathy as a plot device. Todd's shouts continue 'till my voice scratches'; the sibilance sounds painful and again, with the hint of a 'scratched record'; the imagery is drawn from a palette informed by mass communication.

> I turn back to the girl. 'I'm SORRY! I'm sorry this happened to you but I don't know what to do about it AND STOP EFFING ROCKING!'

This is a repetition of his earlier action – turning back, attempting to re-focus on her. As with the content of his dialogue, he only has the internal resources to try the same thing again in the hope it might work this time where it failed last time. I gave a definition of *plot*, in Chapter 2 – the events of a narrative in sequence where one event has a causal connection with the next. In the quoted sentences here, we can see the glimmering emergence of *story* – the effect that the plot will have on the characters on whom we are focused; the way they will change and evolve as a result of their experiences. John Yorke (following Lajos Egri) goes even further and suggests that the evolution of character and the dramatic structure of the narrative are 'inevitably linked' (2013:76). Yorke posits that over the course of a narrative the battle between a character's super-ego and id will bring about either their redemption or their tragedy. Whatever a character wants at the beginning of the story will be an attempt to hide their vulnerabilities; but a showdown with those vulnerabilities, metaphorically speaking, will become necessary by the end. This creates a structure commonly called a 'character arc'. In Todd's case, he begins the story wanting to be a man, but his society has such a narrow definition of what it means to be a man that Todd has to repress crucial parts of himself in order to pass muster. His kindness and compassion are a weakness in the binary boy/man, male/female world he inhabits. However, over the course of the plot, he needs to learn alternative routes to manhood; if he doesn't, he will be psychically destroyed. It is his 'weakness', his compassion, which comes to be his alternate route and so the source of his redemption. This is his character arc, his *story*. Eventually, he will come of age with a better understanding of himself. Here we see that struggle in microcosm. Todd can see Viola's pain, and is sorry for it, but has no idea how to offer comfort and resorts to shouting and swearing. He lacks a language of compassion, and it will take three books to teach it to him.

> 'Yelling, Todd,' Manchee barks.

Here we have a new (to us) character; Manchee is Todd's dog. On New World, it isn't just the men whose thoughts are broadcast, it's the animals too. As Ness states in the following interview, Manchee – or at least a talking dog – was one of the original inspirations for the book. Ness' dislike of 'conventional' anthropomorphic talking animals, which deny animals' alterity and have them conversing with the full communication range of a human, prompted him to wonder: *what would a dog say if it could talk?* In Chapters 1 and 2, we looked at animals as stand-ins for young people. Here, Manchee is as dog-like as Ness was able to make him. DasGupta (2024:7) contends (following Nagel) that it is impossible to disentangle the human from any representation of the animal and that, therefore, the most 'honest' animal writing is that which makes no attempt at verisimilitude and is entirely fantastic – talking animals and all. So, as writers, we may be doomed to failure if 'truth' is our goal, and yet, the puzzle still entices: how might animals, who can't speak, be represented through language? Ness' solution is to limit Manchee's speech acts to monosyllables, devoid of abstract thought. Manchee says what he observes in the moment, in this case he sees 'Yelling'. Moreover, the subjects of his observations almost always revolve around his own bodily needs – food, drink, poos – and his concern for Todd, who is the centre of his world. Here, it is Todd's distress that prompts Manchee to speak, although Ness chooses the verb 'bark' rather than 'speak' in respect to a dog's vocalization.

By giving this one line to Manchee, Ness is taking care of the placing. There have been three characters present in the scene throughout, but, unless they are each given dialogue or an action to complete, they risk being absent. This line 'places' Manchee, giving him a short piece of choreography so that he isn't forgotten by the reader. Additionally, his observation confirms our interpretation of Todd's earlier capitalized sentences as shouting.

> 'Awwghh!' I shout, putting my hands over my face. I take them away and nothing's changed. That's the thing I'm learning about being thrown out on yer own. Nobody does *nothing* for you. If you don't change it it don't get changed.

Todd's inability to articulate comes to its conclusion with a noise rather than a word, the degradation of his communication is complete. He attempts to 'reset' by covering his face for a moment, temporarily hiding himself away, but this fails. We can see here the brevity of Todd's idiolect; each sentence is short, with the subject, verb and object in the conventional syntactic position. There are no adverbs or adjectives. It is Spartan, devoid of rhetoric. Again, character idiolect is connected to upbringing is connected to world-building. Todd is a product of the place that made him and that is evident in every word – or noise – he utters.

Then we have what might be considered a 'guiding principle' for the novel, a statement that can be read as a kind of hypothesis which the plot and story will test. In this way, a novel can be viewed as a narrative thought experiment. Over the course of this coming-of-age novel, Todd will come to learn that he must change himself to survive and thrive; he must accept the parts of himself which he considers the most shameful. He will have to do it for himself, although he will have help and guidance on the way. So, 'If you don't change it it don't get changed' can be read as a manifesto for the story. We will see Todd variously not trying to change, we will see him looking to others for leadership, we will see him expecting others to change while he remains static, we will see him attempt to bring about change without the wherewithal to succeed, we will see him blaming others for not changing, before eventually embracing his own changed understanding of what he must be. In this way, the guiding principle is another means by which an author might structure a story; the testing of the hypothesis in various iterations can provide a central spine for the plot.

> 'We gotta keep going,' I say, picking up my rucksack all angry-like. 'You ain't caught it yet, so maybe just keep yer distance from me and you'll be okay. I don't know but that's all there is so that's what we gotta do.'

This is quite a long speech for Todd. As we have seen, he isn't given to articulating his thoughts – partly due to Noise making it unnecessary, partly because his conception of what it means to be a man is to act without explanation. His idiolect is in evidence again, the non-bookish, non-Standard English of rural America: 'gotta', 'angry-like', 'ain't' and 'yer'. But we also see something of his analytical, logical mind – his natural 'smarts'. Viola hasn't caught the virus yet, so maybe she won't; and what alternative do they have but to stick together anyway.

And so, we leave them, Viola, Manchee and Todd, forced to stick together because, for now, that's all they've got.

Cited Works

DasGupta, P. 2024, 'Representing "Otherness": Animals in "Alice's Adventures in Wonderland", "The Hundred and One Dalmatians", and beyond', *Leaf Journal*, vol. 2, no. 1, pp. 1–9.

Anderson, L. 2005, *Creative Writing: A Workbook with Readings*, 1st edn, Routledge, Abingdon.

Chiaet, J. 2013, Oct 4, *Novel Finding: Reading Literary Fiction Improves Empathy*. Available: https://www.scientificamerican.com/article/novel-finding-reading-literary-fiction-improves-empathy/ [2024, May 8].

Corbett, E. and Phillips, L. 2023, 'Ploughing the Field: Controversy and Censorship in US and UK YA Literature', *International Journal of Young Adult Literature*, vol. 4, no. 1, pp. 1–18.

Kole, M. 2012, *Writing Irresistible Kidlit: The Ultimate Guide to Crafting Fiction for Young Adult and Middle Grade Readers*, Penguin Publishing Group, Cincinnati.

Ness, P. 2008, *The Knife of Never Letting Go*, Walker Books, London.

Penfold, A. 2023, 'The Feminist Quest: Reimagining the Relationship between Language, Gender, and Identity in "The Knife of Never Letting Go" (2008) by Patrick Ness', *International Journal Young Adult Literature*, vol. 4, no. 1, pp. 1–19.

Sangster, M. 2023, *An Introduction to Fantasy*, Cambridge University Press, Cambridge.

Shalvey, K. 2021, Apr 11, *These are the 10 books that made the ALA's most-challenged list for 2020*. Available: https://www.businessinsider.com/american-library-association-publishes-banned-book-list-stories-racism-photos-2021-4 [2024, May 8].

Šnircová, S. 2017, *Girlhood in British Coming-of-Age Novels: The Bildungsroman Heroine Revisited*, Cambridge Scholars Publishing, Newcastle upon Tyne.

Yorke, J. 2013, *Into the Woods: A Five Act Journey into Story*, Penguin Random House, London.

SECTION 2: AN INTERVIEW WITH PATRICK NESS

ELEN: What do you remember about the inception of *The Knife of Never Letting Go*?

PATRICK: When I would go and talk to schools about *The Knife of Never Letting Go*, I would always say – and this is true – it came from two big ideas; one very serious big idea and one very stupid big idea.

The serious big idea was a concern about information overload. About what does that feel like when you're young, when everything you do is recorded? What does that loss of privacy mean? I didn't mean it in a judgemental, finger-wagging way, because I think, you know, the horse has bolted on that one. So, the question now is what do we do with it? What does it mean to lose your privacy? And losing it in the years in which privacy is needed the most, because you are deciding who you are as an individual, separate from your family.

So, I thought: *That's an interesting question*. Just to push it a little farther, I thought: *And what if we had no choice? What if we* had *to share everything?* So that was the big serious idea.

And the big stupid idea, which was just as important, was that I have never liked books about talking dogs. Because I think that they never talk how a dog would actually talk!

I do voices for my dogs and my cats all the time and I think they would only ever talk about food. Dogs would only ever talk about food, shagging and poop. And how much they love you. And, to me, that's hilarious and it's poignant and there's an innocence to it that is funny.

And so, I had these two big ideas. And I also had the idea that I wanted to write something in a [particular] voice. Which I've never done for a great length. That was inspired by Russell Hoban's *Riddley Walker*.

And the thing you find out when you write in voice, and very quickly, was that voice is a lot more fun to write than it ever is to read.

And so, I just kept pushing at it, pushing at it, pushing and thinking: *He's here somewhere, I can feel him, I can feel my narrator.*

And I found him one day. One day he's there, you know; voice is kind of mystical.

That was the point that I really realized it was a YA novel. And I think the wise decision I made – I've made poor decisions in the past, but this was a good one – was where I thought: *Great; that's great.*

That is, I have no fear of that [writing YA fiction], except for the usual, fruitful fear of any book. I thought: *Great, let's run with it.* And, and that's where it began.

ELEN: Maybe I will come back to the idea of that information overload. When did the decision come to gender the Noise? Because that seems so fundamental.

PATRICK: Very early on. And – I really want to stress this – it didn't come from a place of trying to make a statement about men or women. It was coming from a place of trying to make a statement about how we handle *difference*.

I was thinking, what if the difference between the two cis genders …

(My vocabulary has vastly … The world has become vastly richer in the fifteen-odd years since I wrote that book so back then it was [cis men and women]) …

What if the difference between men and women was something that had to be dealt with in every single interaction? If every single time a man and a woman had to communicate, that had to be reckoned with? What would people do? And really that's where it started from.

It was just trying to take an idea of difference, and look at it. Because in the book, and in life, there are great examples of how difference can be handled in healthy ways. And there are terrible, terrible examples. And I think, as a species, we have handled difference very, very poorly. Because we tend to put it in a hierarchy. You know, it's either better than us, so we have to tear it down; or it's less than us, so we can dominate it. The idea of something different simply being different, without a quality applied to it, is almost revolutionary.

So that's really what it was. I was not trying to make a huge statement, that men are obvious, and women are not – because that's not true! It was really about the negotiation of difference.

ELEN: I had assumed that the women were having exactly the same sort of internal thoughts as the men. You know, in terms of violence or anger or repression. They can just do it with a smile.

PATRICK: Yeah, these are the things that come in retrospect. Because when I'm writing, I really try to avoid thinking about 'capital T' themes. I feel like then it becomes like a sermon. But that kind of statement often covers a lot of sins, you know? When people say it's got to be a story first – I absolutely believe it has to be a story first – but lots of people who say that, say that to get themselves off the hook from ever having to think about the themes that accompany their stories.

I think that if I am really responding to a story, and really want to tell it, and there feels like there's richness there, then I have to believe that I'm doing it for a reason.

So, I do believe the story comes first, and I do believe that a plot has to work, etc., etc. But I also believe that my accompanying responsibility is to follow it to its most truthful places.

I can't just ... Nothing can be cheap. Everything has to be earned. Every act of violence has to be felt. Every bit of sadness has to be felt. And so, when I'm writing, I'm really just looking for what is actually true here.

And I, you know, I felt the same way you did. It's not that women weren't thinking these things. It was just that they had – luckily for them – a way to cover it. How would men react to that? Probably not well.

And, also in retrospect, there is an element of 'the closet' to Noise. There is an element of being able to disguise who you are, and what you think, versus being forced to show what you think.

And I look back at it and go: *Huh!* That's only there because I was following a story that I really believed in and was trying to make it as rigorously truthful to itself as I possibly could. So, that's how I think good fiction emerges, versus worthy fiction. Because good fiction can cover every single thing that a worthy novel can. You just have to trust yourself, that you're wanting to tell the story for a reason. And that you're responding to it for a reason and that all the stuff that you love is going to be there.

And then you look back and go: *Oh, wow! Wasn't I genius?* For thinking of all that in advance, you know what I mean?

ELEN: What's a worthy novel?

PATRICK: I used to call them C-BAITs, which is 'crappy books about important things'. And they, in America, they win a lot of awards. And 'twas ever thus. This is not anything new. 'Worthy' in terms of 'here's something historically important', 'here's something that will make you feel better about yourself in a particular kind of way'. And those are fine. They have their place. But to me, they're not novels, really, they are history lessons. And there's nothing wrong with a history lesson, unless you want a novel.

And ... and ... I am 100 per cent aware of my position, saying this as a white guy, because again, the accompanying responsibility, to saying I don't want to tell you a history lesson, is I'd better get my story right. It better be truthful. It better not lie to you. It better question every assumption that I'm gonna put into it. It better question every life assumption that I have just from being who I am.

ELEN: There are so many strong themes: difference, as you've said; gender; genocide; ecology ... Are you writing the story first – or planning a story first, if that's your process – and then seeing a theme and thinking, 'I could turn the volume up on that?'

PATRICK: Sometimes you do, sometimes you do. I mean, mostly though ... So, with the theme of genocide, which you mentioned, that becomes more and more apparent as the books go on. And, I wasn't thinking of the theme of genocide. I was thinking: *What would be the truthful consequences of the situation? What would we do?*

You know, I grew up in the American West. I grew up in Hawaii and the state of Washington, which is on the West Coast. And, for better or worse – which is an interesting question in itself – there is still the feeling of frontier there. Which is such a loaded word and such a loaded question.

It's a question that I've always found interesting, being from the West. Hawaii is a land that was taken from its Polynesian people – who are still there. I lived in a town in Washington called Puyallup, which is named after a tribe, it was tribal land. I have always been particularly interested in the literature of Australia. Because, again, it's the new. What is a new world and who defines what a new world is? It is really interesting to me.

The simplest way to put it is I thought: *Well, if we went to another planet, would we commit the same sins? Probably.*

I didn't want to shy away from that. I didn't want to pretend. I didn't want to put something that I felt was untrue, just because I thought it should be true. I think that's a real losing game. Your reader can smell you a mile away when, when you've lied like that.

So, I thought: *Okay*. What would the consequences of settlement be? What would the consequences of Noise be? How would that split gender? How would those people deal with a native population, particularly one that worked in the Noise easily, because that's their environment?

And so, for me, it comes from answering these questions honestly. Which is not always easy, you know, because the temptation is always to look for reassurance and false hope. I also believe that if you tell the truth about the things that are difficult, then when you do tell the truth about what real hope feels like, and what real connection feels like, then, in a way, it feels more true, because you haven't lied.

And so, I'm not sitting there thinking: *How do I address the issue of genocide?* I'm thinking: *How do I address the issue of genocide, in this environment, in this story, truthfully?*

And sometimes that's quite dark. So, it's really just a matter of trying to be fearless. Or courageous anyway, because fearlessness implies no fear; fear is healthy.

After the first draft and second draft is done, I can look back and go: *Okay. That's interesting*. In the shallowest terms, you know, you get to the end of a draft, and look back and go: *Oh, that's what I meant*. I'm gonna go back and pretend that's what I meant all along. So, that's what I do.

But again, I try not to hit the themes too heavy because then I think you're reading a tome, rather than a book.

ELEN: Can I maybe ask you to talk about Todd's voice as it was such a eureka moment for you?

PATRICK: Very early on, I realized it was important that Todd be illiterate, but not unintelligent. And so, I thought: *Okay, what does that combination look like, and sound like in this world?* Someone who is very, very smart but he has had absolutely no tools to learn with. I heavily misspelled things very early on. But again, it's more fun to write than it is to read.

And I thought: *Okay, why are you doing this?* I just kept simplifying it. Trying to find the balance. Trying to find enough that would suggest, without overly dictating. And I'm not Russell Hoban. That book is a linguistic masterpiece. The various puns and the depths of meanings of different words is extraordinary.

So, I thought: *Okay, that's not what my book's about, you know, but how do I get Todd to sing?* And it took several tries. It really did. And then one day, there he was. It was the double-negatives and … It's really only the '-tion' words that I consistently misspell. Because why would he think they were spelled with '-tion'?

It's a trick you're trying to pull. You are using words to express the mind of a boy who can't read. It's a bit of a magic trick. But I thought: *Okay, what can I suggest that will tell you who he is, without it being a labour?* Because fleetness was very important.

[…]

I thought: *This needs to be fleet-of-foot; this needs to be breathless in a way that isn't empty*. It needs to be his experience. I know there's a lot of talk about first-person present [tense narrators] in YA. People are like, 'Don't use it; I hate it.' [Philip Pullman (2010) has famously objected to its use.] But in itself, it doesn't have a value. It's the use of the thing, you know.

So, I thought: *Okay, how can I earn this?* How can I make this move without losing depth? How can I make it accurate to how he would speak?

There just became a rhythm. The shape of pages emerged. There are lots of one-sentence paragraphs. Which is not what I normally do, you know. Russell Hoban always said that *Riddley Walker* ruined his spelling and I kinda see what he means. For a long while after, I really had to force my paragraphs back into shape because I'd got so used to the breaking.

I have a few writing philosophies which I've slowly come to believe over the years. And one of them is that a book is not a song, a book is the performance of a song. So, pick a good song. But what people want is how you perform it.

I'm always very curious and committed to how my books sing. And this needed to be a bold voice, which was scary.

But he was just there one day, and I thought: *This is the balance*. And off we went. That first sentence was kind of the first thing he ever said. I thought: *There he is. Let's see where that goes; let's see what follows*.

Cited Work

Pullman, P. 2010, Sep 18, *Philip Pullman calls time on the present tense*.
   Available: https://www.theguardian.com/global/2010/sep/18/philip-pullman-author-present-tense [2024, July 27].

SECTION 3: *THE KNIFE OF NEVER LETTING GO*, WRITING EXERCISES

This set of exercises are intended to help you think about genre expectations and how the premise of your work can serve as a tool for plotting.

Exercise A – Genre Tropes

Readers will come to your work with a set of expectations built over many years of reading and absorbing media. Over time, these expectations have come to be understood as genres and readers will tend to align their tastes with particular genres. Writers working within each genre (including literary fiction) should be aware of genre expectations and conventions in order to delight, confound or challenge their readers. *The Knife of Never Letting Go* is both a fantasy/sci-fi novel and a coming-of-age novel. In this exercise, we'll play with some coming-of-age tropes.

1. Imagine a character, on the cusp of adulthood. Without over-thinking, make quick notes on their sex, gender, age, ethnicity, social class, sexuality and any disability. Make notes on their temperament: degrees of positivity, smartness, kindness, courage, etc.
2. Without over-thinking, make quick notes on the setting for your coming of age: contemporary, historical, fantastical, etc. Note down some of the expectations of adulthood your character might have in that society (for example, if you were writing about America, you might note the 'pursuit of happiness' as an expectation of adulthood).
3. Write a scene between your character and their best friend. During the conversation, reveal that the best friend has a different and surprising expectation of adulthood.
4. Imagine you were to continue this scene to the length of a novel. Make a list of some experiences your character might have in the novel to either confirm or challenge their expectations of adulthood – are they or their friend more correct?

Exercise B – High Concept Premise

In his interview, Patrick Ness explained how the plot and world-building for *The Knife of Never Letting Go* unspooled from his high-concept premise. He searched for 'the truthful consequences of the situation'.

1. Pick one from this list of 'high-concept' situations:
   - A bank error deposits £1 million in a teenager's bank account.
   - An AI can predict individual human life-courses, based on an algorithm. It gives teenagers a 90 per cent accurate prediction of their future on their fifteenth birthday.
   - Ghosts are everywhere, one day everyone is able to see them.
   - A girl learns that an active shooter, loose in her high school, is her younger brother.
   - Love can be extracted, bottled and sold.
2. Create a mind-map with 'the truthful consequences of the situation'. Create as many dividing branches as you need. What are the necessary outcomes? The potential outcomes? The wildly unlikely, but still possible outcomes?
3. Choose any point on your mind-map and write a scene inspired by it.

Exercise C – A Guiding Principle

A guiding principle can be seen as a statement that serves as a kind of hypothesis which the plot and story will test. So, for example, the guiding principle of *Romeo and Juliet* might be 'love does not conquer all'. This principle is tested during the play, not just between Romeo and Juliet, but also between the parents and their respective children, between Romeo and Mercutio, between Juliet and the Nurse, and so on. In each case, love is tested and found wanting, in various different ways. Having a guiding principle can be useful in devising which scenes you will need and how you might arrange any subplots (subplots often address the guiding principle, but from a different angle, adding depth to the theme).

1. Pick one from this list of guiding principles:
   - Unity is strength
   - Better to be alone than in bad company
   - It's easier to forgive an enemy than a friend
   - The grass is never greener
   - If you can't love yourself, you can't love anyone else.

2. Make a list of all the elements your guiding principle entails, if you were to use it in a story. For example, with 'love does not conquer all', this necessitates two or more characters in love; a situation where their love is thwarted; a conclusion where their attempts to overcome the thwarting situation fail.
3. Make notes on the characters who will perform your guiding principle. Give them names, ages, situations.
4. Write a short scene in which you bring together at least two of the required elements necessitated by your chosen principle.

Chapter Eight

SECTION 1: *ACE OF SPADES* BY FARIDAH ÀBÍKÉ-ÍYÍMÍDÉ, A CRITICAL DISCUSSION

Note: this chapter contains significant spoilers for *Ace of Spades* by Faridah Àbíké-Íyímídé and discussion of race-based violence.

We conclude this series of discussions with commercial YA and Faridah Àbíké-Íyímídé's *New York Times* bestselling *Ace of Spades*. This novel has been variously categorized as a thriller, a horror and an addition to the growing genre of dark academia. It follows two Black students at an elite private school as a campaign of terror is directed against them by someone known only as Aces; later they will discover a white supremacist conspiracy working to ensure Black students fail. In this extract, one of the two protagonists – Chiamaka – is taking temporary refuge in the girl's bathroom.

Every single night I dream of her. The girl.
But now before those nightmares, I ask myself, *Who is doing this? What will they reveal next?*
'Chiamaka?' I hear a soft voice say, along with the subtle creak of the bathroom door.
I stay quiet, seated sideways on the ground of the stall, looking at my blue plaid skirt spread over my outstretched legs, the thick grey socks that cover most of my thighs, and my brown-heeled brogues pressing against the wall.
'It's Belle', she continues. The bathroom stall next to mine opens and my heart races a little. I hear a slight rattle as Belle pulls at my locked door. She raps at the door three times. I can see her grey suede heels and white frilly socks.
'Are you in there?' she asks. I say nothing. I'm not sure why she's going to such great lengths to be nice. Maybe she's trying to prove a point to Jamie that she's the perfect girl. But I doubt Jamie would notice how Belle treats me, let alone care.
Belle is still and silent, and I almost think she's going to walk away, give up. But then I hear a scraping noise.
I watch the door as the lock slowly starts to turn. There's a sharp *clink* and the door opens.
Belle looks down at me, with wide eyes and a frown. She unzips her bag and hands me a folded tissue.

I don't take it.
(Àbíké-Íyímídé 2021:118–19)

There is much here to talk about: the playfulness with genre, the page-turning quality powered by conflict, and the connection between these things and the physicality of the young women. Let's take our final deep dive into writing for young people!

Every single night I dream of her. The girl.

Once more, we have an internal narrator addressing us in present simple tense ('I dream'). However, the tense in this sentence is tricksy – it is present simple tense being used to describe a habitual event which occurred in the past, the present and, presumably, will carry on into the future. The relentlessness of the event is underscored by the intensifier 'every single'. What is being described here is a repetitive dream which seems to close in from all sides. A nightmare. A haunting.

As I stated earlier, *Ace of Spades* is categorized variously as horror, thriller and dark academia. Here it's displaying these roots with writing in the Gothic mode. We have a young girl haunted by an uncanny Other. The Other in question is a vision of a white girl struck – and presumably killed – in a hit-and-run traffic collision. Chiamaka was a passenger in the car while her friend and crush, Jamie, was driving. They have never confessed to the crime. The threat of an uneasy, revenant past intruding on the present is a dominant theme of the novel, and 'The girl' is just one instance of a symbol being used to reinforce the theme. Her significance is given weight by the syntax. It is not 'I dream of the girl every single night'; rather, 'The girl' is afforded her own sentence and her own line return; she matters.

Pulliam (2010) suggests that there is a special relationship between hauntings and female characters in YA novels in particular. She calls the monstrous Other 'a double with a difference […] whose similarity to the original implies the possibility of resistance to that which has been presented as "natural" and unchangeable' (103). Which is to say that instability in one area of reality (monsters) implies instability *everywhere* (patriarchy, white supremacy and more). This view of the Gothic as space to 'interrogate' the 'social order' is shared by Smith and Moruzi (2021:14). If Pulliam is right, then Chiamaka is being haunted by a girl who is both a threat, but also a promise: Chiamaka doesn't have to accept her place in the world as it is being defined for her, girls can be powerfully monstrous. An interesting possibility for teen readers to encounter.

The girl represents one plot point and one element of conflict – the revenant, guilt-laden past. But, as I have said, this novel is a page-turner. Commonly, in bestselling, commercial fiction, we see *layers* of conflict running concurrently, never allowing the tension or suspense to dip too low. Chiamaka is experiencing both a specific stressor, in that she is being forced to hide in the bathroom because of a lunchtime disagreement with Jamie, but she has also been under sustained stress as a result of the guilt and fear of discovery associated with the hit and run. She is keeping a deadly secret and Àbíké-Íyímídé is using this beat to remind us of that threat.

>But now before those nightmares, I ask myself, *Who is doing this? What will they reveal next?*

The secrets continue into the next sentence. Not as ghostly dreams, but as intrusive fears expressed through interiority, 'I ask myself'. With this tag, our internal narrator clarifies that she is adjusting her psychic distance, moving closer to Chiamaka-the-character rather than Chiamaka-the-narrator. Once this position has been made clear, the thoughts themselves are italicized, indicating a direct thought. This particular arrangement of textual elements removes any ambiguity around the narratorial voice. Again, with commercial fiction, clarity of storytelling allows for a more seamless, uninterrupted reading experience. The plot is delivered as though it were oiled. The phrasing and diction are very clean too. The questions Chiamaka asks begin with 'who' and 'what' making the conflict crystal clear – there is an antagonist who has the power to damage Chiamaka and they aren't afraid to wield that power. So, in these few sentences there are three major conflicts running concurrently: the internal conflict of guilt as Chiamaka wrestles with the fact she didn't help in a hit and run and the external conflict which comes from her discontent with Jamie and from the unknown antagonist who may reveal her guilt to the world.

>'Chiamaka?' I hear a soft voice say, along with the subtle creak of the bathroom door.

We've already noted the unstable present tense in the opening lines of the extract. Now we are in an uncomplicated present simple tense as we move smoothly into the action of the scene. This is a choice which is entirely genre-appropriate. In a thriller, time is limited as the protagonist typically tries to stop something catastrophic from happening; in a horror the writer might want to suggest an uncertain future for their characters. Present simple tense here underscores the precariousness and impermanence of Chiamaka's situation – it all might come crashing down in an instant.

The setting is significant. Chiamaka has taken temporary refuge in a High School bathroom. We encountered the concept of the 'chronotope' in Chapter 5: the space-time of a novel where 'the knots of narrative are tied and untied' (Bakhtin and Holquist 1981:250). The High School is one such chronotope, it is the temporal and spacial locus for significant transition in the lives of young people. The American High School, in particular, with its lockers and sports teams and cafeterias and cheerleaders has become an adolescent lodestone even in countries where none of that paraphernalia form part of the teenage experience. But the flip side to an All-American adolescence is the alienation and fear that is the underbelly of the High School chronotope – for every *Booksmart* there's a *Carrie*, for every *High School Musical* there's a *Scream*. School represents conformity, repression and – at its most extreme – can be a site of violence. High School bathrooms are part of this underbelly. They are coded as a place to escape (think of *Mean Girls*' Cady Heron eating lunch in a stall), but they are also places for secrets – bodily secrets, gossip, bullying, eavesdropping, spaces separated from adult oversight, and even places where predators find their prey. The setting here is laden with genre significance.

In Chapter 5, I shared the concept of 'palette of imagery', which is when a writer draws images and metaphors from material which is thematically relevant. Here, the setting speaks to a teen horror palette. The adjectives in the sentence are pulling in that direction too: 'soft voice', 'subtle creak'. The small sounds suggest the quiet before a jump scare, or the need to be silent to avoid detection.

> I stay quiet, seated sideways on the ground of the stall, looking at my blue plaid skirt spread over my outstretched legs, the thick grey socks that cover most of my thighs, and my brown-heeled brogues pressing against the wall.

This is an interesting beat. It struck me, on first reading, that this was a surprising place to insert a description of what she's wearing; it risks defusing the tension built up by the preceding quiet. However, the beat of description serves an important function in terms of world-building. We have been told earlier in the novel that Chiamaka is one of only two Black students in her year at this predominantly white institution. The uniform of plaid and brogues is associated with private schools (in the USA) and schools with particularly strict uniform codes (in the UK, such as grammar schools or independent schools); places which have traditionally excluded and marginalized Black students. On the face of it, Chiamaka is wearing the signifiers of her own oppression. But 'Ivy' or 'preppy' clothing also has more complex and radical associations with Blackness. Avery Trufelman (2022) in her series *American Ivy* maps out the influence that servicemen, jazz performers and the hip-hop scene had on 'Ivy' fashion as it evolved into American sportswear, until 'preppy' became the default American style. The plaid and brogues that Chiamaka is wearing has an important Black heritage, although that heritage may be obscured and overshadowed by dominant white narratives about the style. The clothes she wears are *both* a reminder that she doesn't belong, and a powerful reclamation of white spaces by Black bodies.

This description then is connected to Ebony Elizabeth Thomas' conception of a 'dark fantastic', stories which are 'working toward a fantastic that is restorative, transformative, and emancipatory' (2019:13). Thomas' definition of the 'fantastic' is deliberately expansive, not limited to genres and settings associated with High Fantasy or the taxonomies we visited in Chapter 3, such as portal fantasy. She includes stories that 'capture [...] the wonder of stepping into a world-that-never-was' (2019:8). Àbíké-Íyímídé has created a setting that is 'a world-that-never-was'. On the surface, this school is plausibly American, but the details reveal it to be something more constructed. It is a place that blends British traditions with American vernacular; the town in which it is based is as walkable as London, yet with gated neighbourhoods in a US style. It is a setting that is nominally 'real' but not mimetic – it is this imaginary setting which speaks to dark academia. In Àbíké-Íyímídé's 'dark fantastic' private school, race and racism serve as the engines for the compulsive thriller plot.

So, the description of Chiamaka's clothes is part of the world-building that supports the plot. But Chiamaka's body is also present here, and it is inflected by the teen horror palette. She is sitting sideways on the ground of a bathroom stall. This is an unpleasant, unsanitary place and an awkward position with her feet 'pressing against the wall'. There is a long history of the female body being used in horror; for example, serving as vessels for evil (e.g. *Rosemary's Baby*, *The Stepford Wives*) or as litmus tests for purity (as we see with virgins surviving as the 'final girl'). Leah Phillips (2023:13–16) suggests an interesting provocation in this context. She posits that, if the traditional male hero is underpinned by 'bodily stability' – he uses his fit, white, able body to shape the world around him – then a female body might have 'fleshy materiality', which indicates her Otherness and so her challenge to the status quo. Through this lens, Chiamaka, a Black girl sitting on a stall floor, is a vulnerable body but, again, not one without power.

> 'It's Belle', she continues. The bathroom stall next to mine opens and my heart races a little.

The person with the 'soft voice' identifies themselves. This is not, then, a jump scare, but rather another student coming to check on Chiamaka. Tonally, the genre blurs for a moment. The name Belle is significant, Beauty. The new arrival opens the empty stall and Chiamaka's 'heart races'. This *could* be the language of horror, but there's an ambiguity here too – this particular noun–verb combination could equally be the language of romance. Later in the novel, Belle will come to be a love interest for Chiamaka and the groundwork for that development is being laid with this subtle foreshadowing.

This is one of many queer relationships in the novel. Research by Jenkins and Cart (2018) and Lo (2018) quoted in Mason (2020:8) demonstrates that queer YA fiction is growing exponentially, from fewer than ten titles in the USA in the 1970s to more than 100 titles a year by 2018. Àbíké-Íyímídé is contributing to the multiplicity of stories being told about queer Black youth, a point she discusses in the following interview.

> I hear a slight rattle as Belle pulls at my locked door. She raps at the door three times.
> I can see her grey suede heels and white frilly socks.

At this stage of the novel, the romance has not yet formed and so we return more firmly to the horror palette here. The door 'rattles', Belle 'raps', noises that evoke a classic haunted house, in the Gothic mode. Belle knocks three times; the 'rule of three' is a common trope of legend and folklore.

Then, as earlier, we are given details of Belle's clothing – this time her shoes and socks. They are, like Chiamaka's, 'preppy', but they are unlikely to be the prescribed uniform (suede heels are very impractical school-wear!). Belle's choice of plausible, yet also fantastical uniform again contributes to the sense of this as a 'real-imagined' setting, halfway between the UK and America. There is an additional tension in this clothing choice – the maturity implied by 'heels' is incongruent with the girlishness of 'white frilly socks'. Belle is perhaps a liminal sort of person, somewhere between innocence and experience. Again, the potential a female body has for being sinner or saint in the Gothic mode is present here. Ultimately, this entangling of good and evil foreshadows the role she eventually plays in the campaign against the Black students: she is an active yet woefully underinformed participant and so the degree of guilt is less than it might otherwise have been.

With this swing from horror to romance and back again we can see how playful Àbíké-Íyímídé is with genre. Todorov (Todorov & Berrong 1976:161) suggests that new forms of writing, new genres, always emerge from older genres 'by inversion, by displacement, by combination' and we can see all three approaches excitingly in evidence in *Ace of Spades*.

We have already seen that Àbíké-Íyímídé is inverting the perspective of the predominantly white institution in terms of the 'dark fantastic', carving out an imaginative space which challenges dominant discourses of Fantasy (with the acknowledgement that, as Sangster says, 'Fantasy has long served as a creative space within which those not comfortable with the status quo can imagine different possibilities' (2023:26)).

She is also expanding and 'displacing' the dominant discourses of dark academia. This is a relatively new genre, with *The Secret History* by Donna

Tartt, published in 1992, generally considered to be a foundational text. It is as much an aesthetic as it is a literary genre. It is characterized by an idealization of traditional academia, its dress and architecture, and a love of the Arts (especially Classical History and Literature). It may or may not include magical systems (the Harry Potter novels and film franchises have contributed to the aesthetic). Maryann Nguyen (2022) suggests the recent popularity of the aesthetic is in part driven by nostalgia for a time when the Arts were valued, in comparison to the contemporary devaluing of Arts and Humanities as a project and the narrowing of access to jobs in the Arts to those with private wealth and connections. Moreover, she suggests that the 'dark' in dark academia arises from the fact that characters in these stories typically defend these traditional enclaves with questionable moral results; 'It becomes a question of "what kind of violence are you willing to commit to maintain your position in an elite, white hegemonic space?"' (2022:63). However, this is not to say that dark academia is inevitably a white hegemonic space. Nguyen identifies *Ace of Spades* as an example of dark academia being used to critique the structures it fetishizes, evolving to ask the question '"what are we trying to protect and why?"' (2022:68). By allowing Chiamaka to defend herself against the threat posed by predominantly white institutions Àbíké-Íyímídé is expanding the genre by displacing its central concerns with her own critique of those same concerns.

Finally, as we have seen in this extract, Àbíké-Íyímídé is combining genres in interesting ways. In the interview that follows, she uses the tagline '*Gossip Girl* meets *Get Out*' to describe the novel. As with *The Knife of Never Letting Go*, this is a high-concept idea from which a myriad implications emanate. These implications include: examinations of privilege, class and wealth; the intersection of these with race; the control, power and dominance that come from these intersections; evolving 'court intrigue' informed by these intersections; that these intrigues will become tangled with love and betrayal; and finally, extreme physical harms are likely as a result of this brew. Both *Gossip Girl* and *Get Out* are significant iterations of their respective genres (school drama and horror) that come with a hinterland of audience expectations. By combining these hinterlands, Àbíké-Íyímídé is able to create new and compelling reader expectations. Furthermore, she has refreshed these stories with a willingness to explore multiple queer romances (although there was a bisexual character in the *Gossip Girl* books, he was removed for the original TV series). This additional layer of representation allows for different narratives to be explored.

'Are you in there?' she asks. I say nothing.

Belle attempts to open communication with Chiamaka by asking this question. We are told Chiamaka's response: she says nothing. It is tight plotting to show the stimulus and the reaction so close together, with any intermediate steps of reflection or evaluation removed. What follows is an explanation of her unwillingness to respond to Belle's overture, but it would have been possible to leave the explanation out completely and ask the reader to deduce Chiamaka's state-of-mind from subtext. As we saw earlier, commercial fiction tends to favour clarity of storytelling. So, Chiamaka's interiority is included,

> I'm not sure why she's going to such great lengths to be nice. Maybe she's trying to prove a point to Jamie that she's the perfect girl. But I doubt Jamie would notice how Belle treats me, let alone care.

Chiamaka's idiolect is notable here. Her private school education is influencing her diction ('such great lengths', 'But I doubt'); there's a confident vocabulary and precision of grammar here, despite the fact that Chiamaka has been brought low and we find her on the floor of the bathroom. Moreover, this idiolect, and its formal structure, reveals something of her character. Despite being in a vulnerable, awkward situation, she actually isn't going to pieces. She brings a clear, analytical mind to the situation. She ascribes Machiavellian motives to Belle, then discards the suspicion as unlikely. Even in despair, Chiamaka remains an astute political thinker.

In plot terms, we can also see yet another layering of conflict, this time interpersonal as Chiamaka and Belle are (at this point in the novel) vying for the attention of the same boy, Jamie. Even as Belle might be read as a potential support for Chiamaka, we are reminded of their rivalry. As readers, the question becomes: to what extent can Belle be trusted in this situation? To what extent can Chiamaka let her guard down? Àbíké-Íyímídé is eschewing subtext for text and, as such, heightens the level of tension and suspense in this thriller.

This romantic triangle is a subplot within the novel. Another contributing factor to the page-turner-ness of *Ace of Spades* is how it handles the plot and subplots and the switches between them. The main plot – the storyline indicated by the snappy tagline *Gossip Girl* meets *Get Out* – is the thriller plot, the need to unmask Aces before irreparable harm is done to Chiamaka and Devon. In scriptwriting terms (see, for example, Burne 2019), this is the 'A' plot and is given the most attention in terms of the number of scenes devoted to it. We considered the concept of the 'guiding principle' in Chapter 7, an organizing statement which the plot 'proves' or 'disproves'. The A plot in *Ace of Spades* might have the guiding principle: 'black students are in danger in white-dominated situations'. From this premise flows the need for: the elite school to serve as the predominantly white situation; the racialized bodies of Chiamaka and Devon in contrast with their all-white peers; guilty secrets which can be used as weapons; the Gothic palette of horror. All this flows from a strong premise.

However, there are other, smaller plots given scene time too. In screenwriting terms, they would be considered the 'B' plot and the 'C' plot. Chiamaka is part of the romantic triangle, as we have seen. Devon has his own new love interest too. Àbíké-Íyímídé regularly shifts between the plot strands, thus increasing the suspense and tension we feel as readers, having to leave one plot on a cliffhanger to head somewhere else. Interestingly, both the B and C plots share elements of the same guiding principle: Black students are in danger in white-dominated situations. Chiamaka is in a romantic triangle with two white people and the degree to which she can trust either of them is a very valid question readers ask again and again throughout the novel. Devon is in a romantic relationship with a Black character, and so, the guiding principle is flipped, 'are black students only safe with each other?' Again, the degree to which Devon's romantic partner can be trusted is a question readers legitimately ask, but – without wanting to give too much away – the novel arrives at a different conclusion than with the A or B plots. Subplots can be entirely separate life events just happening to coincide with the events of the main plot, or, as is the case in *Ace of Spades*, they can be a return to or a revisioning of the themes of the main plot, seen in a new light. By choosing to elide the main and subplots, Àbíké-Íyímídé shines the spotlight even more brightly on the danger her characters are in.

> Belle is still and silent, and I almost think she's going to walk away, give up. But then I hear a scraping noise.
> I watch the door as the lock slowly starts to turn. There's a sharp *clink* and the door opens.

There's a lovely tension here between horror and romance. Belle is 'still and silent' with that hiss-inflected sibilance; we could read this pause as dangerous, as though she were a predator waiting to pounce. The horror motif continues with 'scraping' – the word comes into English from Old Norse and, like many Viking words in English, has a harsh sound and contains echoes of violence. Then, the lock seemingly moving of its own accord, its 'sharp *clink*' is an onomatopoeic sound that might conjure the image of a knife in reader's imaginations. The place of refuge is being violated and safety is falling away.

However, this section is not all horror. Chiamaka gives us a flash of interiority, noting that Belle appears to be about to 'walk away, give up'. There's something in the repetition here that hints at an emotion besides fear: is Chiamaka disappointed that Belle might be so easily dissuaded? Is she sad at the potential loss of an ally or a friend?

Belle looks down at me, with wide eyes and a frown. She unzips her bag and hands me a folded tissue.
I don't take it.

This representation of Belle again contains something of the tension we have seen in her role previously. She 'looks down' at Chiamaka. Of course, this is literally true given the placement of their bodies in the scene. However, it is also thematically relevant – the student body at this elite school is riven with white supremacy and considers Chiamaka and Devon to be inferior despite their multiple achievements. The 'looking down' is literal – is it also figurative? But, Belle looks with 'wide eyes', a feature associated with innocence and childish wonder. Is Belle a scheming foe or potential love interest? The language teeters enticingly on this tightrope; is this enemies-to-lovers or psychotic femme fatal?

On the surface, Belle's action, unzipping her bag and taking out a tissue, is very thoughtful. On the other hand, there's an adult put-together-ness about the sort of young person who is prepared with a neat tissue in times of crisis. Belle is presented to Chiamaka, and so to the reader, in complex terms, with two potential readings of her that are in opposition to each other. Is she someone Chiamaka can trust, or someone she should fear?

In the final line of this extract, Chiamaka chooses self-preservation as a result of her traumatic experience of being in a predominantly white institution; she refuses Belle's offering.

There is horror here, but also attraction. There is defensiveness, but also curiosity. There is guilt and fear, but also empathy. By maintaining these tensions and conflicts throughout the novel, Àbíké-Íyímídé creates a page-turning thriller that also provides a compelling social commentary. Chiamaka may be down, but she is very much not out.

Cited Works

Àbíké-Íyímídé, F. 2021, *Ace of Spades*, Usborne, London.
Bakhtin, M.M. and Holquist, M. 1981, *The Dialogic Imagination: Four Essays*, University of Texas Press, Austin.
Burne, P. 2019, May 23, 'Inside the Story: The ABC of Screenwriting as Demonstrated by ABC's *The Heights*'. Available: https://theconversation.com/inside-the-story-the-abc-of-screenwriting-as-demonstrated-by-abcs-the-heights-115854 [2024, July 22].
Mason, D. 2020, *Queer Anxieties of Young Adult Literature and Culture*, University Press of Mississippi, Jackson, Mississippi.
Nguyen, M. 2022, 'Nostalgia in Dark Academia', *East–West Cultural Passage*, vol. 22, no. 1, pp. 54–72.

Phillips, L. 2023, *Female-Heroes in Young Adult Fantasy Fiction: Reframing Myths of Adolescent Girlhood*, Bloomsbury Academic, London.
Pulliam, J. 2010, *Monstrous Bodies: Femininity and Agency in Young Adult Horror Fiction*, Louisiana State University Press, Baton Rouge.
Sangster, M. 2023, *An Introduction to Fantasy*, Cambridge University Press, Cambridge.
Smith, M.J. and Moruzi, K. 2021, *Young Adult Gothic Fiction: Monstrous Selves/Monstrous Others*, University of Wales Press, Cardiff.
Tartt, D. 1992, *The Secret History*, Penguin Books, London.
Thomas, E.E. 2019, *The Dark Fantastic: Race and the Imagination from Harry Potter to the Hunger Games*, New York University Press, New York.
Todorov, T. and Berrong, R.M. 1976, 'The Origin of Genres', *New Literary History*, vol. 8, no. 1, pp. 159–70.
Trufelman, A. 2022, *Articles of Interest: American Ivy*, Radiotopia.

SECTION 2: AN INTERVIEW WITH FARIDAH ÀBÍKÉ-ÍYÍMÍDÉ

ELEN : Could you say a little bit about the concept behind *Ace of Spades*?

FARIDAH: The way I describe it, I always start with a comparative: *Get Out* meets *Gossip Girl*. Comparative titles obviously come in at the marketing stage. But yeah, from the beginning I had those two titles in mind when I was writing it.

Essentially, it's about two Black students at a predominantly white institution (PWI), who are from very different backgrounds. One of them is upper class. One of them is working class. One of them is Nigerian and Italian. One of them is African American. Or, I guess, African American coded because I didn't want to be too specific about where the story's set. They're both in their last year of high school and they both start being targeted by an anonymous texter, called Aces, who is trying to ruin their reputations and their lives.

ELEN: I know that the seeds of the book came to you when you moved from your familiar home environment, from South London, to your university. I wondered if you could say a little bit about how that change of location shaped you as an artist?

FARIDAH: Yeah. So, I grew up in Croydon, in South London. Obviously, demographically, Croydon is very diverse. It's one of the most diverse areas in London. In fact, I believe that statistically, it's mostly people of colour in Croydon. My high school itself was mostly Black and brown students. I always said, I could probably count on my hands how many white people were in my classes, or in my school halls. So, going from that environment to Aberdeen, in Scotland, was a very big cultural shift. I didn't anticipate it. I didn't even think about what ... When I was thinking of moving to Scotland for university, it didn't even occur to me to think of the cultural difference. I was kind of naive as to how different culture looks in places that aren't London. I'd, kind of, been in my protective bubble before I moved. So that was a big culture shock in many ways. Not just because of race; religion as well. Croydon is also very Muslim, and I'm Muslim. Going from being in that community to university culture, student culture, which is based on going out drinking and whatnot – that was very shocking. That all came into play in my writing of *Ace of Spades*, because the culture shock meant I was experiencing a lot of microaggressions for the first time. When you're the norm or you're the normative face in your environment, you don't really get the same questions as you get when you become the person who is not the norm. So, I never had someone question me so much as a person, as a human being, until I got to Scotland. Then also I was very isolated because I didn't join in with the drinking culture. I really struggled to find community there for a very long time; struggled to make friends and integrate at university. I basically had to be in my room all the time and had to find something to do. And so, I started writing *Ace of Spades*. I was already writing before that, but I gave myself a project to do that would help me get through not having anyone else speak to.

ELEN: Did it feel like a step-change from the writing you'd done before; did this feel like something different because of the move?

FARIDAH: I do think that there was a difference in the sense that my perspective felt like it broadened. I think the big shift in my writing came maybe a year before I went to university. Because I had decided at that point that I really wanted to try and pursue publishing. I already had that shift in the sense of, you know: I wanna get this published. But I think a later shift came in perspective and world view. I realized a lot more about the world. And I saw how unsafe the world could be, and that definitely helped with the thriller elements. I think with *Ace of Spades* a lot of it did come from feeling unsafe, essentially.

ELEN: Did it feel like you were processing what was happening through your writing?

FARIDAH: Yeah, definitely. I think *Ace of Spades*, while I was writing it, didn't feel like a story that felt publishable. Because, at the time, if you looked at the market, thrillers and mysteries weren't really that big. I was writing *Ace of Spades* in 2017/2018. The big YA thrillers that we all think of, like *The Good Girl's Guide to Murder*, hadn't come out yet; that would be 2019. *One of Us is Lying* had just come out around that time, and it had done very well, but it was seen as one of those publishing successes that didn't necessarily mean people were craving the genre. There was no mystery trend yet, so I didn't see anything in the publishing sphere that would make me think that this would be publishable. And also, it was, I feel like, quite a risky topic at the time as well.

And so, really, writing it was almost like self-therapy. Even though I wanted it to be published, I was also processing different interactions with different white people at school through different characters and different scenarios.

ELEN: There's a real feeling, I think, when you're reading the book, that it's a sort of amalgam of worlds; that's its own sort of fantasy. In one interview you called it a 'settingless global North'. I wondered how aware you were you of writing a kind of fantasy setting?

FARIDAH: A lot of readers will say to me, 'What is the setting?' Because, you know, there are some Americanisms to it, but they can't quite pinpoint where in America this could take place. America has a different structure to its cities than in other places, for example. I always reference Grenfell Tower [a London tower block destroyed by a fire in 2017 which killed seventy-two people; residents had warned of the danger years earlier, many remain unhomed years afterwards]. I reference how that was a very big tragedy which impacted immigrants and working-class people, and the tragic part of it was not just that people were killed by the fire, but that this took place in one of the wealthiest boroughs in Europe. That does exist in America, but not with the same closeness, I think, maybe because of the geographical differences in size. London is so small in comparison to the cities in America. You might walk five minutes down the road and find millionaires. Or you can even see millionaires from your bedroom window. In terms of the setting being a fantasy, I wanted it to feel like a place you couldn't pinpoint. I wanted it to feel like this could take place anywhere, and that's almost part of the scariness of it. That it could happen to anyone, anywhere. Because, you know, these systems affect everyone. It's a global thing.

ELEN: I want to ask you about Chiamaka, because on one level, she's quite a stereotypical mean girl, but on a different level, she's a Black girl striving for excellence in a system that's working against her. How would you like readers to think of her?

FARIDAH: Yeah, actually, I'm very happy with any interpretation of Chiamaka. I mean, you know, some people hate her. Some people love her, and that's, kind of, what I intended. I really wanted her to exist as a character who doesn't have the hallmarks of a likeable person. There is the stereotype of the aggressive Black woman. One way that some authors might try to combat that is by doing the opposite: creating a character who is really sweet, showing the diversity of existing as a Black person. But I really wanted to not pander to this invisible person who was going to judge her anyway. I wanted her to almost be radical in her meanness, unapologetic in her meanness. And so, yeah, I like her being read as a mean girl; I think she should be read as a mean girl.

But if people don't like that, I'm okay with them not liking that it. Because I think that the purpose is not for her to be liked anyway. The purpose is that she's unlikeable, but very complex, and there's more to her. But also, I just love the mean girl character in general. I wanted her to be sitting in the same conversations as Regina George.

ELEN: Both of the characters have different kinds of sexual awakenings over the course of the book. They're queer awakenings, for Chiamaka especially. How important was that for you?

FARIDAH: Yeah, so there are a few reasons and angles I want to take with answering this. One of them is casual queerness. A lot of people that come to read the book don't expect queerness, because it's not really part of the main marketing. I like casual queerness; it's something I've always loved when I'm reading or watching something. Because it makes it normative. The other thing as well is that a lot of *Ace of Spades* is meant to be calling back to historical figures or points in time, and a lot of Black, queer figures have been erased, and basically recentring Black queerness in the story was very important to me. But also, I think that queer identity looks different on different people. So, I didn't want only one of them to represent the Black, queer experience. Having them both show how it can manifest was very, very important to me, because I didn't want people to just come away and say, 'Oh, that was kind of a tragic storyline. That's what queerness should be, a tragedy for black people.' I wanted it to look different on purpose, but also for both to have some happiness; not just because they are in a relationship, but internal acceptance as well. That looks different for both of them. With Devon, he got that acceptance from his mum, even though he'd accepted himself, that he was queer. Chiamaka had to come into even knowing that she was queer.

ELEN: Were you aware of the intersection of their class with their queerness? How much were you playing with that?

FARIDAH: I wanted to show how intersectionality in your identity allows you certain freedoms and takes away others. And so, the more privilege you have, I guess, the more you don't have to think about how much space you're taking up, and how much more difficult you're making your life because you have so many other things to fall back on. Which is why you also see queer white characters and how they react to being outed, or how they react to coming into their own sexualities. Basically, how different that looks to Chiamaka and Devon. While you can see Chiamaka probably has a much easier time with her queerness in the story [than Devon], when you compare that to people like Scottie and Belle, they probably have an easier time. You can see the freedom they have, because they can always fall back on their whiteness, or, in Scottie's case, his male privilege, his cis male privilege. So yeah, I like to look at the degrees and the shades of freedom people have based on intersectionality.

ELEN: The complexity of the cast is wonderful, but I think the plot really matters as well. There's always an engine in every scene moving it forward. How much did you plot in advance?

FARIDAH: It was very heavily plotted. I had a 12,000-word outline of *Ace of Spades*. I like to outline the story in a Word document. I literally have, like: Chapter One; and then a bullet-pointed list, an entire page long, of everything that's gonna take place in that scene, or that chapter. And that really helps me look at the story with a bird's-eye view. I can see things that will be dragging the section, or not moving forwards the plotline or character arc.

And also, when I'm writing, I'm often thinking about the type of stories I enjoy. At the time [of writing *Ace of Spades*], I was really enjoying a lot of the teen dramas that I grew up watching. I really enjoyed how everything was so fast paced; there was always a twist or cliffhanger. I was very consciously ending a lot of scenes or chapters on a cliffhanger. And so, in my plan, I would always ask the question: how could I end this scene or this chapter to make the reader come back?

ELEN: What got you to the 12,000-word outline? Were you thinking it through, or trial-writing little bits?

FARIDAH: I think I was scared of actually tackling the book because it was such a big idea. I had the twist in my head first. I was like: *Oh, how am I even gonna accomplish that?* And so, the outline was almost like a 'zero draft', like a skeleton of a draft, almost; 12,000 words is not anywhere near a publishable manuscript, but it almost felt like it was the skeleton of what the story would become. And yeah, I was in my halls of residence in Aberdeen, and I would finish lectures every day, and I would rush home to write a little more, until I finished my skeleton draft. And then my real draft.

ELEN: I wonder if you could say something about being a debut author. Is there anything that has surprised you?

FARIDAH: Yeah, I'm the sort of person who loves being prepared. I love an itinerary; I love being the person that always has all my research done. I had spent years researching publishing. I thought I knew everything about debuting. But I was one of the unlucky people who debuted in the pandemic. So, everything I'd learned went out the window. Everything was a surprise, because everything was unprecedented. Nothing we were doing at that point in time – which was 2021 – had been done before. All my events were virtual. You know, people usually will go out and see their readers to get confirmation that their book is landing well. With [the virtual] audience, there was none of that. And so, my debut year was quite depressing, because I had no confirmation. I didn't even think there were really readers out there. I could see that my sales figures were looking good, but it didn't feel tangible, you know. It just kind of felt like my publishers were being like, 'Oh, yeah, there are people buying your book.' But I couldn't confirm who those people were. I didn't know if what I was doing was actually important – especially when people were dying. I felt like being a writer at that point was, kind of, ridiculous you know; making-up fake stories in your head while real life is happening. And so yeah, I think that was a big surprise for me debuting.

ELEN: But stories were where we all turned. I mean, you know, everyone in 2020 was crafting or making art of some kind.

FARIDAH: Yeah, it's so interesting, because we'd all thought about it in theory, like: *what would you do if the world was ending?* And so now we actually do know what that could look like […] BookTok exploded – no one saw that coming! It completely changed the landscape of publishing, and no one saw it coming! Publishing didn't expect books to be so important. But publishing should expect books to be important!

SECTION 3: *ACE OF SPADES*, WRITING EXERCISES

As we have seen, *Ace of Spades* is a fast-paced commercial thriller with serious themes. In these exercises we look at some of the writing techniques used to create this compelling mix.

Exercise A – Narrative Channels

Commercial fiction tends to deliver its narrative beats in the most efficient and apposite ways, allowing for speedy comprehension and, thus, 'page-turner' qualities. One way to do that is to select narrative channels (sometimes also called 'modes') with care. A useful heuristic is to think of narrative channels as 'ways the narrator might convey a piece of information'. Broadly defined, these are: description, action, dialogue, interiority and exposition.

Any piece of information might be conveyed using any channel.

Let's say that the information the writer wishes to convey is: *Claire is excited about a dance performance she's giving.*

Description Channel: Claire hung the dress above her shoes on the peg. The skirt was a frosting of feathers, white and cream. So many feathers that would fly out in a cloud around her in just a few hours.

Action Channel: Claire hugged herself, bouncing on the soles of her feet at the side of the stage, anticipation fizzing in every nerve.

Dialogue Channel: 'I feel like there are butterflies, and crickets, and a whole field of bugs bouncing in my belly', Claire told Monika.

Interiority Channel: There was no feeling like it in the world, Claire thought, no feeling like stepping out on stage with every eye in the house ready to be entranced.

Exposition Channel: Claire was so excited to be dancing on stage in front of everyone.

There is no 'correct' channel; it is not that one of these is always right and the rest are wrong. Rather, there are times when the writer might want to slow the pace and ask the readers to deduce from inference (e.g. description channel); there are other times when the writer wants to be certain that the key facts have been delivered without fuss (e.g. exposition channel). It is also, of course, possible to blend these channels within a single sentence.

1. Take each of these sentences in turn, rewrite them five times so that the information is conveyed using the five channels (the 'exposition channel' is very likely to look quite similar to the original sentence in each case).
   - Devon fancies Scott.
   - Ali is angry with his dad.
   - Shauna and Mildred are best friends.
   - Bertie and Omar make a good team.
   - Carla feels betrayed by Anna.

Exercise B – Symbolic Palette

We have looked at the use of symbols and the usefulness of genre in previous exercises. Here, I want to combine the two using the metaphor of a 'symbolic palette'. Like an artist, mixing a range of paint colours on a palette, finding the right combination that work together to create an effect, as a writer, you can draw on a complimentary set of symbols – your own palette – to create an effect. In *Ace of Spades* Àbíké-Íyímídé draws on both a Gothic and a Romance palette to create tension for her readers.

1. Write the word 'Gothic' at the centre of a piece of paper.
2. Mind-map out from the centre, following any word associations you have in as many branches as you need.
   (If you are unfamiliar with the Gothic, think of some of its most influential monsters: the vampire, the ghost, Frankenstein's monster and the complicated relationship they have with good/evil).
3. If they are not present already, add associated objects to your mind-map, wherever they might fit.
4. If they are not present already, add associated scents to your mind-map, wherever they might fit.
5. If they are not present already, add associated sounds to your mind-map, wherever they might fit.
6. Use a few of your favourite elements of the mind-map to write a short scene 'in the Gothic mode'. Be aware of how you are drawing from your palette to create any interesting phrases, metaphors, images and so on.

Exercise C – Juggling Conflict to Maintain Tension

We have seen in previous chapters how fruitful conflict can be for creating plot. In this exercise we will consider how juggling different sorts of conflict can be useful for creating suspense and tension.

1. Imagine a teenage character in a high school setting. You can be as real or fantastical as you want. Make very rough notes as you answer the following questions about your character.
2. They are experiencing an interpersonal conflict of some kind. Who is it with? What is at stake if the conflict isn't resolved?
3. They are experiencing an ethical conflict of some kind. What is it? What is at stake if the conflict isn't resolved?
4. They are experiencing a systemic conflict of some kind. What is it? What is at stake if the conflict isn't resolved?
5. They are experiencing an internal conflict of some kind. What is it? What is at stake if the conflict isn't resolved?
6. Write a scene in which your character is aware of at least two of the ongoing conflicts – this might be by thinking about one conflict when another is raised in conversation; an action to resolve one conflict might be attempted, but intrusive thoughts from another might disrupt the attempt, etc.

Note: there are many other types of conflict available: environmental, physical, spiritual, psychological, moral and more. You can swap out the suggestions above for another type of conflict if it feels particularly generative for you.

Bibliography

Àbíké-Íyímídé, F. 2021, *Ace of Spades*, Usborne, London.
Adsit, J. 2017, *Toward an Inclusive Creative Writing: Threshold Concepts to Guide the Literary Curriculum*, Bloomsbury Academic.
Adsit, J. (ed.) 2019, *Critical Creative Writing*, Bloomsbury Academic, London.
Anderson, L. 2005, *Creative Writing: A Workbook with Readings*, 1st edn, Routledge, Abingdon.
Auschwitz Museum 2022, *The Boy in the Striped Pyjamas*. Available: https://x.com/AuschwitzMuseum/status/1487017362675093506?lang=en [2023, June 6].
Bakhtin, M. M. and Holquist, M. 1981, *The Dialogic Imagination: Four Essays*, University of Texas Press, Austin.
Balen, K. 2021, *October, October*, Bloomsbury Publishing, London.
Bang, M. 2016, *Picture This: How Pictures Work*, 25th anniversary edition, Chronicle Books, San Francisco.
Baron, C. and Engel, M. 2010, *Realism/Anti-realism in 20th-Century Literature*, 1st edn, Rodopi, Amsterdam.
Barrington, R. 2024, 'Writing Hopeful Climate Fiction for Middle Grade Readers', *Leaf Journal*, vol. 2, no. 1, pp. 1–15.
Barthes, R. and Heath, S. 1977, *Image, Music, Text*, Fotana, London.
Batty, C. and Taylor, S. 2018, 'Comedy Writing as Method: Reflections on Screenwriting in Creative Practice Research', *New Writing*, vol. 16, no. 3, pp. 374–92.
Booker, C. 2004, *The Seven Basic Plots: Why We Tell Stories*, Continuum, London.
Bowers, M. A. 2004, *Magic(al) Realism*, 1st edn, Routledge, New York.
Bowles, D. 2015, *The Ends of Satire: Legacies of Satire in Postwar German Writing*, Walter de Gruyter, Berlin.
Bradford, C. 2010, 'Race, Ethnicity and Colonialism', in *The Routledge Companion to Children's Literature*, ed. D. Rudd, Routledge, Abingdon; New York, pp. 39–50.
Brayfield, C. and Sprott, D. 2014, *Writing Historical Fiction: A Writers' and Artists' Companion*, 1st edn, Bloomsbury, London.
Burne, P. 2019, May 23, 'Inside the Story: The ABC of Screenwriting as Demonstrated by ABC's *The Heights*'. Available: https://theconversation.com/inside-the-story-the-abc-of-screenwriting-as-demonstrated-by-abcs-the-heights-115854 [2024, July 22].
Bush, E. 2019, '*Other Words for Home* by Jasmine Warga', *Bulletin of the Center for Children's Books*, vol. 72, no. 10, pp. 455–65.
Campbell, J. 1949, *The Hero with a Thousand Faces*, 2nd edn (1968) Princeton University Press, Princeton.
Carriger, G. 2020, *The Heroine's Journey*, Gail Carriger, Milton Keynes.

BIBLIOGRAPHY

Chang, H. 2021, 'Women, Coming-of-Age and Secrets in Jamaica Kincaid's "Annie John"', *Children's Literature in Education*, vol. 54, no. 1, pp. 1–16.

Chen, S. 2022, 'Autism, Representation and Culture in Mark Haddon's "The Curious Incident of the Dog in the Night-Time" and Yonghong Hu's "My Running Shadow"', *Neohelicon*, vol. 49, no. 2, pp. 789–800.

Chiaet, J. 2013, Oct 4, *Novel Finding: Reading Literary Fiction Improves Empathy*. Available: https://www.scientificamerican.com/article/novel-finding-reading-literary-fiction-improves-empathy/ [2024, May 8].

Child, L. 2000, *I Will Not Ever Never Eat a Tomato*, Orchard Books, London.

CLPE 2023, *Reflecting Realities: Survey of Ethnic Representation within UK Children's Literature 2022*, Centre for Literacy in Primary Education, London.

CLPE 2018, *Reflecting Realities: Survey of Ethnic Representation within UK Children's Literature 2017*, Centre for Literacy in Primary Education, London.

Coats, K. 2017, *The Bloomsbury Introduction to Children's and Young Adult Literature*, Bloomsbury Publishing, London.

Coker, C. 2018, 'Reviews: "A Quest of Her Own: Essays on the Female Hero in Modern Fantasy" and "Feminine Power in Young Adult Horror Fiction"', *Journal of the Fantastic in the Arts*, vol. 29, no. 3, pp. 449–52.

Cooperative Childrens Book Centear 2024, *Books by and/or about Black, Indigenous and People of Color (All Years)*. Available: https://ccbc.education.wisc.edu/literature-resources/ccbc-diversity-statistics/books-by-about-poc-fnn/ [2024, July 24].

Corbett, E. and Phillips, L. 2023, 'Ploughing the Field: Controversy and Censorship in US and UK YA Literature', *International Journal of Young Adult Literature*, vol. 4, no. 1, pp. 1–18.

Crisp, T., Napoli, M., Yenika-Agbaw, V. and Zapata, A. 2020, 'The Complexities of #OwnVoices in Children's Literature', *Journal of Children's Literature*, vol. 46, no. 2, pp. 5–7.

Dalal, S. 2023, 'Migration and Melancholia: In Search of Self through Jasmine Warga's *Other Words for Home*', vol. 14, no. 2, pp. 147–59.

Darwin, E. 2010, *Psychic Distance: What It Is And How To Use It*. Available: https://emmadarwin.typepad.com/thisitchofwriting/psychic-distance-what-it-is-and-how-to-use-it.html [2024, July 7].

DasGupta, P. 2024, '"All Children, Except One, Grow Up": Adultification in Alex Wheatle's "Crongton Knights" and Jewell Parker Rhodes' "Ghost Boys"', *On Writing for Young People* Bristol, UK, Nov 2023.

DasGupta, P. 2024, 'Representing "Otherness": Animals in "Alice's Adventures in Wonderland", "The Hundred and One Dalmatians", and Beyond', *Leaf Journal*, vol. 2, no. 1, pp. 1–9.

Day, S. K. 2014, 'Docile Bodies, Dangerous Bodies: Sexual Awakening and Social Resistance in Young Adult Dystopian Novels', in *Female Rebellion in Young Adult Dystopian Fiction*, ed. S. K. Day, Routledge, London and New York, pp. 75–92.

Dehart, J. D., Rigell, A., Banack, A. and Songey, C. 2022, 'Verse Novels as Transitional and Identity-Forming Spaces for Young Adolescents', *Voices From the Middle*, vol. 30, no. 1, pp. 29–32.

Doherty, P. 2022, 'Reading Children's Literature in the Anthropocene: The Representation of "Nature" in Ursula K. Le Guin's Earthsea Fiction', *Children's Literature in Education*, vol. 55, no. 2, pp. 248–62.

Duyvis, C. 2015, *#ownvoices*. Available: https://twitter.com/corinneduyvis/status/640584099208503296 [2024, July 19].

Falconer, R. 2010, 'Young Adult Fiction and the Crossover Phenomenon', in *The Routledge Companion to Children's Literature*, ed. D. Rudd, Routledge, Abingdon; New York, pp. 87–99.

Fisher, T. 2023, 'Under the Hood of the Verse Novel: A Consideration of Variation in Form and Technique in the Contemporary Verse Novel for Young Adults', *Leaf Journal*, vol. 1, no. 2, pp. 1–29.

Friesner, B. 2016, *The Verse Novel in Young Adult Literature*, Rowman & Littlefield Publishers, Incorporated, Lanham.

Gamble, N. 2019, *Exploring Children's Literature: Reading for Knowledge, Understanding and Pleasure*, 4th edn, SAGE Publications, London.

Gardner, J. 1991, *The Art of Fiction*, Vintage Books, New York.

Gibson, M. 2010, 'Picturebooks, Comics and Graphic Novels', in *The Routledge Companion to Children's Literature*, ed. D. Rudd, Routledge, Abingdon; New York, pp. 100–11.

Green, J. 2023, 'On Writing for Young People Conference 2023, Keynote Speech', *Leaf Journal*, vol. 1, no. 2, pp. 1–8.

Groys, B., Matusov, E. and Marjanovic-Shane, A. 2017, 'Between Stalin and Dionysus: Bakhtin's Theory of the Carnival', *Dialogic Pedagogy: An International Online Journal*, vol. 5, pp. 1–5.

Gubar, M. 2016, 'The Hermeneutics of Recuperation: What a Kinship-Model Approach to Children's Agency Could Do for Children's Literature and Childhood Studies', *Jeunesse, Young People, Texts, Cultures*, vol. 8, no. 1, pp. 291–310.

Haddow, S. and Dempsey, S. 2016, *Dave Pigeon*, Faber and Faber, London.

Harris, M. 2006, '"A History Not Then Taught in History Books": (Re)Writing Reconstruction in Historical Fiction for Children and Young Adults', *The Lion and the Unicorn (Brooklyn)*, vol. 30, no. 1, pp. 94–116.

Heilker, P. and Yergeau, M. 2011, 'Autism and Rhetoric', *College English*, vol. 73, no. 5, pp. 485–97.

Horton, A. 2000, *Laughing Out Loud: Writing the Comedy-Centered Screenplay*, University of California Press, Berkeley.

Hutton, R. 2019, 'The Wild Hunt in the Modern British Imagination', *Folklore*, vol. 130, no. 2, pp. 175–91.

Jahn, M. 2021, Jun-last update, *A Guide to the Theory of Narrative*. Available: https://www.uni-koeln.de/~ame02/pppn.pdf [2023, May 12].

Johnston, I. 2012, 'The Chronotope of the Threshold in Contemporary Canadian Literature for Young Adults', *Jeunesse*, vol. 4, no. 2, pp. 139–50.

Jones, O. 2002, 'Naturally Not! Childhood, the Urban and Romanticism', *Human Ecology Review*, vol. 9, no. 2, pp. 17–30.

Kennedy, V. 2017, '"Chick Noir": Shopaholic Meets Double Indemnity', *American, British and Canadian Studies Journal*, vol. 28, no. 1, pp. 19–38.

Kennon, P. 2017, 'Monsters of Men: Masculinity and the Other in Patrick Ness's Chaos Walking Series', *Psychoanalytic Inquiry*, vol. 37, no. 1, pp. 25–34.

Kertzer, A. 2012, 'Pathways' End: The Space of Trauma in Patrick Ness's "Chaos Walking"', *Bookbird*, vol. 50, no. 1, pp. 10–19.

Kessler, L. 2021, *When the World Was Ours*, Simon & Schuster, London.

Kidd, D. C. and Castano, E. 2013, 'Reading Literary Fiction Improves Theory of Mind', *Science (American Association for the Advancement of Science)*, vol. 342, no. 6156, pp. 377–80.

Klassen, J. 2012, *This Is Not My Hat*, Walker Books, London.

BIBLIOGRAPHY

Klassen, J. 2023, *Jon Klassen in Conversation with Peter Lord.*

Kokkola, L. 2013, *Fictions of Adolescent Carnality Sexy Sinners and Delinquent Deviants*, John Benjamins Pub. Co., Amsterdam.

Kole, M. 2012, *Writing Irresistible Kidlit: The Ultimate Guide to Crafting Fiction for Young Adult and Middle Grade Readers*, Penguin Publishing Group, Cincinnati.

Koning, L. 2021, *The Dishonest Woman: An Ekphrastic Novel with a Critical Reflection on Bruegel, Bourdieu and Writing Historical Fiction*, Dissertation, University of Winchester.

Lapinski, L.D. 2020, *The Strangeworlds Travel Agency*, Orion Children's Books, London.

Lavoie, F. 2021, *Why We Need Diverse Books Is No Longer Using the Term #OwnVoices.* Available: https://diversebooks.org/why-we-need-diverse-books-is-no-longer-using-the-term-ownvoices/ [2024, July 19].

Le Guin, U. K. 2009, *Cheek by Jowl*, Aqueduct Press, Seattle.

Lee, C. 2023, 'More than Just a Thing with Feathers: The Importance of Hope in Middle Grade Fiction', *Leaf Journal*, vol. 1, no. 1, pp. 1–10.

Lewis, D. 2001, *Reading Contemporary Picturebooks: Picturing Text*, Routledge, London.

Mantel, H. 2020, *Hilary Mantel on How Writers Learn to Trust Themselves.* Available: https://lithub.com/hilary-mantel-on-how-writers-learn-to-trust-themselves/?fbclid=IwAR0BbhvgbT036WqNY_iG_1o21SwoV_UJsS5Fwx8kfFYgVhcJOmWpml3alVo [2024, July 14].

Mason, D. 2020, *Queer Anxieties of Young Adult Literature and Culture*, University Press of Mississippi, Jackson.

MasterClass 2021, Oct 26, *13 Types of Comedy: Popular Types of Comedic Performance.* Available: https://www.masterclass.com/articles/types-of-comedy [2024, April 11].

Mendlesohn, F. 2008, *The Rhetorics of Fantasy*, Wesleyan University Press, Connecticut.

Mills, C. 2012, 'Rousseau Redux: Romantic Re-Visions of Nature and Freedom in Recent Children's Literature about Homeschooling', in *Time of Beauty, Time of Fear: The Romantic Legacy in the Literature of Childhood*, ed. James Holt McGavran, University of Iowa Press, Iowa City, pp. 169–83.

Ness, P. 2008, *The Knife of Never Letting Go*, Walker Books, London.

Nguyen, M. 2022, 'Nostalgia in Dark Academia', *East–West Cultural Passage*, vol. 22, no. 1, pp. 54–72.

Nosy Crow, *Nosy Crow About Us.* Available: https://nosycrow.com/about-us/ [2024, April 10].

Owen, G. 2023, 'Impossible Relations, Ethical Relations: The Stakes of #OwnVoices Representation in LGBTQ Young Adult Fiction', *International Journal of Young Adult Literature*, vol. 4, no. 1, pp. 1–21.

Pantaleo, S. 2014, 'The Metafictive Nature of Postmodern Picturebooks', *The Reading Teacher*, vol. 67, no. 5, pp. 324–32.

Patterson, C. W. 2022, 'Towards a Manumissive Black Fantastic in Fandom, Fantasy, and Literature for Young People, or: A Case for the Black Hermione', *The International Journal of Young Adult Literature*, vol. 3, no. 1, pp. 1–29.

Penfold, A. 2023, 'The Feminist Quest: Reimagining the Relationship between Language, Gender, and Identity in "The Knife of Never Letting Go" (2008) by Patrick Ness', *International Journal Young Adult Literature*, vol. 4, no. 1, pp. 1–19.

Phillips, L. 2023, *Female-Heroes in Young Adult Fantasy Fiction: Reframing Myths of Adolescent Girlhood*, Bloomsbury Academic, London.

Price Gardner, R. 2020, 'The Present Past: Black Authors and the Anti-Black Selective Tradition in Children's Literature', *Journal of Children's Literature*, vol. 46, no. 2, pp. 8–18.

Prose, F. 2006, *Reading Like A Writer*, Aurum, London.

Pulliam, J. 2010, *Monstrous Bodies: Femininity and Agency in Young Adult Horror Fiction*, Louisiana State University Press, Baton Rouge.

Pullman, P. 2010, Sep 18, *Philip Pullman calls time on the present tense.* Available: https://www.theguardian.com/global/2010/sep/18/philip-pullman-author-present-tense [2024, July 27].

Pullman, P. 2017, *Daemon Voices*, David Fickling Books, Oxford.

Rosenzweig-Ziff, D. 2020, Mar 26, *Chatting with ... Jasmine Warga*. Available: https://magazine.northwestern.edu/exclusives/chatting-with-jasmine-warga/ [2024, June 27].

Rozema, R. 2014, 'The Problem of Autism in Young Adult Fiction', *Language Arts Journal of Michigan*, vol. 30, no. 1, pp. 26–31.

Rudd, D. 2010, *The Routledge Companion to Children's Literature*, Routledge, Abingdon; New York.

Russell Williams, I. 2019, May 9, *'Toffee' by Sarah Crossan review – A Profoundly Moving YA Novel in Verse*. Available: https://www.theguardian.com/books/2019/may/09/toffee-sarah-crossan-review [2024, May 31].

Sands-O'Connor, K. 2024, *'The Repeating Island?' Racial Diversity in Young Adult Publishing*, Goldsmiths University, London.

Sangster, M. 2023, *An Introduction to Fantasy*, Cambridge University Press, Cambridge.

Scholastic 2019, *Kids & Family Reading Report*. Available: www.scholastic.com/newsroom/online-press-kits/kids-and-family-reading-report.html [2025, June 17].

Selden, S. 2022, '"I Wonder What They Do Teach Them in These Schools": The Chronicles of Narnia and Nature-Deficit Disorder', *Children's Literature in Education*, vol. 55, no. 3, pp. 449–64.

Serafini, F. 2010, 'Reading Multimodal Texts: Perceptual, Structural and Ideological Perspectives', *Children's Literature in Education*, vol. 41, no. 2, pp. 85–104.

Shalvey, K. 2021, Apr 11, *These are the 10 books that made the ALA's most-challenged list for 2020*. Available: https://www.businessinsider.com/american-library-association-publishes-banned-book-list-stories-racism-photos-2021-4 [2024, May 8].

Simon & Schuster 2024, *When The World Was Ours*. Available: https://www.simonandschuster.co.uk/books/When-The-World-Was-Ours/Liz-Kessler/9781471196812 [2024, July 18].

Sims Bishop, R. 1982, *Shadow and Substance: Afro-American Experience in Contemporary Children's Fiction*, National Council of Teachers of English, Urbana.

Sims Bishop, R. 1990, *Mirrors, Windows and Sliding Glass Doors*. Available: https://scenicregional.org/wp-content/uploads/2017/08/Mirrors-Windows-and-Sliding-Glass-Doors.pdf [2024, July 17].

Singh, S. 2022, Jan 6, *Sunny Singh On Writing*. Available: https://x.com/profsunnysingh/status/1479043500691841025?s=12&t=NMasUqVrBkKscUhC08VH1w [2024, July 19].

Smith, M.J. and Moruzi, K. 2021, *Young Adult Gothic Fiction: Monstrous Selves/Monstrous Others*, University of Wales Press, Cardiff.
Smulders, S. 2024, 'Penguin Parables: Picturebooks, Interspecies Companionship, and Ecoliteracy', *Bookbird*, vol. 62, no. 1, pp. 32–40.
Šnircová, S. 2017, *Girlhood in British Coming-of-Age Novels: The Bildungsroman Heroine Revisited*, Cambridge Scholars Publishing, Newcastle upon Tyne.
Snyder, B. 2005, *Save the Cat!: The Only Book on Screenwriting You'll Ever Need*, Michael Wiese Productions, Los Angeles.
Soyinka, B. 2015, *Presentation to Stockholm Symposium on Transnational Creativity*.
Thebo, M. 2023, "Thebo, Mimi, 'Talking Tigers: Concepts of Representational Ethics Applied to Non-Human Characters in Writing Children's Fiction"', *Leaf Journal*, vol. 1, no. 1, pp. 1–8.
Thom, J. A. 2017, *Once Upon a Time It Was Now: The Art and Craft of Writing Historical Fiction*, Blue River Press, Indianapolis.
Thomas, E.E. 2019, *The Dark Fantastic: Race and the Imagination from Harry Potter to the Hunger Games*, New York University Press, New York.
Todorov, T. and Berrong, R. M. 1976, 'The Origin of Genre', *New Literary History*, vol. 8, no. 1, pp. 159–70.
Tolkien, J.R.R., Flieger, V. and Anderson, D. A. 2008, *On Fairy-Stories*, HarperCollins, London.
Trufelman, A. 2022, *Articles of Interest: American Ivy*, Radiotopia
Walsh, R. 1997, 'Who Is the Narrator?', *Poetics Today*, vol. 18, no. 4, pp. 495–513.
Warga, J. 2019, *Other Words for Home*, Balzer + Bray, New York.
Warwick, A. 2007, 'Feeling Gothicky?', *Gothic Studies*, vol. 9, no. 1, pp. 5–15.
Weisz, N. 2023, 'The Niagara Effect: Reimagining Emotional Intensity in Young Adult Writing', *Leaf Journal*, vol. 1, no. 1, pp. 1–13.
Weste, L. 2020, *Inside the Verse Novel: Writers on Writing*, Australian Scholarly, North Melbourne.
Wickens, C. M. and Junco, E. 2021, '"Every Person is a Possibility": A Post-Postmodern Analysis of LGBTQ Young Adult Novel "Every Day"', *Children's Literature Association Quarterly*, vol. 46, no. 2, pp. 160–77.
Wilkie, C. 1997, 'Digging Up "The Secret Garden": Noble Innocents or Little Savages?', *Children's Literature in Education*, vol. 28, no. 2, pp. 73–83.
Yeh, J. and O'Reilly, S. 2022, *Creative Writing: A Workbook with Readings*, 2nd edn, Taylor & Francis Group, Abingdon.
Yergeau, M. 2022, 'Authoring Autism: on Rhetoric and Neurological Queerness', *Neohelicon*, vol. 49, pp. 789–800.
Yorke, J. 2013, *Into the Woods: A Five Act Journey into Story*, Penguin Random House, London.
You, C. 2019, 'Representing Zoo Animals: The Other-than-Anthropocentric in Anthony Browne's Picture Books', *The Lion and the Unicorn*, vol. 43, pp. 22–41.
Yuliati, R. 2021, 'Oppression to Empowerment: Syrian Refugee Women in Warga's *Other Words for Home*', *CaLLs: Journal of Culture, Arts, Literature, and Linguistics*, vol. 7, no. 1, pp. 28–38.

Index

act structure (*see* structure)
adultification 57, 58
alliteration (*see* rhetoric)
allusion (*see* rhetoric)
antagonist, force of antagonism 25, 38, 40, 49–50
anthropomorphism 18, 32, 34–5, 44, 147–8
attentive writing 123, 124–5, 136
authorial point of view 15, 16, 39, 88, 126, 131, 174
anaphora (*see* rhetoric)
archetype 33–4, 37, 38, 39, 49
authenticity, accuracy 110–11, 123, 131, 136

character
  arc 114, 147
  primary (*see* protagonist)
  secondary and tertiary 34
  techniques for revealing 55, 56, 70, 76, 92, 114–15, 121, 132, 143
chronotope 101–2, 114, 164–5
class (*see* social class)
colonialism, empire 56, 57–8, 67–8, 154
coming-of-age (*see* genre)
conceptions of childhood 15
  commonality, kinship model 15–16, 17, 23–4, 46
  corruptible 142–3
  idealized 25–6, 114, 126
  liminal 103
  minoritized 35, 57, 58, 101, 104
  moral education 16, 17–18, 39
  noble savage 78
  redemptive 78–9
  Romantic, natural world 75–6, 78–9, 86
  socialization, period of 36, 157
  urban childhood 44, 58, 79, 86
conflict 13, 38, 100, 105, 164, 169, 181

dark academia (*see* genre)
diction 145, 164, 169
discourse framework, Serafini's 10, 15
dramatic irony 15, 16, 24, 120, 121

early readers 30–1, 36, 44, 48, 50
external narrator (*see* narrator)

focalizing character 60, 119, 135
foreshadow 122, 166
free indirect style (*see* narrator)

gatekeeping 143
gender 56, 142, 144, 147, 152
genre
  blending 168
  comedy 33, 45
  coming-of-age 141–2, 157
  commercial 163–4, 169, 179
  dark academia 167–8
  Gothic 17, 163, 167
  historical 122–3, 129, 131
  horror 17, 165–6, 170
  quest 53, 54, 58
  noir 45
guiding principle 148–9, 158, 169–70

hamartia 39, 40
Hero's Journey 53, 54, 57, 61, 70, 102
Heroine's Journey 76–7, 79, 80
high-concept 145, 158, 168
hook 64, 120
humour 9, 32, 37, 45, 50, 58
hyperbole (*see* rhetoric)

ideology (*see* authorial point of view)
idiolect 54, 60, 70, 80, 92–3, 145, 148, 169
interiority 39, 55, 70, 89
intertextuality (*see* rhetoric, allusion)
irony (*see* rhetoric)

INDEX

LGBTQ+ (*see* queer)

metaphor (*see* rhetoric)
methodologies
    praxis 3
    reading-as-a-writer 1, 8, 11, 12
metonymy (*see* rhetoric)
mimetic fiction 74, 166
middle grade 52, 74, 96, 100, 110
multi-modal narrative 9, 13, 27, 40, 145

narrative time 103, 104
narrator
    choice of 81
    close third 55–6, 58–9, 60, 68, 132
    dramatic monologue 14, 21, 23, 97
    external 54, 60, 71
    free indirect style 55, 60
    homodiegetic (*see* narrator, internal)
    internal 14, 76, 103, 120–1, 132
    omniscient 55
    polyphonic 54, 119, 135
    reliable 54, 55, 102
    unreliable 14–15, 82, 121
neurodiversity, neurodivergence 74, 82, 87

#ownvoices (*see also* authenticity) 123–4, 136

pace 12, 32, 48, 179
paratext 9, 119, 120, 123, 137
parechesis (*see* rhetoric)
parody (*see* rhetoric)
past tense (*see* tense)
peritext (*see* paratext)
personification (*see* rhetoric)
phase space, Pullman's 12, 15, 18, 36, 41
picturebook 8, 9, 46–7
picturebook, elements of
    audio 9
    double-page spread 8, 9, 10, 28
    gutter 10
    layout 12
    signature 10, 16
    structures 11
placing 148
plausibility (*see* authenticity)

plot 38, 43–4, 49, 64, 88, 100, 109, 147, 149, 169–70, 181
portal fantasy 52, 53, 54, 57, 58, 61, 67–8
positionality 3, 11, 115, 131, 135–6
postmodernism 14, 33, 40–1
premise 17, 52, 145, 158, 169
present tense (*see* tense)
process
    drafting 21, 43, 46, 64, 85, 87, 107, 111–12, 177
    edits, editing 4, 22, 45, 64, 71, 88, 128–9, 152, 154–5
    flow 4, 129
    plotting 87–8, 130, 177
    roughs 20
    weaknesses 11, 43, 87, 89–90, 109
protagonist 49–50, 70, 88, 132
psychic distance 55–6, 57, 60, 71, 120–1, 164
publishing 21, 43–4, 66–7, 88–9, 108, 119, 124–5, 132–3, 174, 177–8

queer 56, 66–7, 153, 166–7, 176
quest (*see* genre)

race 60, 101, 102, 107, 108–9, 166, 173
Reflecting Realities Report (*see also* ownvoices) 35
reported speech 82
rhetoric
    alliteration 83, 91
    allusion 17, 34, 80
    anaphora – Balen (definition given), contranym 78
    hyperbole 80
    imagery 77, 80, 145, 146–7, 165
    irony 14
    metaphor 33, 50, 76
    metonymy 76, 80, 105
    parechesis 81, 83, 91
    parody 34
    personification 61, 80
    polysyndeton 75, 77, 81, 91
    rhythm 83, 100
    sibilance 99
    symbol 80–1, 82–3, 92, 122–3, 141–2, 180
    tricolon 146
rhythm (*see* rhetoric)

setting (*see* world-building)
social class 57, 58, 60, 65–6, 104, 110, 176
story 147, 149
Structure
    beats 21–2, 49, 98, 113, 122
    guiding principle 149
    questions 109, 154
    refrain 28
    rising tension 28, 169–70
    scene 40
    three act structure 28, 38, 39
    verse 97–8
style 11, 12, 77, 87, 91
subplot 158–9, 169–70
subtext 14, 169
suspense, tension 120, 164, 169–70, 181
symbol (*see* rhetoric)

teen (*see* young adult)
tense

past tense 55, 132
present tense 75, 98, 132, 142, 163–4
theme 103, 109–10, 141, 152, 154
theory of mind 15, 77
transnational writing 101, 102–4, 111, 115

verse novel 97–8, 99, 101, 111–12, 113
vignette 98, 99
villain (*see* antagonist)
voice 2, 75, 91, 155

world-building 54, 59, 61, 64–5, 142, 146, 148, 165–6, 175
writing process (*see* process)

young adult 118, 122, 141, 144, 165